The Rebirth
of Liberty

OTHER BOOKS BY CLARENCE B. CARSON:

The Fateful Turn
The American Tradition
The Flight from Reality
The War on the Poor
Throttling the Railroads

THE REBIRTH OF LIBERTY

The Founding of The American Republic 1760-1800

Clarence B. Carson

ARLINGTON HOUSE New Rochelle, N.Y.

for
MELISSA

Contents

Appendices

Preface

This work had been in my mind a half dozen years before I undertook to write it. I had only a general theme in mind when I first conceived it, and that was to treat the period in American history from 1760 to 1800, or thereabouts, as an epic whole. Any shorter period of time would not encompass the founding of the United States, although many works have attempted to do just this. I did not have a clear conception of how to treat both the many controversies of the time and the numerous controversies among historians in interpreting various developments. I knew that some of them would have to be taken up, but I had not formed hard and fast conceptions about how to deal with them. I knew in advance, for example, that I would not make an interpretation based on economic determinism. Nor did it seem likely that in my research I should become privy to the inner motivations of the men of this period. In this, I was right. But I was quite uncertain as to what I would do about such interpretations.

As the work proceeded, my approach began to take shape. I would, as it turned out, largely ignore the controversies among historians over the years. Moreover, I would deal with the controversies of the time within the framework in which they occurred, not imposing any scheme upon them, but viewing them, generally, as differences among men of good will. The great advantage of doing this is that the focus is then upon *their* ideas and beliefs, and upon *their* differences. To accept them largely on their terms is to treat men, events, ideas, and beliefs as important. This is what I have attempted to do.

I started, too, with the notion that this is a dramatic and potentially exciting period in history, though years of teaching have made me all too aware that most frequently the drama and excitement are in the eye of the teacher beholder only. Yet the drama was there: the buildup toward revolt, the clash of British and American thinkers, the development of an American justification for revolt, the decisive battles of a war, the great men who led the armies and the populace, the experiments with government, the debates of conventions, the shaping and establishment of a Constitution, and the rebirth of liberty. There were in much that happened cautionary lessons to be learned as well as worthy examples to be imitated. Those to whom such history is not alive are only partly alive themselves. My task was to convey this idea. It is for those who read it to say whether I have done so.

I wish I could assure my colleagues in history that my preparation for doing this work made me the inevitable candidate for the job. But candor requires that I report that my preparation has been more casual and haphazard than they would wish. I became interested in this period by studying intellectual history. My early interest was in the European Enlightenment and how and to what extent Americans were influenced by it. Later, I became interested in economic history. I then tried to master the more general works on the period and to study the public documents. Whatever advantages there might be to extensive specialization in some aspect of this period, I have not had them. It is my hope that my long-term interest in this period will compensate, at least in part, for such deficiencies.

I have relied heavily upon the work done by others in making this account. Thus, I am much indebted to those who have made specialized studies, compiled documents, and interpreted the events. I have found that it is frequently the case that a work whose interpretation is rejected may be nonetheless a mine of information. My debt to these historians and writers is partially paid by footnote citation; the remainder, I hope, will be in the reward they receive knowing that they have been helpful to others.

It gives me special pleasure to acknowledge the more direct help I have had in doing this work. It first appeared serially in *The Freeman*, and my premier obligation is to its editor, Dr. Paul L. Poirot, who during its writing provided me with encouragement, editorial assistance, and helpful comments. He is without peer in promptness, kindliness, and decisiveness. David Franke of Arlington House has rendered the kinds of aid in making the book without which the writer is only a scribbler of disconnected words. Carmen Schultz rendered timely aid by doing a superb job of typing on short notice.

My greatest debt, however, is to my wife, Myrtice Sears Carson. She has not only coped with the difficult task of keeping a house but also with the even more difficult one of having a writer in residence for a considerable while. Hers has been the largely thankless task of maintaining peaceful surroundings for my work, and I herewith thank

10

her. She rendered even more direct aid by reading copy, some of it several times, and insisting that it make sense.

Of course, none of these people are responsible for any errors of fact, infelicities of expression, or misinterpretations which may be discovered herein. That responsibility is mine alone, and I accept it, albeit with some foreboding.

Clarence B. Carson

April 1973

The Rebirth of Liberty

1

Prologue:
The American Epic —
1760-1800

Several years ago, I introduced and undertook to teach a college course called "The Founding of the American Republic." Several things moved me to do it. One was my long term interest in the period. Another was the belief that such a course would offer one of the best means for covering the basic political principles on which these United States were founded, covering them with sufficient detail that they would be more likely to be remembered by students than the usual much briefer coverage in broader courses. Yet another reason was an idea that there was some sort of unity within these years that warranted treating them in a separate course.

One difficulty, of sorts, presented itself to offering such a course effectively. There was not a textbook which dealt with the period I had in mind in a unitary fashion. This could be attributed, in part, to the fact that I proposed to take the course down to the year 1800. Books which looked by their titles as if they might be appropriate did not do this. For example, Merrill Jensen's *The Founding of a Nation* covers the years 1763-1776, while Forrest McDonald's *The Formation of the American Republic* deals mainly with the years 1776-1790. Books which treat the American Revolution mostly deal in detail with only a small portion of the period. Richard B. Morris's *The American Revolution* concentrates on the years 1763-1783, and John R. Alden's *The American Revolution* covers the years 1775-1783. Books of readings cover a shorter period, too, as a rule. For example, Jack P. Greene has edited two extensive anthologies—*Colonies to Nation* and *The Reinterpretation of the American Revolution*—both of which are for the years 1763-1789.

There are numerous books that deal with some aspect of this period: the background to it, the coming of the revolt, the Declaration of Independence, the War for Independence, the years under the Articles of Confederation, the Constitutional Convention, and the early years of the Republic. In addition there are biographies of most of the leading figures of the period, numerous monographs on such specialized subjects as religion, economics, ideas, and so on. It may well be the most written about period of American history; most certainly, the period has been most extensively mined for documents to collect and reprint. A few titles will suggest something of the depth in which it has been covered: Max Savelle, *Seeds of Liberty* and *The Colonial Origins of American Thought*; Robert A. Rutland, *The Birth of the Bill of Rights*; Nathan Schachner, *The Founding Fathers*; Leslie F. S. Upton, *Revolutionary versus Loyalist*; Peter N. Carroll, ed., *Religion and the Coming of the American Revolution*; Douglas S. Freeman, *George Washington* in seven volumes.

Moreover, the events, movements, developments, and men of this time have been the subject of a great variety of interpretations and some of the most active controversies among historians. Professor Greene divides the older interpretations into three broad categories: the Whig Conception, the Imperial Conception, and the Progressive Conception. To this, he would add a panorama of interpretations that have come since World War II, many of which are revisions of earlier interpretations.

He says that the "new investigations have focused upon seven major problems: (1) the nature of the relationship between Britain and the colonies prior to 1763; (2) the nature of social and political life within the colonies and its relationship to the coming of the Revolution; (3) the reasons for the estrangement of the colonies from Britain between 1763 and 1776; (4) the explanations for the behavior of the British government and its supporters in the colonies between 1763 and the loss of the colonies in 1783; (5) the revolutionary consequences of the Revolution; (6) the character of the movement for the Constitution of 1787 and its relationship to the Revolution; (7) the nature and meaning of the Revolution to the men who lived through it."[1]

This list shows, too, how fragmented and specialized the study of this period has become. Interpretations have not generally been of the whole period but of some briefer span within it. Such questions as the following have been subjected to intensive study. What was the impact of British mercantilism on the American movement for independence? How many people from what areas and which segments of the population voted for delegations to ratification conventions in the states? What was the role of merchants in fomenting revolt against the British?

Just to touch upon the outlines of some of the interpretations that have been made will suggest some of the angles from which the happenings of these years have been viewed. Many of these focus upon why

16

the colonies broke from England, and upon the years 1763-1776. The oldest and most enduring interpretation is that it was a movement for liberty and from British oppression—a view that is sometimes called the Whig theory. There is a mercantile thesis, which may include the idea that the British followed a policy of "salutary neglect" during most of the colonial period, only to reverse this policy a decade or so before the revolt. Or, the mercantile theory may deal much more complexly with the inner contradictions of mercantilism, their adverse effects on trade and relations among nations. There is the maturity thesis—vigorously set forth by Lawrence H. Gipson—which holds that many of the American colonies had reached such a level of political and economic maturity that they no longer needed or wanted the British connection.

A major effort has been made to subsume the whole of this epoch into a class struggle theory. The inception of the conflict is particularly difficult to place in this framework, but there is something to go on in pitting the British landed class against the merchant class both in England and America. From some such point of view, the struggle might have arisen from the efforts of Americans both to resist mercantile restrictions and the payment of their debts. Much more fertile, for class struggle theorists, was the conflict within individual colonies between tidewater aristocrats and piedmont yeomen, particularly in North Carolina. On this view the revolt from England was accompanied by a civil war within the colonies. The contest continued over the years and involved such questions as easy money, a moratorium on debts, the powers of the states versus the Confederation, and eventually split the country over the question of ratifying the Constitution.

Many historians in the twentieth century have insisted upon telling the story of the years 1763-1800 in the context of a series of contests between Liberals and Conservatives. The terms were not in use at the time, and those who pursue their use must have some of their characters reversing their positions from time to time in ways that the men need not have been conscious of doing, if they did. Still, those who wanted to break from England in 1774-1776 must be, by these writers, denominated "Liberals," while those favoring continuing the British connection would be "Conservatives." Those who favored ratification of the Constitution of 1787 would be "Conservatives," while those opposing it would be "Liberals."

There have been other interpretations, but the above examples give some idea of what has gone on. The epic character of the founding period of American history has frequently been obscured by the attention focused on contending interpretations, by the dredging up of selected facts which serve as grist for the mills for some partial view, by the concentration on minutiae which results in losing sight of the

17

forest amidst the trees and shrubs, by the amplification of debates which had frequently long since been decently interred before the participants were themselves, by the quest for failings among great men and the search for imperfections among people, and by the fragmenting into parts of something which has a basic unity.

Many of these tendencies have been aggravated by the tendency among historians toward empirical data unillumined by philosophy but given its meaning by ideology. This is not to be taken to mean that facts are not indispensable to history, nor that the work of finding and substantiating details is not valuable, nor that anyone attempting to write an account of these years can be anything but grateful for the scholarship that has gone before. It is rather to observe that the fruits of research and study have so often been presented in such a way that the mind loses hold or does not grasp much that is momentous about the founding of these United States.

There is no need, of course, to go to the opposite extreme, to ignore the debates and the divisions, to glorify riotous behavior, to describe the Founders as if they had no personal interests involved in their decisions, or to pretend that there was unity where there was diversity. The epic character of these years does not depend upon the purity of all the participants nor the disinterestedness of their behavior. It depends upon grasping what they wrought by pursuing a course over the period of a generation despite their imperfections, their divisions, their selfishness, and their shortsightedness. By their fruits ye shall know them, we are told in Scripture, and it is these fruits which give unity to an era and an epic cast to what was done.

The American epic occurred between 1763-1800, with a background laid before that time and some filling out occurring after. The political foundations of these United States were set during these years. Seventeen eighty-nine does not make a good terminal date for the founding of the Republic; the Constitution was at that point only a "piece of paper." It had not yet had the breath of life breathed into it by the determination and actions of men; it did not even have a Bill of Rights. An experiment began to become an actuality within the next decade or so, and the story needs to be continued for several years beyond the inauguration of the government in 1789.

Strictly speaking, there is no American epic, or, if there is, it is according to the fifth meaning in the *American College Dictionary*, i. e., "something worthy to form the subject of an epic." An epic, essentially, is a "poetic composition in which a series of heroic achievements or events, usually of a hero, is dealt with at length as a continuous narrative in elevated style." The models for the epic in Western Civilization are the *Iliad* and the *Odyssey*. Epics frequently have as their subject the founding of a city, a nation, or the coalescing of a people. They usually have to do with legends and myths, with early accounts of a people that go back before any historical record, accounts that have been passed along by word of mouth.

But this serves mainly to point up the differences between the founding of the United States and most countries which had preceded it in history. The origins of most nations are available to us mainly in myths and legends; they go back to a time when the memory of man does not run contrary to their existence. Little enough is known of the coming of the Anglo-Saxon peoples to what then became England, much less about their antecedents on the continent. The establishment of English monarchy is, for us, a tangled web of chronicle, legend, lore, and historical glimpses of shadowy figures who had acquired such sobriquets as Ethelred the Redeless. Even more so was this the case with Rome and Greece, and it is only somewhat less so with France and Spain.

These United States, by contrast, came into being in what are for us modern times with what that connotes of literary record, events substantiated from many independent sources, and the characters definitely historical ones with not even a shadow of a doubt that some of them might have been mythical or combinations of several actual persons.

Poetry has rough going in dealing with prosaic factual materials. Heroes can hardly surface or survive the minute probing of their lives by modern biographical techniques. Elegant language requires an informing vision which has not fared well in the midst of a naturalistic outlook. Prosaic history under the tutelage of professionals has replaced epic poetry; irreducible facts which will stand careful scrutiny have tended to supplant elegantly worded narratives. We have gained in exact knowledge quite often at the expense of impoverishing the spirit; those who seek sustenance from the past have asked for bread and been tendered a stone instead.

Even so, there are the makings of an epic in the men, events, documents, and developments of the years 1763-1800. Every schoolboy once learned the rudiments of the stuff of epics: "Give me liberty or give me death"; the midnight ride of Paul Revere; "the shot heard 'round the world"; "Taxation without representation is tyranny"; the making of the flag by Betsy Ross; Nathan Hale's "I regret that I have but one life to give for my country"; the heroism of George Washington: at Kip's Bay, crossing the Delaware, at Valley Forge; the villainous treason of Benedict Arnold; "millions for defense but not one cent for tribute," and so on.

An epic is not for schoolboys alone; hence, it must probe more deeply into the background of a people. These years had an unusual crop of men, major and minor characters who would fit well amidst the elegant language of an epic: James Otis, Patrick Henry, Samuel Adams, John Dickinson, Benjamin Franklin, George Washington, John Hancock, Thomas Paine, Thomas Jefferson, Gouverneur Morris, Horatio Gates, Baron von Steuben, Marquis de Lafayette, James Madison, John Adams, Alexander Hamilton, John Marshall, and many, many others who have been well called Founding Fathers.

Events abound, many of which have a symbolic ring to them, events which call to mind crises, resolutions, and climaxes, such as: the Stamp Act, the Stamp Act Congress, the Boston Massacre, the Tea Act, the Boston Tea Party, the Coercive Acts, Lexington and Concord, the meeting of the Second Continental Congress, the declaring of independence, the Battle of Saratoga, the Franco-American Alliance, the Battle of Yorktown, the Treaty of Paris, Shay's Rebellion, the Constitutional Convention, the XYZ Affair.

Even the documents of these years have an epic quality to them: the elegance of the language, their philosophical tone, and the vision with which they call an imperial rule to account as well as set forth the new direction for a people. The story of these years is encapsulated in the documents for which these titles stand: the Suffolk Resolves, the Circular Letters, *Letters from a Pennsylvania Farmer*, the *Novanglus Letters*, the Olive Branch Petition, *Summary View of the Rights of British America, Common Sense*, the Declaration of Independence, *The Crisis*, the Articles of Confederation, the Virginia Bill of Religious Liberty, the Constitution, the *Federalist*, Hamilton's Report on Manufactures, Washington's Farewell Address, and the Virginia and Kentucky Resolutions.

What gives dramatic character to any series of episodes which make up an epic is conflict. Of conflicts, there were more than enough during these years: Parliament versus colonial assemblies, King against American congresses, the opposition of loyalists to revolutionaries, Redcoats against Continentals, Federalists versus anti-Federalists, Conservatives (or whatever they should be called) against Jacobins, the partisan conflict between Federalists and Jeffersonian Republicans, and nationalists versus states-righters, not to mention such more subtle conflicts as those between establishmentarians (or antidisestablishmentarians) and disestablishmentarians or between mercantilists and proponents of laissez-faire. What was right and who wrong may not always have been as clear as partisans liked to think, but many of the conflicts were worthy of the combatants.

What takes these men, events, documents, developments, and conflicts out of the ordinary and raises them to epic proportions are the great ideas which were espoused, which informed and enlivened them. Professor Clinton Rossiter has noted the habit the people of this time had "of 'recurring to first principles,' of appealing to basic doctrines. . . . Few men were willing to argue about a specific issue . . . without first calling upon rules of justice that were considered to apply to all men everywhere."[2] The following are some of these ideas: natural law, natural rights, balance of power, separation of power, limited government, freedom of conscience, free trade, federalism, and republican forms of government. As Rossiter says, "The great political philosophy of the Western world enjoyed one of its proudest seasons in this time of resistance and revolution."[3] To which should be added, it had its finest season in the laying of the political foundations during the constitution-making years.

Perhaps the greatest wonder of all during these years is what these men wrought out of revolution. The modern era has had revolutions aplenty, and then some. All too often they have followed what is by now a familiar pattern, that is, great proclamations of liberty and fraternity, the casting off of the old rules and restrictions, the subsequent loosening of authority, the disintegration of the society, and the turning to a dictator to bring a more confining order. Though some have tried to tell the story of America during these years along such lines, the interpretations are always strained. Clearly, the Americans avoided most of the excesses associated with revolutions.

Many things may help to explain this, but one thing is essential to any explanation. Americans did not cut themselves off from their past experience, from ideas and practices of long standing, or from older traditions and institutions. In their building they relied extensively upon ancient and modern history and that which had come to them through the ages. What separates this as an epic from abortive revolutions is that these men brought to a fertile junction their heritage—which contained several great streams, namely, the Classical, the Christian, and the English— their experience, and contemporary ideas. The Founders stood on the shoulders of giants, though it sometimes requires giants also to attain such heights.

An epic poem might well ignore these antecedents in order to attribute all that was accomplished to the heroes of the time. An historical account—even one which acknowledges the epic proportions of what occurred—cannot well do so.

Thus, it is appropriate now to relate something of the heritage and experience which went into the founding of the American Republic.

2

The English Heritage

One of the major elements in the complex of experience and background which the Americans brought to their founding activities was their English heritage. The majority of the colonists were of English lineage, and they were preponderantly British in origin, since the latter designation would include those of Scotch and Irish descent. What the Americans constructed when they got the opportunity were mainly alterations and reshapings of their English heritage.

Nonetheless, there was considerable ambiguity in the attitude of the colonists toward their English background. Indeed, this ambiguity has attended the attitudes of those who have come from Europe over the centuries to settle in America. On the one hand, they have rejected the Old World, the most obvious sort of rejection being their very coming to the New World. Many who came have fled from one kind or another of persecution or oppression. The Old World has often been described by those who betook themselves to the New as a seat of persecution and corruption. Certainly, American colonists of the latter part of the eighteenth century readily identified the English Church and government with corruption—the Church with its pampered hierarchy and impoverished parish priests, and the government with its rotten boroughs and members of Parliament whose votes were bought by the monarch with sinecures.

And yet, however ambiguous their attitude toward it may have been at times, the Americans did not basically reject their English heritage. Instead, they valued it essentially, made great efforts to preserve it, treasured its outlines, and, when the time came, builded upon it. From first to last, over a colonial period of a little less than two hundred years these settlers showed their attachment to and dependence upon England. Fathers who could afford it frequently sent their sons to be educated in England. They read English books, watched English plays, if any, and consumed English-produced goods.

In many ways, the settlers showed their preference for things English, both in words and deeds. Professor Samuel E. Morison says that two early New England writers, Nathaniel Morton and Edward Winslow, declared that one of the main reasons the Pilgrims left Holland for the New World was the fear that their children would lose their language and nationality.[1] One historian has recently shown how devoted the Puritans were to their English background. He says, "They were hardly more worried that their laws should be 'scriptural,' that is approved by the Bible, than that they should be sufficiently English; and that any changes in English laws should have ample warrant in local needs."[2] Even more strongly, he declares:

> Scholarly dispute as to whether early New England law was primarily scriptural or primarily English is beside the point. For early New Englanders these two turned out to be pretty much the same. Very little of their early legal literature attempted to construct new institutions from Biblical materials. They were trying, for the most part, to demonstrate the coincidence between what the scriptures required and what English law had already provided.[3]

A case could be made, however, that the New Englanders were among the least devoted to their English heritage of the American colonists. They were dissenters from the Church, developed a considerable literature of their own, were opposed to such things as plays, had colleges of their own, and had more latitude than was usual in developing their governments. Certainly, many of the other colonies conformed much more closely to English ways. A Virginian, writing in 1728, contrasted that colony with others, and proclaimed that "Virginia may be justly esteemed the happy Retreat of *true Britons* and true Churchmen."[4] Statements affirming the connection between Britain and America can be found in abundance all the way up to the Declaration of Independence.

Not all the affirmations of admiration for things English nor all the reliance on Britain should be taken at face value as indicating the real state of sentiment or that everything that was done was voluntary. Colonists were under a variety of pressures and restraints which bent them toward such conformity. The charters under which they were supposed to operate usually required that their laws not be contrary to English law. For example, the General Court of Massachusetts was authorized by the charter to make laws for the inhabitants, with the proviso that they be "not contrairie to the Lawes of this our Realme of England."[5] The Maryland charter provided that the proprietor "was to make no laws incompatible with those of England, and none without the consent of the freemen or their representatives."[6] Since others usually had similar provisions, colonists found it in their interest not only to conform to the British pattern but to profess to do so as well.

A dependence on Britain for many things was engendered by British regulations. In general, they were encouraged over the years to buy various products from the mother country because of restrictions on their manufacture in the colonies. Such restriction definitely hampered the development of an American literature by limiting printing opportunities. An American printer could rarely undertake the publication of a book because of the scarcity of type. "In England the supply had been limited as part of the control of the press; a Star Chamber Decree of 1637 allowed only four persons, each with a limited number of apprentices, to operate type-foundries at any one time. Not until the Revolution could American printers buy type of American manufacture."[7] In the late seventeenth century, the King provided the Governor of Virginia with orders "that no person be permitted to use any press for printing upon any occasion whatsoever."[8] Not all the dependence of the colonies upon England was by choice, it is clear.

Even so, the Americans did revere the essentials of their English heritage. They could hardly have done otherwise; to reject it out of hand would have been to repudiate much of themselves as they were. The furniture of their minds was made up largely of British conceptions. Their angle of vision was set to see things the way one of such descendance would see them. The best proof that they revered the heritage, however, is that they kept so much of it when they had an opportunity following the revolt to dispense with it. To see that this was so, it will be useful to call up the outlines of the English systems and ways.

A profound ingredient of the English heritage is the conservative cast of mind. In a general sense, this may not distinguish British peoples from most others. It is quite likely that most peoples at most times have been preponderantly conservative, though not necessarily in a discriminating way. It could even be argued that man is by nature conservative (as are also the lower animals) in that he usually prefers to continue to do things in the same way he has done them. Small children tend to be conservative in insisting on ritualizing activities and in their intolerance toward things or people that are different. Such conservatism is undifferentiated in its posture toward things familiar, reveres them for their familiarity alone.

British conservatism is something different from and more than what might well be called "brute conservatism." If it were not, it should hardly have come to our attention, for it would only be a universal condition, one which would be no more worthwhile to announce than that Englishmen have two legs. The particularities of British conservatism took shape over many centuries of experience, took shape in the Middle Ages as a people defended their ways against Danish and Norman monarchs, as the classes battled against arbitrary and despotic kings, as the thrust of change was blunted by the persistent clinging to ancient rights and privileges.

British conservatism was a reality long before Edmund Burke so elegantly gave it a set of articulated concepts and a language. Englishmen over many centuries harked back to the Magna Charta as the fount of their privileges. Parliament for its first several centuries did not claim to legislate; it claimed only the power to participate in declaring what the law *was*, and the law was, most frequently, what it had been since the memory of man runneth not to the contrary. When the English Church broke from the Roman Church, the least changes were made in it of all the churches born out of the Protestant Reformation. The English had a revolution, of sorts, in the middle of the seventeenth century, but in short order they returned to their older arrangements. This is not to say that the British did not change; it is rather to affirm that when they changed they kept much more than they changed, and they were given to defending their changes on the grounds that they were restoring an earlier condition. It was this that the Americans inherited and brought with them to their constitution-making and their attitudes toward institutions.

One of the most important of the things the colonists derived from England was the literary heritage. The vehicle through which it was transmitted was the English language, which became the tongue of the continental colonies. It is easy to ignore the significance of so common a thing as language, to imagine that what language one uses does not matter. It is quite otherwise, of course, for each language has its nuances, shades of meaning, rhythms, and tones. A language embodies much of the history and experience of a people; it embraces their values and transmits their culture.

The English language was just becoming an effective literary language when the English colonies were settled in the seventeenth century. The Renaissance and Reformation were the major movements out of which English was developed into a literary language. Latin had been the language used by peoples of Western Europe for formal and elegant secular writings, as well as those of the Church. The break with the Roman Church hastened the development of national languages, and the Renaissance gave great impetus to growth of an imaginative and scientific literature. The English language came into its own with

Elizabethan poets and dramatists, the King James Version of the Bible (1611), and the scientific writings of the seventeenth century. Hence, Englishmen going forth into the wilderness of the New World brought with them a potent and virile vehicle of communication.

It was through this language, too, that they imbibed the literature. One historian of ideas notes that "Americans shared with Great Britain the balladry and the more formal literature of the motherland. But the literary legacy was greater than this, for it was through English and Scotch channels that the Graeco-Roman classics and the literature of the Renaissance were transmitted to the American people. . . . The British newspaper, pamphlet, broadside, and magazine likewise provided colonial Americans with models."[9]

By the time of the American revolt, they had at the least four major categories of literary influence from Britain. The first of these to reach its fruition was that of the English Renaissance. Outstanding works were produced by Thomas More, Edmund Spenser, Thomas Kyd, Christopher Marlowe, and, pre-eminently, William Shakespeare. Spanning a much greater period of time and encompassing a much more diverse bounty of offerings was the English Reformation literature. It ranges from the writings of John Wyclif in the late fourteenth century to John Wesley in the late eighteenth century, and includes those of Hugh Latimer, Miles Coverdale, John Tyndale, Robert Browne, Richard Hooker, John Bunyan, John Milton, George Fox, and so forth. A third category was the seventeenth century philosophical and scientific literature which included the works of Francis Bacon, Thomas Hobbes, Isaac Newton, Roger Boyle, Edmund Halley, and John Locke. The literary heritage which had the most direct impact on founding the American Republic was that of political writings. This was a rich literature indeed, for it included the contributions of James Harrington, Edward Coke, Thomas Hobbes (not much referred to by Americans but an essential part of the justification of government because of the nature of man), Algernon Sidney, John Lilburne, John Milton, John Locke, John Trenchard, Earl of Shaftesbury, Thomas Gordon, William Blackstone, and Joseph Addison, among many others.

The British tradition included a complex of social arrangements, customs, institutions, and mores. Some of these had the sanction of law, and in some cases there were attempts to establish and maintain these relationships by law. Indeed, it would be difficult to name an institution that was not in some way buttressed by the power of government in seventeenth century England. The Church was established, supported by taxation, and attendance at its services required. Economic organizations were usually chartered by government, given monopolies for trade or manufacture in some jurisdiction, their activities viewed as adjuncts

27

of government. Manufactures were restricted as to where they might be carried on, wages controlled (usually in an attempt to keep them lower than the market price), and prices of goods frequently fixed. The development of libertarian ideas in America (as well as in England) is given greater meaning with such a background in mind.

Marriage, the family, and property were tangled in a web of restrictions and prescriptions. According to law, the landed inheritance must go to the eldest son, a system known as primogeniture. In like manner, estates were frequently entailed so as to prevent their being broken up and disposed of during the lifetime of the owner. Both these practices were widely established in the American colonies. Moreover, in England, according to ancient practice, tenants had claims, in perpetuity, to the lands which they rented. A strong case could be made that these, and similar practices, buttressed the family as an institution. Not only did the eldest son inherit the estate (or other claims to property) but also the responsibilities of the father, such as to look after the widowed mother, to take care of unattached females in the family and any others who might not be able to provide for themselves.

Probably, though, these regulations and prescriptions had much more directly the purpose of maintaining a class system. Certainly, England had a class system in the seventeenth and eighteenth centuries, though it had become more flexible, more subtle, and more complex than it had been in earlier centuries. There was an aristocracy made up of the titled nobility and the upper clergy, whose members had the privilege and responsibility of sitting in the House of Lords. There was what has been most commonly referred to as a middle class composed of the landed gentry and merchants and tradesmen. The gentry were reckoned by their rent rolls, but the merchants were not so formally recognized. The merchants were a class primarily because they had been granted government privileges, patents, and monopolies in trade and manufacture. There were assorted other free men beneath these in the scale, yeoman farmers, mechanics, parish priests, and so on. Below these were the disfranchised, those who did not have the basic political privileges and had insufficient economic privileges to be independent. An attempt was made to transfer the outlines of this system to America.

There were all sorts of institutions which derived from England, but perhaps the main outlines and character of many of them can be suggested by the idea of the corporation. A corporation, most basically, is some organization authorized by the sovereign. It might be a political organization such as the town, an economic one such as a trading company, or an educational one such as a college. The monarch authorized such organizations by granting to them charters or patents which spelled out their privileges, the scope of their activities, and might include various limitations. Such corporations were relics of the Middle Ages, but they were given new vitality at the time of the settling of America by the founding of colonies on the basis of such charters. The tendency of this method of establishing organizations was to make all activity hinge on government and be controlled by government.

British political institutions and practices had the most direct bearing on the founding of the United States, and it was from these that the most extensive borrowings were made. The most basic of these was the constitution itself. Some examination of it will clarify the relation between British and American political organizations.

It is no simple matter to describe the English constitution. It cannot be read in a single document as can the United States Constitution. Indeed, much of it is nowhere written down in a document or collection of documents. It is a combination of several sorts of things: the first of these is the way things are done in government, the procedures, practices, and customs; the second would be great acts which have altered these or fixed them more firmly, such as the Act of Supremacy of 1534 which placed the leadership of the Church in the hands of the monarch, or the Restoration Settlement of 1660 and the immediately succeeding years; a third kind would be great documents which have limited the king, such as the Magna Charta, the Petition of Right, and the Bill of Rights; fourth, would be court decisions which built up a body of law.

What the Americans learned or deduced from the existence of the English Constitution was a particular fortification of the idea of a higher law. There were other sources of the American belief in the higher law than the British constitution, but this was the main embodiment of it with which they were familiar. Americans learned over a long colonial period how one set of laws could be used to limit and restrict their own governments. Many of them did not miss the point, either, that such restrictions could be protective of their rights and privileges, for however much the colonists might resent certain restrictions, the requirements that their laws must conform to British laws secured to them their rights and privileges as citizens within an empire. The best proof of this is that some of the same ways they had been restrained as colonies under the English constitution were reintroduced as restraints on the states in the United States Constitution.

The principle of separation and balance of power among the branches was embodied in British government for Americans, as it was for the Frenchman, Montesquieu. Of the three branches, it might be supposed that Americans were least attracted to monarchy. So they were, if monarchy be considered only in its manifestation of the trappings of royalty, the apex of an aristocratic structure, and hereditary

29

rule. Such trappings are only historical accidents, an Aristotelian might say; the essence of monarchy is rule by one. Americans did not abandon the monarchical principle, as we shall see; they trimmed away the superficial aspects of it, kept it under different guises or names, and counterbalanced it with other principles of disposing of power. Rule by one—limited by being circumscribed—was kept in the office of governor and president.

Not only did Americans keep the monarchical principle, but they kept many of the functions that the English monarch had performed. In England, the king was chief executive; so are the governor and the President. The king appointed officers under him, took the leadership in forming and executing foreign policy, was in control of the military forces, and had the prerogative of mercy, as well as being ceremonial head of state. All these powers the President may exercise. Of course, there are some which were sloughed off, such as head of a state church and all those that have to do with the hereditary principle.

The debt of Americans to the English legislative system is much better known than that to the monarchical principle. The most obvious borrowing is of the two-house legislature. In like manner, there are similarities between the House of Commons and the United States House of Representatives: each is composed of members elected by district, each is the more numerous body, and each has the power of origination of revenue measures. The House of Lords and the Senate have both similarities and differences: the Lords are hereditary largely, while the members of the Senate were originally chosen by state legislatures and still have fixed terms; each body is the smaller of the two; the Lords had more court functions, while the Senate has more to do with appointments in the executive branch. One court function of Parliament is preserved for Congress in the power of impeachment, another in the investigative powers.

Much of the English legal system was established in the American colonies and some of it continued after the break. The most basic principle of justice, which the British had long labored to establish, was government by law. It is frequently described as a government of laws rather than of men. The fundamental requirement for this to prevail is that men be tried by standing laws, that they lose life, liberty, or property only after having been convicted of violating some law which was on the books preceding the committing of the act.

A variety of procedures in English law supported this principle. The underlying one was the right to a writ of habeas corpus, the right of a person being held to demand that he be charged with violating some law or be released. As one historian notes, "Meant to serve as an effective check on arbitrary power, the writ was clearly established by Parliament in the late seventeenth century as a means of releasing a person unlawfully imprisoned."[10]

Another English principle which influenced Americans was that of having an independent judiciary. This principle was fairly well established before the end of the seventeenth century. The main threat to the independence of the judiciary had been the monarch, who had from time immemorial tried to use the courts as extensions and instruments of himself. The way to do this was through the power of appointment and dismissal. Several of the Stuart kings were notorious for subduing the courts by these devices. Following the Glorious Revolution (1688-89), monarchs could no longer dismiss judges, and in the course of the eighteenth century kings abandoned the practice of appointing new judges upon their accession to the throne. England had an independent judiciary; judges could serve during good behavior, subject to dismissal only by both houses of Parliament.

The cornerstone of English law was the common law. The common law had taken shape during the Middle Ages as a result of decisions of the king's courts who sought to find the common elements in the diverse customs and practices among the English people. It arose as an edifice from judicial decisions over many centuries and was a depository of legal experience for a people. Undoubtedly, the common law was, and is, a mixed bag; one can find somewhere in it rulings along almost any line sought. It is ordinarily seen as having much more consistency than that, however, because in any given era the rulings fall into a pattern. It is profoundly conservative, for the law is resistant to change; courts are ordinarily considered to be bound by precedents, and legislative enactments are usually only frivolously suggestive and tentative beside it. By the time the judges have brought a legislative act within the confines of existing law, any radical character which the act might have had originally will usually have been lost. The common law is the main device by which the courts counterbalance legislatures in the English system. Among the protections of individuals under the common law, were the following, according to one account: "due process of law, habeas corpus, and an admonition 'that no man ought to be imprisoned, but for some certain cause. . . .' The common law also offered accused persons the expectation that they would readily be 'tried in the county where the fact is committed.' Double jeopardy for the accused was forbidden. . . ."[11]

Trial by jury was common practice in England long before Europeans became aware of the Americas. Courts are, after all, instruments of government, judges frequently appointed by the executive power. Juries, by contrast, are made up of private citizens, people in like condition to whoever is being tried in that they are of the ruled. They are charged with determination of the facts, but these must ever be viewed in the light of the penalty to be assessed if the person is found guilty. The jury may also have most directly in mind the future peace of the community. Hence, trial by jury was venerated both by the English and their American descendants.

The English heritage, then, was a rich one. Many had left England to come to America for one reason or another. Yet, their coming they would rarely construe as a repudiation of their heritage. Those things that drove them from England could be and usually were thought of as aberrations from the traditions. The Church of England was a corruption of original Christianity; therefore, it needed to be purified. The tyrannies of monarchs were violations of the constitution. In this view, the colonists were frequently joined by a numerous body of the English people and could find their ideas substantiated by British thinkers.

Of course, the Americans made innovations in the English heritage. They grew away from the English system in many ways and, at the least, became devoted to their interpretation of it. What they chose to preserve of it was that attenuation of it that prevailed in America, that which had become a part of themselves out of long experience. It is time now to examine that experience.

3

The Colonial
Religious Experience

The English heritage was modified and transfigured by colonists out of nearly 170 years of experience. It is frequently asserted that the United States is a young nation, as such things go, and the people are sometimes described as being in their youth. Such notions, if taken to mean that Americans are short on experience, will not hold up on examination. Americans have had not only the experience of the human race before them—such of it as they carried with them as furniture in their minds or recalled in the literature with which they were familiar—but also a broader and more cosmopolitan experience than a homogeneous people who have remained in their homeland. Moreover, they had a long colonial experience which was quite varied since the colonies grew up distinct from one another. The two facets of that experience to have most direct bearing on the founding of the United States were the religious and the political.

The religious background and experience will be taken up first because it is most basic. A reading of the United States Constitution, however, could easily mislead anyone as to the religious disposition of the Founders. There is nowhere in it even a mention of God. The only direct references to religion are those prohibiting the establishment of religion and prohibiting religious tests for office—both negative in character. In addition, a case could be made that several of the leaders among the Founders were Deists—that is, held only such residues of religious beliefs as they could square with human reason. One historian notes the importance of religion in the coming of the revolt in this way: "Yet if we realize that the eighteenth century, for all its enlightened rationalism, remained an age of faith, the religious background of the Revolution becomes instructive. This is not to say, of course, that religious grievances or religious ideology *caused* the Revolution. . . . But

33

the subterranean forces which motivate political behavior can be found within the more general atmosphere of the times. On the eve of the Revolution, the Protestant religion constituted a fundamental aspect of American culture."[1] To which needs to be added that the religious framework not only underlay the move for independence but undergirded the way it was done, the statements of the day, the constitutions that were drawn, and the Republic that was founded. How fundamental religion was to them can be made clearer by examining a little into the background.

It is widely held that the American Revolution was not very revolutionary—a view to which this writer subscribes— that in comparison with the French Revolution, the Bolshevik Revolution, or even the Puritan Revolution in England in the seventeenth century, the American one was not nearly so radical or was basically conservative. What contributed to this, as already indicated, was a considerable reliance on the English heritage, as well as a general dependence on experience and experienced men. But there was something else which made Americans shy about radical experiments in social reconstruction. It has not been put this way before, I think, and a new thesis deserves more extensive treatment, but it is very germane to this background.

Let it be stated baldly, then. Americans had already had their try at revolution before they came to break with England. Now I do not mean what Clinton Rossiter meant when he referred to *The First American Revolution*.[2] His meaning was that a revolution in outlook in the decades before 1776 preceded the declaring of independence. What I mean is that when some of the colonists left England and arrived in America they attempted a revolutionary reconstruction of the social and political order. This could be conceived as a revolution only by contrasting what they attempted to do in America with the order that prevailed in the land from which they came. Ordinarily, historians think of a revolution in terms of a prior situation in some country in contrast with what was done in that same country. This may account for their not perceiving the revolutionary content of the changes between England and America during the earlier colonial period. Be that as it may, there were some rather drastic experiments attempted in America in several colonies. They failed, by and large, and their failure meant that the bulk of Americans were not inclined toward radical reconstruction when they broke with England.

What has impressed many historians in more recent times has been the impact of the physical environment of America on settlers from Europe. The thesis regarding this impact is known as the frontier thesis. The frontier thesis was first most persuasively presented by Frederick

34

Jackson Turner in the 1890's. It holds that American culture can be explained largely in terms of a succession of encounters with the moving frontier. Undoubtedly, those who came to the New World had to contend with the physical environment, and, undoubtedly, they developed ways which were different in some respects from those of Europe in dealing with it. (Those who have held to the frontier thesis have meant much more than this, of course, for they have generally been determinists, holding that the environment actually shaped Americans.) Yet many of the early settlers struggled with something much less plastic than the physical environment, and from their unsuccessful wrestling with it must have drawn conclusions which joined them once again to the age-old experience of man. In several of the early communities, those who came wrestled with human nature itself, conceived and elaborated systems which would eventuate in new societies. They were much more impressed with the potentialities of a cultural frontier than of a physical one. What they discovered—perhaps, better, came to accept—was the Old Adam in man which is not exorcised by a new setting. This needs to be filled out with some particulars, but first the religious background needs to be covered.

Those Europeans who came to settle in America were preponderantly Christians, nominally, habitually, or devoutly. The few who were not were probably theists and people of the Book, i.e., Jews. They were Christians whose churches and sects were known by such varied names as Baptists, Brownists, Moravians, Quakers, Presbyterians, Congregationalists, and Catholics. Though it was their differences which stood out at the time and over which they wrangled, they nonetheless shared a basic outlook which transcended their differences and evidenced their common heritage.

As Christians, they accepted God as Creator, as Provider, and as Disposer. Life was viewed within a dualistic framework of Time and Eternity. Time was that dimension within which man lived out his allotted years; however brief they might be, they were fraught with ultimate significance as the span within which the decision for eternity was made. Christians had, and have, a historical framework implicit in their religion, one which is bounded by time and is marked off by several transcendent events: the Creation, the Fall, the Incarnation, the Second Coming and the Last Judgment. These are the great landmarks of sacred history, past and future. Not everyone who has gone by the name of Christian has felt the impact of their deeper meaning, yet to be Christian has meant, to say the least, the acceptance of the Incarnation as the entering of God more directly into history through Jesus Christ, the providing of a way of salvation through His grace, and the setting in motion of events which will culminate with His return. To be a Christian has ever meant, too, that man does not give meaning to his life; instead, God gives meaning to it.

The Founders of these United States would have rejected out of hand any suggestion that they write any such credo into the Constitution. Yet their rejection of it would not have signified in most cases that they rejected the beliefs involved. Indeed, they conceived themselves to be doing something much less than and different from pronouncing upon theological questions: they were erecting a frame of government. The kind of government they erected, however, was undergirded and informed by theistic and Christian concepts. It was a government which did not have as its object the salvation of man, the bringing of Heaven to earth, or anything of the sort. These things could well be left to their own realm and men could be left free regarding them because they were in the domain and hands of God. Men without such a faith can leave no area of freedom, for to be free without God is a chaos of wills.

Most of those who came to America from Europe in the first two centuries of settlement along the East coast were Protestants. To speak of a Protestant faith or doctrine is to speak loosely, for Protestants have their doctrines and beliefs within particular churches and sects, and these differ greatly from one another. Yet, here again there is a common bond, acknowledged by the very use of the term, Protestant, and it goes beyond opposition to the Roman Catholic Church, though it is usually defined in contrast with that body.

The seventeenth century settlement of America occurred while the tides from the Protestant Reformation were still flowing strongly. The religious wars, spawned by the Reformation and Counter-Reformation, took place in the midst of the seventeenth century. Doctrines were still picking up adherents; there was a great vitality to religious matters, and many men were deeply concerned about correct belief. This is to say that at the time of the early settlements there was profound interest in and concern about religion. Several currents of ideas were sweeping toward their crests. This was true of those called Puritans as well as a host of sectarians.

One thing that Protestants generally shared was an emphasis on the Bible as the sole source of their beliefs. This was in contrast with the Roman Catholic Church which used in addition to the Bible such other sources as church tradition and the writings of the Church Fathers. Undoubtedly, Protestants subsumed much of this tradition into their versions of Christianity. The Anglican Church kept a goodly amount of the older tradition. But Protestants in general insisted upon a biblical foundation for their beliefs. This central role of the Bible pro-

36

vided a major underlying support to the idea of having a written constitution. By analogy, the English constitution was like the Roman Catholic Church in relying mainly on tradition; the United States Constitution is Protestantlike in being the written word.

Another most important difference between Protestants and Catholics was in the position toward monasticism. In the Catholic Church, a person with a religious vocation went into one of the religious orders: if he was a man, he became a member of the secular clergy—those who served in such capacities as pastors and priests to the laity—or the regular clergy—those living under rules as monks; if a woman, she became a nun. Protestants renounced, denounced, and, where they could, abolished monasticism. Though Anglicans differed from other Protestants in many respects, on this issue they were agreed. Renouncing the world, to Protestants, was a renouncing of the duties and responsibilities God had placed on men when they were born into it; it was a retreat from the necessary engagement with the Adversary who tested one's mettle.

To devout Protestants, the things of the world are a snare and a delusion. Yet, we are called to grapple with them, possess them, live out our lives in the midst of them, and keep them in their proper perspectives—as things to be used rather than to be used by them. Out of this subtle and somewhat ambiguous attitude toward life in the world came the Protestant ethic, an ethic frequently referred to as the Puritan ethic but actually one shared by most Protestants, though less tenaciously by Anglicans and Lutherans at times. This ethic involved a particular posture toward the workaday world. It is seen most clearly in the Puritan Doctrine of the Calling. According to this doctrine, God calls to useful employment all those whom He elects to salvation. This calling might be any lawful undertaking which compensated not only the person engaged in it but served others as well. One showed forth the character of his faith by the quality of his work. Though other denominations might be less explicit, the whole Protestant movement was permeated by the drive to perform well by the fact that most religious people were engaged in worldly undertakings rather than withdrawing from them into a life apart.

Personal piety tended to replace for committed Protestants the personal devotions of the religious among Roman Catholics. This is often mistaken for a rigid moral posture toward everything both by observers and undoubtedly by some of the practitioners. Piety, however, is a vesting of all things and all acceptable activities with religious significance, a significance that derives from their impact on the condition of the soul of the person involved with them. Anything that cannot be done to the glory of God cannot be rightfully done. Protestants tended to repudiate the specializations of the Catholic Church: special orders of religious people, holy days (Puritans castigated a great variety of Christmas activities as pagan), numerous sacraments, the collection of religious relics, and so on. No day was more holy than any other (except, the critic may observe, the Sabbath, which was the major Protestant concession to specialization, a day set aside for religious devotion, that which, in general, Protestants had downgraded), no work more a calling than any other, no thing more worthy of veneration than another. This was the tendency of the Protestant movement, and the outreaches were experienced in vigorous trade and productive activities, insistence on public and private virtue, and a great deal of fervor going into many undertakings which those who discriminated according to a different ethos would reckon to be of little account. That much of this fervor would be obnoxious and repugnant to those of a different faith should be obvious, though men do not ordinarily concede that differences which do not attract them may derive from a great faith, but anyone who would understand American history must come to grips with this moving vitality which stems from a pious attitude toward the Creation.

English settlements in America grew up separate from one another, as a rule. These settlements were originally called plantations, came to be known as colonies, and most of them eventually became states within the United States. The separation was owing in part to the accident of the location of grants from the king, in part to the difficulties of land travel in those days, in part to British mercantile policy, and in considerable part to religious differences. Most seventeenth century colonies were conceived of and took shape as religious communities, though those who came to them may have had a variety of motives. That they were conceived as religious communities means that they were to be made up of people of the same faith (with a few notable exceptions) and that religion was believed to be the glue that held them together as well as sometimes that which distinguished them from the others.

There may be, there undoubtedly is, a strong individualistic strain in Christianity. Individuals are saved, not communities nor nations, according to Christian teaching. Protestants were more individualistic than Catholics, at least in their insistence upon a direct relationship between God and man, one which neither required nor could use a human intermediary. Moreover, Christianity is a missionary religion, that is, the Gospel is to be preached to all nations and peoples. It is not an exclusive religion as is, say, the Hebrew religion. Therefore, religious community in an exclusive or collective sense would be alien to Christianity or to the main thrust of it. Of course, congregations or communities within organizations universal in their purported extent would not be alien.

The Protestant Reformation eventuated in the breakup of the unity of Western Christendom and in the founding of numerous denominations. The initial direction was the founding of national churches as the religion of the people was dictated by the religion of the prince. These national churches were sometimes distinct from any other, most notably the Church of England, and usually required that all those within the country adhere to them. Religion was probably more deeply entangled with political power than it had been before the Reformation. At any rate, to be able to practice any religion freely, it was necessary almost everywhere to hold political power.

Hardly anyone could conceive of a community or nation existing at the beginning of the seventeenth century which did not have one established religion and did not proscribe all others. After all, religion undergirded all institutions, laws, and other establishments. One might as well speak of a people living together under several different systems of laws as with several different religions, so people generally thought. In such a framework, the freedom to practice one's particular religion entailed the lack of freedom of anyone else to practice his in the same community.

The Protestant Reformation not only spawned national churches but also a great deal of religious questioning and vigorous searches for the one true religion. Once a man had discovered the true religion—or the true doctrines and practices within the Christian religion—he must needs live according to his belief, else his soul would surely be forfeit. America was a land of opportunity in the seventeenth as well as later centuries, a land where converts of the true faith might come and set up communities where their faith could prevail.

It was this character of some of the settlements in America which made their coming and their activities in America a revolution, of sorts. Several religious groups in England revolted, in effect, against the Church of England. The Separatists, of whom the Pilgrims who came to Plymouth were a branch, definitely would not accept worship in the Church of England. The Puritans, when pressed to conform, were in tacit revolt against the established church. Something of the same could be said for the Quakers and a goodly number of members of other sects not only in England but also in other lands. Those who came to America were usually successful in their revolt, in that they were able to practice their religion in the New World.

What was more revolutionary than this was the kind of society some of them tried to set up. The example which comes most readily to mind is that of the Puritans who settled in Massachusetts in large number in the 1630's. These had greater opportunity than did most settlers to innovate because they brought their charter with them and a controlling group of stockholders as well. The Puritans were not utopians, nor were they redistributionists by doctrine. They did, however, conceive of the good society as one ruled by the saints, that is, ruled by the elect. They were Calvinists in derivation, and believed in the doctrine that God has elected some to salvation and the rest to damnation. It is His will, so they thought, that the redeemed, so far as they could be discovered, should rule. And, in their rule, they tried to run the government and order society so as to remove all wrongdoing and leave men free only to do good.

The Puritans established their church in Massachusetts, and branch-offs from it were established in other places in New England, with the notable exception of Rhode Island. The church was supported by taxation, attendance upon its services was required of all inhabitants, and the moral prohibitions enforced by the civil authorities. The Puritans enforced an orthodoxy in public utterance as well as in moral behavior. Those who would not conform were banished from the colony. They had not come, they said, to form a debating society.

The Puritans' insistence on orthodoxy may have had political sources, in part. They had a difficult time in justifying the rule of the saints and the prescription of the same regimen for both saved and damned. Since all of their theologians could agree that a moral life could in no wise attain salvation for one, it was not at all clear why the saints should concern themselves with church attendance and what are ordinarily referred to as the private morals of the unredeemed. The Massachusetts Puritans had a dogma to fill this apparent vacuum; it was known as "preparation for salvation."[3] This was the doctrine that one could be prepared for the receiving of grace for salvation by hearing sermons, attending church, and good conduct. This justified, in their minds, the use of force or power in religious matters; it provided an ultimate sanction to the mundane business of intertwining church and state.

The Puritan experiment failed; everyone seems to agree on this point. Their preachers never tired of telling their congregations that they had fallen away from the zeal of their fathers. Their small farming towns founded on an abstraction of the manor failed to contain a population, much of which turned to the sea for a livelihood. A Half-way Covenant in the latter part of the seventeenth century admitted the children of the "saints" to church membership and political participation without requiring of them all the signs of election. The charter was revoked in the 1680's. The witchcraft persecutions of the 1690's made many doubt the validity of theocracy. The Congregational church was not finally and fully disestablished in Massachusetts until the 1830's, but the theocratic concept of a Holy Commonwealth had long been abandoned. There were, of course, powerful residues from it. The covenant idea went into a stream of ideas which supported a written constitution as a pact between the governors and the governed. The idea of reconstructing society for the good of all has not died, either; it has gone through many mutations in American history. But many New Englanders had enough of such drastic experiments by the eighteenth century.

There is not space here to discuss in any detail the many different community experiments of the colonial period; it would take a good sized book to do so. There were experiments in communal storehouses and disposal of land. The earliest of these was at Jamestown; it was such a dismal failure that it was very shortly abandoned. A similar fate met the Plymouth experiment in the 1620's. This did not deter the founders of Georgia from attempting an even more extensive experiment along these lines in the 1730's and 1740's. They attempted to plan the economy and control the morals of the inhabitants: small parcels of land were distributed to householders; an attempt was made to produce silk; they selected the inhabitants according to need and other criteria; and an act of 1735 declared that "no Rum, Brandies, Spirits or Strong Waters" could be imported or sold in the colony.[4] By mid-century just about everyone had had enough of this experiment, including the trustees. Of this experiment in philanthropy, historian Daniel Boorstin notes that "a project which had been lavishly supported by individual charity and public philanthropy, had come to a dismal end. It is uncertain how much of the population had deserted Georgia for the freer opportunities of Carolina and the other colonies by the middle of the century. . . . But many had left, and there was more than romance or malice in the notion that Georgia was on the way to becoming a deserted colony."[5]

These were not strictly religious experiments, but the effort of the Quaker colony of Pennsylvania was more nearly so. The Quakers departed radically from Christian tradition. They abandoned the inherited forms of Christianity, indeed, professed to despise them, eschewed liturgy, theology, or a specialized clergy, believed that each man was illumined by an inner light, and were confirmed pacifists. Also, in the early years, their zeal was almost unbounded, as is illustrated by the determination of some of their number to be martyred in Massachusetts. (The authorities there finally decided to oblige them.) They refused to be sworn in courts or take oaths of office in conventional manner. They believed that if the Indians were treated fairly there would be no trouble with them.

How such a people with such beliefs could govern is difficult to fathom. Government has to do with monopolizing and using force, if it is to be employed at all. Yet here were a people loath to bear arms.

41

Boorstin observes that "almost from the beginning the Quakers realized that their religious doctrines . . . would put difficulties in the way of running a government. It was one thing to live by Quaker principles, quite another to rule by them."[6] Over a good many years in the mid-eighteenth century Quaker legislators hampered the government from preparing to defend against Indians on the frontier. The matter came to a head during the French and Indian War when Indians rampaged over western Pennsylvania. After much debate and soul searching, most of the Quakers who adhered to a rigid pacifism withdrew from political activities in 1756. Most of those who remained in the legislature were willing to compromise on the issue.[7]

By the middle of the eighteenth century most Americans had been weaned away from visionary ideas; their experience in the New World had brought them closer to that of the Old World, even as they were growing away from political connections with the old. Many were of a mind to learn from the wisdom of the ages.

American experience was tending to wean people away from established churches, too. The most generally established body was the Church of England. It was most vigorously established by law in Virginia, where it was not only supported by taxation but other denominations were scarcely tolerated. This attempt to make the church not only the cement of community but also the support of monarchy and other aristocratic establishments had largely failed. Many Virginians disliked having such an establishment, held the clergy in low esteem, and were quite willing to part with it when the opportunity offered itself. In many of the other colonies the established church was only one among many other denominations. In such circumstances, it was not very convincing to argue that all the people of a commonwealth must be of the same faith else the community would fall apart. This was clearly not the case. Several colonies did not even have an established church, and some of these were as cohesive as those which did.

There was more to the tendency away from established churches, however, than an unfavorable experience with them. There were principled objections which eventuated in new conceptions of the relation between government and religion and between the individual and society. The two major sources of these were the sectarian denominations and the Great Awakening.

The American population in the colonial period could be divided into two major religious groupings: the churchly people and the sectarians. Churchly people were those who had or sought to have an established church. Sectarians were those who neither had nor in principle desired an established church. The first of the sectarians to hold power was Roger Williams in Rhode Island. Williams denied that there was any efficacy to enforced religion. God chose whom he would and rejected the others; no good works or any other human agency or action could affect God's choice. Both the saved and the damned must live in society with one another, and government was necessary to that end. But it would be an abomination to attempt to enforce the dictates of religion on those not elected; it would disturb the peace of the community, give decision over religious matters to unqualified men in government, and would dangerously intertwine matters of this world and the next that should be kept separate.[8]

There were other sectarians, some of whom did not trace from Calvinism. The Quakers were the most prominent. They did not believe that religion should be forced, and where they had authority there was religious toleration. Many German sectarians came over in the eighteenth century to settle in the areas where they would not be bothered or where there was religious toleration. Among them were Moravians, Mennonites, Amish, and so on.

The Great Awakening, however, played an even more prominent role in the breakdown of the ties between church and state. The Great Awakening was a revival movement which swept through the colonies in the 1740's and whose impetus continued through the latter part of the eighteenth century. The most prominent preachers were George Whitefield, Jonathan Edwards, and Gilbert Tennent. Whitefield was an Englishman who preached throughout the colonies with great impact. It was through this movement that evangelical piety began its move to become the dominant mode of American religion.

The evangelical movement took the emphasis away from doctrine, from forms, from ritual, and from what may be called in more general terms "churchiness." What was essential was not outward conformity to religious prescripts but inward conversion, a new heart, and a new man. To such an outlook, an established church tended to be only so much dead weight. The revival movement stressed individual conversion and individual piety and the improvement of society by way of improved individuals. The way to community was not through government power but by changed men. The Great Awakening divided the older churches between those who accepted the new revivalist emphasis and those who championed the rational approach. An established church became, quite often, an anachronism, when what was no longer involved was a single church. Moreover, the Great Awakening cut across the bounds of colonies and religion to provide a common ground in religion to inhabitants throughout the colonies.

By the latter part of the eighteenth century, then, men were chastened by their experience with attempts at reconstructing society, by the use of government to achieve some religious end. They had also

43

been enlivened by a new concept of the role of religion in society. For some Americans, religion may have become less important than it was to their forebears. To many others, it was still of utmost importance, so important that it should not be corrupted and stinted by the expediency of the exercise of power. To virtually all Americans, their religious background provided the framework through which they winnowed their ideas and in terms of which they builded.

4

The Colonial
Political Experience

I have often asked a class at the beginning of a course in history if they have heard the saying, "Experience is the best teacher." Usually, all or most of them indicate that they have. To confound them, I tell them that what they have heard is most likely a debasement of an older and possibly much wiser epigram. Benjamin Franklin gave this formulation to it: "Experience keeps a dear school; the fool will learn in no other." This is a prelude to making a case for the study of history to my classes. The point is that it is quite costly to learn by personal experience, while it is much less expensive to learn from the experience of others.

Actually, however, the case for vicarious historical versus personal experience is not as conclusive as I tend to make it. Personal experience usually makes a much stronger and lasting impression than do accounts of the experience of others. Any retelling of an experience is to a large extent an abstraction which leaves out the warp and woof of life. The difference between vicarious and personal experience is quite often like the difference between travel folders on an area and the actual vacation experience—a chasm of considerable dimensions. Still, there is much that has to be learned, if it is to be learned at all, from the experiences of others because of the limited career of an individual and because some things—e. g., drowning—are likely to be experienced only once, and all experience ceases.

Political experience—both vicarious and personal—is of particular urgency for those who would erect governments and govern. This is so because government is both essential and potentially man's most dangerous instrument, most dangerous because it can muster all other instruments and bring them to bear in the pursuit of whatever end those who govern may have. Government is that body charged with the monopoly of the use of force in a given jurisdiction. Politics is the arena of contest over who shall employ the force for what ends. Each of us is prey to the notion that if we had power we would exercise it only for the good of those who fell within our jurisdiction. Without experience, we can easily concoct plans whose fulfillment we would achieve if we could get the reins of power. The plans may have all the beauty of any abstraction, but they usually ignore the reality of the contest of wills by which power is actually gained and exercised, contests in which the man with a vision imputes evil to those of a different view, seeks power at first for the good he would do, then seeks power because he thinks he is good, and eventually seeks power for itself alone. There is a human tendency for anyone in power to concentrate it in his hands and absolutize it.

There is, however, a counter tendency at work in most governments at most times. It arises, in the first place, out of the difficulty which any ruler experiences of putting into effect personally his edicts. Authority must be parceled out. Those who exercise it incline to arrogate to themselves that particular authority. Moreover, it is easier to do anything if it is made into a routine. Routines become customs, and customs assume the character of law in the course of time. Hence, power is balanced and constrained to some extent and as a rule at most times and in most places. This can be prevented from happening only by relentless terror, a terror of a kind which is unusual.

Political experience is experience of the contest of many wills, of routine and custom become law, of devices by which power is constrained, of compromise, of the gap between conception and execution because both those who rule and those who are ruled have wills. A deep reading of history may acquaint one with these processes and actualities; personal experience will be even more likely to do so.

Americans in the colonies had a goodly amount of political experience before they broke from England, experience with the uses and abuses of power. They had it in what is probably the best way to gain experience with the use of power; the power at their disposal was limited and constrained. The colonists gained experience within the confines of the English constitution, in the first place. Their laws were supposed to conform to those of England. To make sure that they did, the system provided that court cases could be appealed to the Privy Council in England.

The colonists were restricted in what they could do also by their charters. Most of the colonies had originally been founded as commercial ventures, though a few were founded as proprietaries which harked back to the feudal system for models, and one—Georgia—was a trust. In any case, they were founded on the basis of charters. These spelled out the territory to be occupied, the financial arrangements, and the rights and privileges of the settlers. Ordinarily, the settlers were permitted to participate in the making of laws, and such laws as were passed had to be in keeping with and not contrary to English law. It would be correct to say that the colonists were both restrained and enfranchised by their charters.

The colonies were restricted also in that they were a part of the British Empire. In that capacity, they fell under the authority of the government of England (after 1707, the United Kingdom) and were subject to certain of the acts of the Crown-in-Parliament.

Before discussing this relationship, however, it will be useful to note some major changes that had occurred in the English government in the last years of the seventeenth century, the changes associated with the Glorious Revolution. These changes raised questions about the extent of parliamentary authority over the colonies under the constitution as it had developed, questions that were not finally pushed to the point of irreconcilable contradiction until the 1770's.

At the time when most of the colonies were chartered and founded, England was more or less of an absolute monarchy. Parliament was, for the Tudors and the early Stuarts, an auxiliary to them in the exercise of their power. In theory, and usually in practice, Parliament was that body which enabled the monarch to make alterations from time to time in the contract with his subjects whom he ruled by Divine right. Ordinarily, he could and did rule without consultations with Parliament. If some change were wanted by the monarch—e. g., a new tax measure —then he might call a session in order to get the needed legislation. If he could get by on established revenues and laws, he had usually foregone the nuisance of having Parliament meet.

The Stuart kings and Parliament were at odds for most of the seventeenth century over their respective powers. The issues were resolved by the Glorious Revolution and its aftermath, resolved in favor of Parliament. As one historian summarizes the consequences of this Revolution, it "demolished the doctrine of the divine right of kings. . . . After that momentous victory Parliament slowly and gradually, yet remorselessly and irresistibly, extended its power in all directions."[1] Another sums up the changes this way:

> William III began his reign with a clear recognition on his part that the royal office had been shorn of extensive powers. As it has been expressed by a distinguished historian of the constitution: "The king was distinctly below statute; he was to have no power to suspend statutes or to dispense with statutes; he could not by his proclamations create any new offence; he could not keep a standing army in the realm in

47

time of peace without the consent of parliament; parliament had begun to appropriate supplies; the military tenures were gone; he had no powers of purveyance and preemption; he could not try men by martial law; the judges were no longer to hold office during his good pleasure. . . ." We may add: he could make no laws without the consent of the nation's representatives; he could lay no taxes; he could claim no kingship by divine right. . . .[2]

In short, Parliament had come to occupy much of the ground formerly held by the monarch and would in the course of the eighteenth century gain much more control over affairs. England had a constitutional monarchy.

These changes affected Americans in two most important ways. One of them is that Parliament's powers were neither clearly delineated nor restricted. The British had spent much energy over the centuries in limiting the king. This was now as well accomplished as it might be without making him impotent. In doing so, however, a new power had been loosed—Parliament. It is true that the House of Commons is restrained by having its members stand for election. This was so, however, only for England and then the United Kingdom.

The other import of this for Americans was related, for it had to do with what the power of Parliament over colonials would be. The colonists had no representatives in the House of Commons, nor were there any American bishops or nobles sitting in the House of Lords. Moreover, nothing comparable to the Glorious Revolution occurred in the colonies. Parliament proceeded to pass acts affecting the colonies, though there was now doubtful constitutional warrant for such measures. For a long time the issue was not pushed with vigor by either side; it lay dormant ready to spring to life when differences between the colonists and the mother country rose to the point where constitutional questions would come into focus.

One reason that the issue did not come to the fore was that Parliament exercised restraint in legislating for the colonies until the 1760's. Parliamentary acts known as statutes of the realm usually applied only to England, Wales, and to Scotland after 1707. "Inasmuch as both Parliament and the colonial assemblies exercised the lawmaking power, a rather indefinite distinction between internal and external legislation was allowed to develop. Parliament generally confined itself to the regulation of the external affairs of the colonies (trade, currency, etc.) and permitted the colonial assemblies to legislate for domestic concerns."[3] This policy is sometimes referred to as one of "salutary neglect." Why it should be so called except by a partisan of British rule and Parliament is not clear; it suggests that the colonies were neglected and that Parliament had the authority to impose its will over the colonies—both doubtful propositions.

If there was "neglect," it was in the neglectful manner of the founding of the colonies, not so much in their later governance. The Stuart kings probably had two prime motives in authorizing plantations. One was to benefit England commercially; the other was to be rid of troublesome, undesirable, or, in the case of Roman Catholics to whom they were sympathetic, persecuted elements. The latitude that many of them were given in matters of religion suggests that the monarchs did not expect the growth of large, peaceful societies under their dominion. At any rate, a strong case can be made that over the years the British government was less and less "neglectful" and more and more concerned to tie the colonies close to England and make them conform to the British pattern. It is certain that over the years more and more laws were passed, and more and more attention was given to imposing the British will over the colonies.

One way to see the trend toward greater British control is to look at the types of colonial governments and changes in them. There were three types of governments in the colonies: royal or crown, proprietary, and charter. A royal colony was one in which the colony fell directly under the king: the governor was appointed by the monarch; he was an agent of the king, in effect, acted in the place of the king, and he, in turn, appointed lesser officers. A proprietary colony was one in which the proprietor appointed the governor and otherwise had authority reminiscent of a feudal lord. He, in turn, was a kind of vassal of the king. A charter colony was one operating on the basis of a charter; in effect, the members of the colony were members of a corporation, and the electors among them controlled the government on the basis of the charter.

The trend over the years was for England to extinguish the charters and proprietorships, which the original colonies had been, and to make of them royal colonies. By the middle of the eighteenth century, there were only three proprietary colonies and two charter colonies. The meaning of this is made clearer by this contemporary comment on the power of the people in the charter colonies: "The people in these Colonies chuse their Governors, Judges, Assemblymen, Counsellors, and all the rest of their Officers; and the King and Parliament have as much influence there as in the wilds of Tartary."[4] This is an exaggeration, but it does indicate that the trend toward royal colonies was a trend toward greater British control.

Despite the fact that the colonies had grown up to considerable degree separate from one another, they had a similar form of government to one another and to that of England. Each of them had a governor, whose powers were modeled on those of the English monarch. The extent to which the English attempted to gain or maintain control of colonial development is indicated both by the fact that most colonies were made royal colonies and by the extensive powers of the governor. He "was the personal representative of the king and the symbol of the empire in the colony, 'endowed with vice-regal powers, analogous though inferior in degree to those of the monarch.' As such he was the commander-in-chief of the military forces in the colony and the chief among the agents of the crown. He had the power to appoint judges in the vice-admiralty court, where there was such a court in his colony, and judges, justices of the peace, and sheriffs in the administration of civil justice. He also had the power to nominate members of the executive council . . . , and the power to veto acts passed by the legislature. . . ."[5] He could summon, adjourn, and dissolve the legislature, and he could pardon those who had been convicted of offenses. "The governor's powers were thus fourfold, for he was at once a Crown agent and the effective head of the executive, the legislative, and the judicial arms of government."[6]

A colony ordinarily had one or more councils, but usually there was a single council which served in several capacities. These were men chosen from among natives who were usually men of wealth and position in their communities. In one of their capacities, they were a sort of governor's cabinet, assisting him in governing by advice and in other ways. In another capacity, they might serve as a court of appeals. And, they were the nearest thing to an upper house of the legislature that the colonies had. In this capacity, they were analogous to the House of Lords. Many colonials got experience in governing by serving on councils.

However, most of the colonial political experience was gained by serving in the legislative assembly. This body was known by different names from colony to colony—i. e., House of Delegates, General Court, House of Burgesses, and so forth—but each of the colonies had one. It was the fount of popular government in the colonies, the only body at the level of colony that was chosen by the freeholders. In theory, it was subordinate to the governor in royal and proprietary colonies, awaiting on his call, subject to his dismissal, even subject to being dissolved in favor of the election of a new one, and its acts subject to his absolute veto. It could almost be said that it existed at the pleasure of the governor.

Theory is often one thing, however, practice another, and this was certainly so for the colonial assemblies. In their service in assemblies colonials learned the subtleties by which power is counterbalanced and the maneuvers by which power can be gained. The way they worked, in general, is described by one scholar in this passage:

> One is impressed with the rather prosaic manner in which the lower houses went about the task of extending their authority, with the infrequency of dramatic conflict. They gained much of their power in the course of routine business, quietly and simply extending and consolidating their authority by passing laws and establishing practices, the implications of which escaped both colonial executive and imperial authorities and were not always fully recognized even by the lower houses themselves. In this way they gradually extended their financial authority to include the powers to audit accounts of all public officers, to share in disbursing public funds, and eventually even to appoint officials concerned in collecting and handling revenues.[7]

Some of the devices by which they gained power are interesting and were quite valuable experience for colonists. One position from which they gained leverage over governors was that the salary of most of the governors was paid by their respective colonies. This meant that the legislature had to appropriate it. If they would only appropriate it on an annual basis, the governor would find it expedient to call the legislature into session each year. If they made the appropriation of his salary the last item of business before they were ready to adjourn, he could be, and was, effectively stripped of his powers to prorogue the assembly. "Not content with reducing the governors' legislative power, the assemblies . . . used their control over the purse to usurp many executive functions, insisting that certain conditions be met before appropriation bills were sanctioned. Thus the assemblies extended their sway over financial matters by stating in detail how money was to be spent, by appointing provincial treasurers . . . , by naming collectors of the revenues . . . , and by setting up committees to supervise the spending of money appropriated."[8]

Colonists got political experience at two other levels than that of colony. One level that did not involve many people directly but was nonetheless important was as agent for a colony to the government in England. An agent was sent from most colonies toward the end of the colonial period to England to explain to various governing bodies the situation in the particular colony, the attitudes of the inhabitants, and the effects laws and other English actions might have. Sometimes both a governor and a legislature would send such an agent. He would have no official standing in England, but he would be valued for his service both by the mother countries and the colonies and would gain much valuable experience. Benjamin Franklin undoubtedly got the most experience as agent, for he represented several colonies at one time; through this experience, he was prepared for the yeoman work he would later perform as diplomat for the United States.

The other level was local governments. Of their importance, Clinton Rossiter says: "In general, the central governments of the colonies exercised even less control over local institutions than did the mother country over the colonies."[9] That is, they managed most governmental affairs locally by institutions that were in keeping with the locale. In New England, town government was the most important level, and the town meeting the device by which the electorate directed affairs. In other parts of the country, county and parish government handled most local affairs. These were the features of local governments Rossiter thought particularly worthy of note: "the broader suffrage for local than for colony-wide elections; the multiplicity of unpaid offices and duties, a system under which a much larger percentage of citizens performed some sort of public duty than is the case today. . . ." In short, a large number of colonists had political experience while they were under nominal British control.

The British government did not neglect the colonists in the last hundred years or so of the colonial period. They set over most of them an arrangement that should, in theory, have brought them under the will of those who governed in England. There were governors with comprehensive appointive powers, numerous agents of a variety of boards and committees were sent to America, and Americans were in some ways more clearly under the dominion of the king than were the inhabitants of the United Kingdom. Short of taking from the Americans their institutions of government, it is not clear how they could have been prevented from developing as they did.

Nonetheless, the American colonies did evolve away from the British pattern, even as, to a lesser extent, the government in the homeland was evolving away from its older pattern. Americans today do not feel great unfamiliarity with colonial institutions and practices as they had developed by 1765. They would, however, if they understood them, find most of the institutions that were originally transplanted unfamiliar and foreign. Many of these institutions were medieval in character when they had been set up. For example, a town was a corporation with definite bounds, with privileges for its inhabitants, with powers to exclude others from them, with monopolistic powers, with an exclusive and delimited character. This had so far broken down by the end of the colonial period that men could generally come and go, move in or out, and go about their business without much onerous restriction.

52

In a similar and related manner, there was an attempt to maintain class arrangements and prescriptions in America. In the middle of the seventeenth century, the General Court of Massachusetts forbade the wearing of certain clothing to the lower orders. Yet, such efforts were of little avail, and long before the end of the colonial period it was commonly observed that respect for and distinctions among classes were disappearing.

When confronted with the Puritan demands for the abolition of episcopacy, James I declared, "No bishop, no king." His prophecy proved correct for America. Though there were several colonies in which the Anglican Church was established, there was never a bishop in America. The Bishop of London was appointed over the American colonies, and he was represented from time to time in particular colonies by a commissary, a man appointed to perform some of the overseeing functions of the bishop. But there was no clerical hierarchy that amounted to anything in America. Hence, even in Anglican colonies, the control of church affairs tended to slip out of the hands of the clergy and into that of the vestry. Of course, in several of the colonies, the prevailing denominations neither had any hierarchy nor approved of it as an institution. The religious supports for rule by an hierarchical order were missing.

In the same manner, there was never any titled nobility in the colonies to speak of. There is a saying that "Dukes don't migrate," and it is substantially true. For decades on end most Americans never saw a titled noble, and if they did, he was most likely a royal governor. No native Americans were ever raised to such rank, to my knowledge, nor is it likely that they aspired to it. Americans who acquired extensive possessions aspired to the life of a country gentleman, so far as we can tell, and would have been aliens in their own country had they been titled.

The effect of this is that Americans turned away from the old sources of authority and political power even more than did their counterparts in England. Authority, for them, did not extend from the top downward; it derived from the place they were accorded by their peers. Americans looked up to men who had acquired possessions by their own efforts or that of their immediate forebears and, among these, to those who showed ability at managing their affairs. Birth counted for little; achievement counted most.

Probably, Americans had more extensive experience in governing in legislatures, in towns, in counties, and as councilors than did any people anywhere in the world at that time. True, it was limited experience. They had little experience as chief executives or in foreign affairs, and they operated within the limitations of the British constitution and the empire. Even so, they were probably better prepared for popular government than anyone else, unless it was the English people themselves.

It is possible, however, to overrate experience. There are experienced thieves and murderers. There are experienced demagogues, and there are politicians with a vast amount of experience at gaining more and more power by plundering the populace. Experience can be useful in attaining any end, but it does not discriminate among ends. That is determined by what a people, or some portion of them, value. And values are a resultant of ideas held and cherished. It was not enough for Americans that their experience had turned them away from monarchy, from hierarchies, and from authoritarian government. If their experience was to stand them in good stead, they must be drawn to something constructive to take the place of these things. Americans were, and developments in ideas prepared the way for this shift.

5

The Enlightenment Impetus

From the early 1760's to the mid-1770's, as colonial resistance to British rule mounted, ebbed, and flowed, colonists referred over and over again to the British constitution, to the rights of Englishmen, to the charters on which the colonies were founded, and so on. This they could do so long as they were attempting to alter British policy and retain existing relationships. But once they decided to break the connection with England they could no longer hinge their action on the British constitution nor any longer support their institutions with it. Experience could be utilized; forms and practices could be abstracted from the British pattern; but all these would have to have a new foundation and new justifications.

The new foundation on which they built was the natural law philosophy. This is not to say that the natural law philosophy was new or that Americans had just become acquainted with it. On the contrary, the natural law philosophy, or its underpinnings, is nearly as old as Western civilization; it had been greatly revived in English political discourse in the seventeenth century; and American thinkers were widely familiar with it long before the break from England. But it had got new impetus behind it in the past century and a half, and the doctrines out of it were being brought to a fruition at just the time that Americans turned to it to justify their actions and undergird their institutions. If James Madison had been aware of intellectual history in this way, he might have remarked about the occurrence of this fruition of the natural law philosophy at just this juncture of history in the same vein he did about another matter in these words: "It is impossible for the man of pious reflection not to perceive in it a finger of that Almighty hand which has been so frequently and signally extended to our relief in the critical stages of the revolution."

Documents, writings, and addresses of the revolutionary period are replete with references to the natural law philosophy and ideas derived from it. Jefferson based his argument in the Declaration of Independence on "Nature's laws." Thomas Paine argued both that independence was called for as a natural right and that the resulting country should be founded on underlying law. State constitutions frequently listed a number of rights which were "natural." The United States Constitution was implicitly framed from an order explicit in the natural law philosophy. As Clinton Rossiter has said: "The principles in which they placed their special trust were . . . those of . . . the school of natural law." They "sought limits [on political power] more universal than those staked out in laws, charters, and constitutions. The great philosophy that preached the reality of moral restraints on power had always been a part of their Anglo-Christian heritage. Now, in their time of trial, the colonists summoned it to their defense."[1]

The natural law philosophy is grounded in metaphysics. That is, it is grounded in something beyond the physical; it is not accessible to the senses directly. No one can see, hear, taste, feel (tactilely), or smell natural laws. If they are real, their reality is vouchsafed in some fashion other than through direct sensual contact. Their reality should not be understood as a becoming, either, as made up of ideals which may be fulfilled in the course of time. The founders of these United States were not idealists in this sense; they did not conceive of natural laws as something it would be desirable to see established. On the contrary, they were understood as being already everywhere established, inviolable, and finished.

Intellectual developments since the eighteenth century have made it increasingly difficult to understand the natural law philosophy, and the meaning of this is that it has become increasingly difficult to understand that on which these United States were founded. The difficulty can be exposed by examining a familiar phrase from the Declaration of Independence, the one which reads: "We hold these truths to be self-evident, that all men are created equal. . . ." The phrase has been so often heard and seen that it has attained that status for us of an idea which is so familiar that it neither shocks nor calls forth any examination of it. Probably, in our day, most people hear not the words but a translation of them which would go something like this: We hold it as an ideal that all men should be made equal. Yet, that is not what the words say, nor is it reasonable to render them in this fashion.

In the first place, what does it mean that "these truths" are "self-evident"? Today, the phrase "self-evident" is often used as if it were a synonym of "obvious" or "apparent." This is probably a way, unconsciously adopted, of avoiding the difficulty for us of the term. "Self-evident" means that the statement contains its own evidence. To turn it around, it means that there is no external evidence for the truth of the statement, or that none is being adduced. It can be made clear that in the instant case no evidence either is or can be adduced for the validity of the statement. All the evidence that I know of indicates that all men are *not* created equal. Each person is different from every other at birth, different in appearance, different in capacities, different in circumstance, and different in what he inherits. Jefferson's statement is one which, if true, must be "self-evident."

This is not to say that there is no evidence for the reality of natural laws; it is rather to affirm that such evidence as there is is indirect. Thomas Jefferson was working out of a long-established philosophical tradition when he wrote the Declaration of Independence. This tradition was dualistic, holding that there are two realms of being. They can most directly be described as the realms of the physical and the metaphysical. The physical realm may also be described as the realm of the existential, the changing, the historical, and of appearances. The metaphysical may be called the realm of forms, of essences, of fixities, and of the real. It is, of course, the realm of natural law. It is that underlying order which gives shape, form, predictability, and their character to things.

The philosophical roots of the natural law philosophy reach down deeply into Western thought from its early beginnings. The Greek thinkers of classical antiquity were early taken up with the difference between appearance and reality. To appearance, all things seemed to change; indeed, all physical objects undergo alteration and corruption with the passage of time. This led some men to conclude, such as Heraclitus, that all is flux, that there is only change. Others held, however, that the changing is only an appearance, that underlying it is fixity and order.

Philosophy, as we understand it, had its beginnings with efforts to find the primal stuff from which all else comes. It was commonly believed for a long time that there were four elements—earth, air, fire, and water—from which all else is made. This search begot yet another one, the search for that which gives form and order to things, to that which causes them to assume the shapes that they do, to follow the course that they do in their development, and to behave as they do when impinged upon by something else. Men have, for as long as they have had settled modes of living at the least, been aware of numerous regularities and predictabilities in the world about them. Philosophy—by which is meant here its most abstruse branch—has been concerned with trying to make a coherent explanation of these.

Metaphysical thought reached a plateau with a line of Greeks which commences with Socrates, goes through Plato, and culminates with Aristotle, a plateau which it has ever since been difficult to reach or to rise above. New reaches in philosophy were only one of the achievements in the ancient world, of course, though these may have been the keystone. The Greek achievements were spread about the Mediterranean in what has since been known as the Hellenistic Age, and were taken up by the Romans who expanded and developed that portion of Greek culture which appealed to them. Roman thinkers were the first to set forth the natural law philosophy extensively. They did so both to undergird the edifice of Roman law and to justify the spread of that law over a vast empire. Their acquaintance with a multiplicity of peoples of diverse cultures led some of them to seek for common features underlying the differences which would be of the order of law everywhere applicable.

So impressive were the varied achievements of the Ancients that men refused to forget them even after the empires fell and Europe broke up once again. There were many revivals and renascences over the years. Two major efforts to revive the learning of the Greeks and Romans occurred in the Middle Ages: the first is known as the Carolingian Renaissance, and the second took place in the twelfth and thirteenth centuries. There was an almost continuous renaissance in the modern era from the fifteenth into the eighteenth century. There was a neoclassical revival in literature in the seventeenth century, and the music of the eighteenth century is frequently described as classical. If what is meant by classical is an emphasis upon order, harmony, balance, moderation, reason, and form, then the eighteenth century was the preeminent neoclassical age of our era.

The natural law philosophy was revived in Europe in the seventeenth century. On the continent exponents of it in the political and legal realm included Hugo Grotius, Jean Bodin, and Samuel Pufendorf. English writers in this stream would include Thomas Hooker, Harry Vane, Richard Hooker, James Harrington, Algernon Sidney, and John Locke. Much of the English thought was produced during the constitutional struggles of the seventeenth century, struggles which culminated in the Glorious Revolution. This body of thought was most useful to Americans when they came to revolt, because they were able to hinge much of their case on English thinkers.

The natural law philosophy in general got a great boost in the seventeenth century from what we call scientific developments. These developments which are associated with the names of Francis Bacon, René Descartes, Galileo, Johannes Kepler, Leibniz, Spinoza, and Isaac Newton were both spawned by the revived natural law philosophy and gave new impetus to it. The central features of this development were the emphasis upon the rationality of the universe, the rationality of man, and mathematically expressible laws governing the behavior of objects. Ways were worked out for discovering the laws, and these and other men experienced phenomenal success in the work of exposing them. Alexander Pope wrote:

> Nature, and nature's laws lay hid in night,
> God said, Let Newton be, and all was light.

So impressive was the natural order revealed by scientists that renewed efforts were made to discover more precisely the natural order as it applied to man and his affairs. The effort to do this in the political, social, economic, religious, and artistic realms has come generally to be called the Enlightenment of the eighteenth century. The title contains a considerable measure of presumption in it: it suggests that men were coming to be enlightened while those who had gone before had been in the dark. This is pointed up, too, by the conscious sloughing off of the reliance on the ancient thinkers and attempts to discredit them. A case can be made that the thought of the Enlightenment was deeply influenced by classical antiquity even as that age was no longer venerated. An equally strong case can be made that there was in the Enlightenment a potentially fundamental break with tradition which would cut men off from their past. Both these things are true.

It was with some trepidation that I used the term Enlightenment in the title of this chapter. There is no doubt that Americans at the time of their revolt were under the sway of the natural law philosophy, but there is reason to doubt that they were under the sway of the Enlightenment. This doubt is occasioned, I think, because of the course of developments in France. Many historians of the Enlightenment have focused on French thinkers, on Voltaire, Diderot, Quesnay, Montesquieu, d'Alembert, Rousseau, and so forth. The French were the most dramatic proponents of the Enlightenment, the most daring and iconoclastic of thinkers, the ones who broke most emphatically with the past. In France, too, centuries-old anticlericalism shifted toward opposition to all the formal religions and became, for some, outright atheism. The repute of the Enlightenment has been tarnished, too, because in its wake came the French Revolution with all that entailed.

Now some Americans were influenced by French thinkers. Probably all Americans who knew of it were favorably influenced by Montesquieu's arguments for a separation and balance of powers in *The Spirit of the Laws*. The affinities between the French and Benjamin Franklin, Thomas Jefferson, and Thomas Paine, as major examples, are well enough established. But the Enlightenment was not an exclusively French affair, nor the direction in which some of the French took it an inevitable one. The Enlightenment can be considered a much broader development encompassing the emphasis on reason, natural law, and balanced with a thrust toward liberty. In this sense, Americans shared in its fruits, and used the ideas associated with it. The bulk of Americans did not accept the more radical breaks with the past nor become antireligious as a result of their thinking. Americans tended to counterbalance abstract ideas with reference to experience and by the use of common sense.

There are several concepts basic to the natural law philosophy. The most basic concept is that of a *state of nature*. Thinkers in the seventeenth and eighteenth centuries were given to beginning some statement with the phrase, "Man, in a state of nature. . . ." Anthropologists of the nineteenth and twentieth centuries have pointed out that man is nowhere discoverable in a state of nature, that, on the contrary, he always exists in a social state. As is frequently the case when men of one era take on those of another in controversy, those of a later date have misunderstood the position, whether intentionally or not we do not know. The thinkers of an earlier day did not mean that man had ever existed in a state of nature historically, or that he could somewhere be found in that state at any time. The concept is essential, hypothetical, and imaginary. To know the nature of anything, it is necessary to strip away all that is peculiar and particular to that thing, all that has been accidentally added, and view it in terms of the common features it shares with all others of its kind.

To know the nature of man, then, is to know him in a state of nature, that is, to know him stripped of all cultural accretions. Stripped of his culture, a creature is only *potentially* a man, of course. It is a work of the imagination to discover man in a state of nature. It is an hypothesis from which to reason to other conclusions. It is man reduced to his essence that is discovered in this fashion. It is, as understood by the men about whom we have been talking, man as he really is. Thus, it can be affirmed that man is a rational animal—i. e., that he is capable of reason, that his potentiality for reason separates him from other creatures. If reason were something acquired from the culture, then all other creatures in the culture could acquire it.

The state of nature concept, then, is used to discover the nature of things. Everything has its nature, men of the Enlightenment held, has its form, shape, and potentialities. This could be affirmed of government, of society, of economy, and so on. Nor was the state of nature a neutral concept in the Enlightenment. The nature of a thing was believed to be implanted there by God, and it behooved man and all institutions to conform to their natures. On this view, everything is either natural or artificial. Herein lies the most revolutionary side of the natural law philosophy. One can follow a line of reasoning that all culture and all artifice violates nature and must be destroyed. (This was the tendency of Rousseau's thought.) Or, this line of thinking may be followed in a more discriminating fashion and lead to conclusions that some cultural developments run athwart the nature of the thing—such as mercantile regulations, for example, while others do not, as, for example, the institution of marriage. The founders of these United States tended to be quite conservative in their interpretation of the relation of their institutions to the nature of things.

Another basic concept of the natural law philosophy could form a counterblance to the revolutionary tendency of the state of nature concept. This is the concept of the *social contract* or *compact*. It will be useful here to distinguish between the essential and the existential social contract, even though such a distinction was not usually carefully employed in the eighteenth century. The essential social contract is timeless and universal; it is that contract which must exist if men are to live at peace in society. It is an enduring contract which one perforce enters at birth and quits only when he leaves society. As I have noted elsewhere, the social contract "is that tacit, essential, and necessary agreement which binds man to man, members of a family to one another, members of communities together, binds generation to generation, binds people to government and government to people. It is everyman's tacit agreement not to use violence to get his way, to leave others to the enjoyment of the fruits of their labor, not to trespass upon the property of others, to fulfill the terms of his individually entered into agreements, to honor his parents, to succor his children, to keep his word, to meet his obligations— to family, to community, to country—, to keep all treaties, and to observe the amenities of his culture."[2] It should be clear that the acceptance of such a social contract would mean that drastic changes would not be made in the social fabric, for to do so would be to violate the social contract. Americans accepted some such conception, as most peoples at most times do, whether they are aware of it or not.

The existential social contract is the particular one which prevails in a given society. When men referred to it they had in mind usually the compact between the governed and the governors. Any constitution would be such a contract, whether it had been written out or not, and whether or not both parties had formally ratified it. Americans in 1775 had a considerable history of dealing with such compacts. There was the British constitution, the colonial charters, the Mayflower Compact, the Fundamental Orders of Connecticut. In the natural law philosophy, if the rulers violated the existing social compact basically and consistently, a people could revert to their condition prior to their rulers

61

and work out some new agreement. This is what Jefferson argued in the Declaration of Independence.

Probably the most potent concept derived from natural law theory for the American colonists was the doctrine of *natural rights*. This is the doctrine that men have by nature, and as a gift of God, certain rights. They have been most commonly categorized as the right to life, liberty, and property. John Adams described the position this way:

> All men are born free and *independent*, and have certain natural, essential, and unalienable rights, among which may be reckoned the right of enjoying and defending their lives and liberties; that of acquiring, possessing, and protecting property; in fine, that of seeking and obtaining their safety and happiness.[3]

It was in their claim to rights that Jefferson was saying all men are created equal in the Declaration of Independence. He followed his famous phrase about equality with this one: "that they are endowed by their Creator with certain unalienable rights. . . ." It should be clear that this statement cannot be validated by an appeal to historical evidence. History is replete with instances of violations of the rights of individuals to their life, liberty, and property. Murder, suppression, and trespass have been all too common throughout history, nor would surveys anywhere at any time have been likely to turn up the fact that all were equally protected in the enjoyment of their rights.

But Jefferson did not appeal to historical evidence; he said that the truth of the position is "self-evident." The effective meaning of this is that the truth of the statement follows from the nature of man and of conditions on earth. What does it mean that one is entitled to life? It means that no one has a prior claim to it, that no one may take it without provocation, that it is his to whom it has been given. In the nature of things it is clear that no one could have established a claim on the life of another at birth or thereafter.

In a similar manner, man has a natural right to liberty, that is, to the free use of his faculties (with the commonly stated proviso that he do no injury to others in his use of them). In the very nature of things, no one may constructively employ the mind, the senses, and the limbs of a person but that person himself. It follows that he to whom they belong does so by prior right which it is impossible for him to alienate. The right to property is shorthand for the right to the fruits of one's labor. It is self-evident that a person who has produced something by his own labor with his materials on his own time has a rightful claim to it. The right to property is the better phrase, however, for

62

it encompasses the subtleties of distribution by which the fruits of one's labor may be determined in complex situations which usually prevail.

The natural law philosophy mightily buttressed a belief in liberty. It also provided methods for discovering liberties and the means for establishing and maintaining them. The Enlightenment gave added impetus to making such discoveries and an urgency to acting upon them.

The concept of an ordered universe provided the most profound basis for liberty. Seventeenth century scientists had affirmed that the universe was governed by laws capable of precise formulation. Newton's statement of the law of gravity explained how the great bodies in the solar system are kept in their orbits by a combination of the motion of freely falling bodies and the attraction of the bodies to one another. All sorts of other phenomena were shown to operate according to law. These laws were believed to be the creation of God and to be immutable.

As thinkers extended their activities into the social realm they discovered a natural order there as well. It is an order modified, however, by the free will of man. Man not only can reason but he can will as well, and he can will to do wrong to others. Hence, government is necessary, and certain prohibitions by it are essential to enable men to live fruitfully in society. But the existence of an order prior to government means that the role of government can be limited and restrained. It is not to be expected that everything will come apart if some human agency does not control and direct it; on the contrary, things will operate as they are supposed to ordinarily without some compulsive force.

To restrain government to its proper role, power must be separated into its various functions, and powers must be counterblanced against one another to prevent those who govern from exceeding their bounds. The separation and balance of powers concept was a paradigm of Newton's description of the universe itself. The heavenly bodies are kept from flying off into space by mutual attraction. On the other hand, they are prevented by their own motion from being drawn into the sun and consumed. A basic separation and a delicate balance between thrusts and pulls holds them in their orbit. This is one of the models for the separation of powers in government by which it may be kept to its task.

There is not space here to describe in detail the arguments for and justifications of liberty that derived from this outlook. Some of them will be described at other points. Suffice it to say that Americans were impressed wherever they looked with the felicitous possibilities for liberty. The broad lines of the insight went something like this: Compulsion is not necessary to make men sociable; man is a social creature by nature. He needs the society of others to satisfy his wants and will seek out the company of others. To have that company, he will be under pressure to behave in ways acceptable to others. There is an economic order which men willingly take part in without being compelled to do so or without being told what to do. Man is religious by nature. He cannot be compelled to believe what he does not believe. By nature this is impossible. But he might be expected to worship with others of like mind if left to his own devices.

By the time the crisis between Britain and America came, Americans were prepared by the natural law philosophy in three most important ways. With it they had ready to hand a foundation to substitute for the British constitution, one which undergirded that institution and transcended it in its universal validity. And they were impelled toward liberty as a temporal object. The diversity of the colonies had once had the unity of a common British background. When they struck off the British connection they kept much of their diversity but thrust to a new unity on the basis of the natural law philosophy. Independence, liberty, unity, and diversity found shelter within the broad framework of natural law.

6

The Mercantile Impasse

What provoked the American colonists to resist British acts, to rebel against restrictions placed upon them, and eventually to declare and effect their independence? To put the matter in more conventional terms: What caused the American revolution?

Men who have spent years studying the questions propound different answers. Some hold that the British mercantile system provided the provocation to revolt. Others have held that the American colonists benefited from mercantilism and that, this being so, mercantilism was hardly at the root of the difficulty. Another thesis that has been argued, most persuasively by Lawrence Henry Gipson, is that the American colonies had attained a level of maturity that made them no longer dependent upon Britain and no longer desirous of the connection. Some historians have gone so far as to charge that American debtors with the desire to rid themselves of pressing British creditors stirred up resistance and brought off a revolution. Those looking for a class struggle explanation of the conflict have tried to make the revolt against Britain a part of an internal struggle between the haves and have-nots. In short, almost every interpretation that could be imagined has been offered, and many of these have been buttressed by impressive arguments and such evidence as fitted them.

One thing is about as clear as such things can ever be: mercantilist acts did not provoke the initial resistance in the mid-1760's. The Stamp Act of 1765 was not a mercantilist act, nor was the Sugar Act of 1764 primarily mercantilistic. Indeed, the Sugar Act altered some of the original mercantilist features of the Molasses Act of an earlier date. Moreover, there had been mercantilist restrictions on the American colonists for more than a century, and none of these had provoked violent resistance. There can be no doubt that colonists were long since used to mercantilist restrictions, and peoples are unlikely to revolt against that to which they have become accustomed. The fact is that when representatives of the colonists gathered at the Stamp Act Congress to air their grievances, they announced that what they fundamentally opposed was "taxation without representation," a thing contrary to the British constitution. They readily granted—at first—that Britain had the right to regulate their commerce. It follows, then, that the immediate provocation to resistance was not mercantilist measures.

But this is only to look at things from the surface and to wrench them out of a much broader historical context where they belong. Suppose that instead of asking why and what the colonists resisted we ask why the British persisted in passing measures which provoked the colonists. More directly, why did Parliament attempt to raise revenues from the colonies in ways that departed from custom and long established policy? Why did they lay direct and indirect taxes on the colonies?

The answers to these questions are not far to seek. The British government was in dire need of new sources of revenue. The wars of the eighteenth century had been highly expensive, and the indebtedness of the government was mounting. The debt in 1755—just prior to the Seven Year's War (or French and Indian War as it was known in America)—stood at about £75,000,000. By 1766 it had mounted to £133,000,000.[1] The British people were heavily taxed, and new taxes were being added. The reaction in the mother country to an added tax on domestic cider is instructive. "The news of the passing of the cider act was the signal for 'tumults and riots' in the apple-growing countries of England, and many producers of cider threatened to cut down their orchards if the excise were collected."[2] In short, the heavily taxed British were in no mood to accept additional burdens.

By contrast, American colonists were generally lightly taxed, and several colonies had no government debt to speak of. For example, one historian describes the situation in Pennsylvania in this way: "Not only were the inhabitants relieved of all *ordinary* charges of government during the years 1760-63 but, aside from a revived excise tax on liquors, they also enjoyed such relief during the remainder of the period down to the Revolution. Moreover, the personal and estate taxes . . . represented a per capita levy of less than one shilling . . ." by 1775.[3] A report from Maryland in 1767 indicated that "all levies for the support of the provincial government—in contrast to those for the support of the clergy, the schools, and other county and parish charges—amounted to less than £5,500, an annual per capita tax of about a shilling."[4] Though not all the colonies had such a pleasant tax situation, neither was it generally unpleasant. On top of this, colonial governments had been reimbursed for their military outlays during the French and Indian War.

If these conditions be accepted at face value, if there be no looking behind them, it would appear that the case of Britain's taxing the colonists would certainly be understandable and probably justifiable. But the situation does warrant an examination of the background. British taxation of the colonists broke a long-term contract with them—so the colonists said—and heralded a major policy turn. Back of this policy shift were the mercantilistic policies and practices which had produced a domestic crisis for the British which their government tried to relieve by bringing pressure on the colonies.

The contradictions of mercantilism had produced a long harvest of bitter fruit, some of which the British government and people were no longer willing to accept. No more, in justice, could the American colonists to expected to accept them. It is true that the debates of the 1760's and 1770's were not usually conducted in terms of mercantile policy. The contradictions were there, however, and policy changes should be viewed in the light of them. During this time, Adam Smith was putting together his monumental work, *The Wealth of Nations*, which laid bare the fallacies and contradictions of mercantilism. It may be accounted appropriate, too, that this work appeared in print in 1776, the same year as the Declaration of Independence. A little examination into British mercantilism will show its role in producing an impasse between Britain and America.

Mercantilism was a composite of ideas and practices which had grown helter-skelter over a couple of centuries before the revolt in the American colonies. Most of the ideas were formulated in the seventeenth and eighteenth centuries, but some of the practices associated with it are much older. The theory of mercantilism was the first faltering effort at devising a general theory of economics in the modern era. As some thinkers cut loose from a Christian framework and attempted to look at things naturally, they devised a crude economics to fit new preconceptions. The theory was weighted down with two assumptions, however, which were cultural in origin rather than natural.

The first of these assumptions was made up largely of what is commonly called the bullion theory. Bullionism is the notion that wealth consists of precious metals, particularly gold, and that the value of everything else derives from the fact that precious metals will be exchanged for it. It is understandable that men should have come to think in this way. Gold was the most universally acceptable medium of exchange in both East and West. It hardly deteriorates; it weighs little in proportion to its exchange value for other things; it has many practical uses; and it is malleable. Men ever and again mistake money, because it can be exchanged for goods, for the source of the value which their demand gives to the goods. Small wonder, then, they should make this confusion about gold when gold is valued as a commodity as well as a medium of exchange.

The second major assumption of mercantilism was nationalistic. That is, mercantilists thought exclusively about how a single nation might enhance its wealth by increasing its supply of gold. One nation's wealth, as they saw it, was usually gained at the expense of another nation. Ordinarily, one nation gains gold from another nation which is losing its supply. (It is interesting to speculate that mercantilistic theory and practice may well have been born out of the intense desire of many countries to separate the Spanish from the great hordes of gold they had found in the Americas.) According to the bullion theory, then, one nation's wealth is increased by diminishing that of another.

The thrust of mercantilism was to make trade into a contest among the governments of nations. This was so because trade was now conceived of as a potential means for increasing the bullion holdings of a nation. This would be accomplished, according to mercantilists, by way of a favorable balance of trade. A favorable balance of trade is said to exist when the goods and services which one nation sells to another exceeds those bought from the other. In brief, a nation had a favorable balance of trade when exports exceeded imports. This was thought to be "favorable" because the difference would be made up in gold and the "wealth" of the nation thus favored would be augmented. A nation which imported more than it exported would, of course, have an unfavorable balance of trade.

Numerous practices which might help a nation to get a favorable balance of trade were contrived or justified by this theory. The practices were usually aimed at increasing exports and decreasing imports. Imports could be decreased if more of the goods consumed in a country were produced there. To that end governments encouraged manufacturing by special charters and encouraged the growing of certain crops by subsidies and bounties. Of course, imports were more directly discouraged by tariffs, quotas, and discriminatory charges levied against foreign suppliers. Similar practices also might help a country to increase its exports.

Colonies were conceived of as being particularly valuable in enhancing the wealth of a nation. Frequently wanted were raw materials for manufacturing as well as produce which could not be grown economically at home. If such exotic products could be acquired from colonies they need not be imported from some other country. In addition to this, a colony might have an unfavorable balance of trade with the mother country and thus be a source of the precious metals it would send to make up the trade deficit.

The American continental colonies were part of a British empire which had been shaped in the seventeenth and eighteenth centuries as a result of the mercantile policies of England. Initially, the kings of England had attempted to plant and benefit from colonies by granting them as monopolies to private companies and proprietors. These companies and individuals were empowered to regulate the activities of those who came over so that the undertakings would benefit the owners and, perchance, enhance the wealth and power of England. Things did not work out that way very consistently. Colonists frequently cared little enough about whether they benefited the original charter holders or not; instead, they concentrated their efforts on doing what was to their own benefit. Moreover, as colonists gained some measure of control over their governments, they often enacted their own mercantile policies with the intent of making a colony self-sufficient.[5] Such action ran counter to British aims, of course.

By the mid-seventeenth century, then, Britain was ready to begin to impose a general system of mercantile restrictions on the colonists.

The most general of the mercantile acts are those known as the Navigation Acts. A series of these acts was passed over the years from 1651 through 1663. The number of acts passed was increased because legislation passed in the 1650's was considered invalid after the restoration of monarchy in 1660. This being the case, the later acts are the only ones that need concern us here. The Navigation Act of 1660—reenacted in 1661—required that all trade with the colonies be carried in English-built ships which were manned predominantly by Englishmen. "English" was defined for this purpose to include the inhabitants of the colonies. All foreign merchants were excluded from the commerce of the English colonies, and certain enumerated articles, e. g., tobacco, could be exported from the colonies only to Britain or British possessions. The Staple Act of 1663 provided that goods to be exported from European countries to English colonies must first be shipped to England.

"These acts intended to give England a monopoly of the trade of her colonies," one historian notes:

—not a monopoly to particular persons, but a national monopoly in which all English merchants should share. The Staple Act meant not only that English merchants would get the business of selling to the colonies but also that English manufacturers might dispose of their wares at an advantage in that the foreign goods which had to pass through England en route to the colonies might be taxed, thereby raising their prices and enabling English goods to undersell them. Similarly, the enumerated article principle assured that most of the colonial staples important to England would be exported by English merchants, who were also guaranteed employment for their vessels through the exclusion of foreign vessels from the English colonies.[6]

Parliament passed another Navigation Act in 1696, but it was only an effort to tighten the administration of existing law rather than to add new features.[7]

British legislation also attempted to prevent certain kinds of manufacturing and trade from developing in the colonies. The Woolens Act of 1699 prohibited the export of wool or woolen goods from a colony either to other colonies or to other countries. The Hat Act of 1732 prohibited the exportation of hats from the colony in which they were made, and limited the number of apprentices a hatmaker might have. The Molasses Act of 1733 placed high duties on molasses, sugar, and rum imported into the colonies from any source other than British colonies. This was an attempt to give the British West Indies a virtual monopoly of the trade. It may also have been intended to increase income from the tariff or to reduce the shipping activities of New Englanders. The Iron Act of 1750 permitted pig iron to be exported from the colonies to England duty free but prohibited the erection of new iron mills for the finishing of products in the colonies.

There were other types of mercantile regulations than those above. Over the years, it was usually illegal for specie (gold coins) to be exported from England to the colonies. The British tried to encourage production of wanted goods in the colonies by paying bounties. For example, the British government paid these premiums to importers of colonial naval stores: "£4 a ton for pitch and tar; £3 a ton for resin and turpentine; £6 a ton for hemp; and £1 a ton for masts, yards, and bowsprits."[8]

The purpose of all these regulations and restrictions was to make the colonies profitable to Britain, of course. To that end, the colonists were encouraged to produce goods which could not be competitively produced in England, discouraged to compete with the mother country, encouraged to send specie to England, discouraged from receiving specie from that country, and discouraged from developing markets in America which could serve either England or other countries. There were, however, many unwanted side effects of these policies. They are commonly referred to as the inner contradictions of mercantilism.

The most dire result of mercantilism was war. Indeed, some believe that mercantilism did not so much lead to war as war led to mercantilism. One writer says that the "needs of constant warfare, especially its costs, had encouraged every power to develop and marshall its resources, attempting to become self-sufficient, especially in the sinews of war. . . . This economic nationalism, generally described as *mercantilism*, is less a theory than a weapon—the use of economic means to serve political ends."[9] There is no doubt that mercantilist methods were used sometimes in warfare, but the usual causal relation is the other way around. Mercantilism ranges government power behind the commercial activities of a nation, uses government power to support the merchants of a nation against those of other nations, prohibits trade activities of foreigners in order to give advantages to native tradesmen. In order to support or protect their tradesmen, other nations retaliated with similar restrictions and sought colonies which would be protected trade areas for their people. If trade is free, competition is peaceful, but mercantilism shifts the contest into the realm of governmental power. When governments contest for advantage in this way they are moving in the direction of the ultimate recourse—war.

Such were the results of mercantilism in the seventeenth and eighteenth centuries. War followed upon war with monotonous regularity as naval and colonial powers contested with one another for dominance and advantages. The wars between the British and Dutch in the mid-seventeenth century were clearly mercantile in origin and character. Nettels notes that the Navigation Act of 1651 "precipitated the First Anglo-Dutch War of 1652-54."[10] Further, he says that the "acts of 1660-63 threatened to exclude the Dutch completely from the English colonies and consequently new fuel was added to the old rivalry. In 1664 occurred the Second Anglo-Dutch War. . . ."[11] It was not simply incidental, either, that during this conflict the English gained control of the Middle Colonies in America. A third war broke out in 1672. "Although a Dutch fleet recaptured New Amsterdam in August 1673 the treaty of peace in 1674 once more restored it to England—an act which marked the passing of the Dutch menace to England's North American trade."[12]

Unfortunately, it did not end the rivalry in North America nor the train of mercantilistic wars. France was now emerging in the latter part of the seventeenth century as a major power under the aggressive leadership of Louis XIV. Louis courted English monarchs so that they would allow him room to operate to fulfill his ambitions on the continent of Europe. The courtship may have been the undoing of Charles II and James II; at any rate, it came to an end with the Glorious Revolution in 1688. A Dutchman, William of Orange, became William III of England and joint ruler with his wife Mary during the rest of her lifetime. In very short order, Britain went to war with France (King William's War) and by so doing began a series of conflicts with that nation which did not finally end until the Congress of Vienna in 1815. Since other nations and their possessions were usually involved in these conflicts between England and France, these wars may well be called world wars.

While King William's War of the 1690's was ostensibly fought to maintain a balance of power in Europe, the colonies were at stake, also, at least potentially. One history indicates that in issuing his declaration of war "William took cognizance of the offenses of Louis' subjects in America against the English colonies there—in Newfoundland, in Hudson Bay, in the West Indies, in New York, and in Nova Scotia."[13] Though there was considerable fighting in America, there were no significant territorial changes as a result of that war.

Maps of North America showing territorial possessions of European powers and changes in them from 1700-1763 indicate something of the bearing of the colonial situation on the great wars of this period. In 1700, the English held only a relatively narrow strip of the eastern coast of North America from New England to Georgia, with claims running back to the Appalachian mountain chain generally. Most of the territory which is now Canada was then claimed by France, along with the vast hinterland region drained by the Mississippi River. South and west of these were the extensive Spanish possessions. The English hold on the continent was still precarious, and the colonies were surrounded except on the side of the Atlantic Ocean by territory claimed by other European powers. This situation would be dramatically altered by 1763 as a result of the wars.

The War of the Spanish Succession (1702-13, known in England as Queen Anne's War) was fought over issues which were tied to the question of who would dominate the Americas. Louis XIV was determined that his grandson should become king of Spain immediately and should eventually succeed him to the throne of France. This would not only bring under one person two great powers in Europe but would also link two massive empires in America. This was an intolerable prospect for England. As one history puts the matter: "For Holland and England, it was a war over colonies and trade. These two countries were determined to prevent a union of the French and Spanish crowns; but they were above all determined to prevent France from getting into a position to block their own commercial and territorial ambitions in America."[14] At the conclusion of the war, provisions were made for perpetual separation of the French and Spanish crowns, and Britain gained new territory in America: Newfoundland, Acadia, and the Hudson Bay territory.

England got involved in war with Spain in 1739, known as the War of Jenkin's Ear, and a part of the struggle was over possession of Georgia. There was some fighting in America, but it was very limited, for the conflict shifted to Europe and the more general convulsion known as the War of the Austrian Succession (1740-48). This war did not result in any territorial changes, though there were changes in alliances on the continent of Europe which affected future events.

The peace that followed this second of world wars in the eighteenth century was unusually brief. The French and Indian War broke out in America, 1754; it involved most basically a contest over territory in what is now western Pennsylvania between the French and Indians on the one hand and the British and English Americans on the other. As an extension of this conflict, a general war broke out in Europe in 1756, known as the Seven Year's War. A major conflict continued in America, reaching its climax with the Battle of Quebec in 1759. There the British forces decisively defeated the French. By the Treaty of Paris of 1763, the British got all the French Canadian holdings and French and Spanish territory east of the Mississippi.

The British had apparently emerged triumphant in these wars against France. The American colonies now had an extensive domain to be opened up and exploited; it was a long way to the frontiers of any other European colonial power. A vast British empire had been acquired and was ready for the shaping.

So it may have looked to an imperialist, but the British Parliament and people were confronted with grave difficulties in the wake of the apparent triumph. There was, as earlier told, a huge debt in England in 1763 as a result of the wars. It was a debt of a size that would most likely dwarf all the profits gained thus far from mercantilist policies. But even if the balance books had stood otherwise, the contradictions of mercantilism would still, most likely, have produced an impasse.

One of the fallacies of mercantilism is that the wealth within a nation constitutes the wealth of a nation. Wealth in Britain was not distributed among the inhabitants equally but individually possessed. Undoubtedly, some merchants, manufacturers, shippers, and tradesmen extracted great wealth as a result of special favors within the mercantile system. But this need not have increased the wealth of the populace in general. Indeed, when it is understood that mercantile policies restricted the entry of goods from other lands and raised their prices, it becomes clear that the populace in general frequently suffered rather than benefited from mercantilism. When the burden of taxes to pay for mercantile wars was added to this—taxes levied on the populace in general—it is easy to understand why there was widespread dissatisfaction in Britain.

Of course, the British government did not proclaim mercantilism a failure. Even if this had been clearly understood at the time, it is doubtful that those in power would have reversed their policies. At any rate, they did not do so. Instead, they laid the blame for difficulties on American evasion of mercantile restrictions, determined to enforce them more vigorously, and declared that the Americans must be taxed to help pay for the wars, a portion of which had been fought in their defense.

This course of action seemed eminently fair to many Englishmen. After all, the colonists had been prime beneficiaries of British protection. Moreover, many Americans were reported to be living well if not luxuriously. Not only that, but to make matters worse, these colonists paid very little by way of taxes. Such expenses as they had incurred in the recent French and Indian War had been reimbursed from the British treasury. Surely, there could be no reasonable objection to mild taxation of the colonists. As a matter of fact, there could and would be, but we have not yet come to that part of the story.

What is most relevant here is the impact of mercantilism on the American colonies. The question has been raised by some historians as to whether the colonists were not really the beneficiaries of British mercantilism rather than the victims. The fact that many Americans prospered under the system is submitted as evidence that they benefited from the system. There is also negative evidence that Americans had rough going economically after the break from England. The reasoning underlying this argument confuses *because of* with *in spite of*. The thrust of mercantilism is not such that it would produce prosperity in general for those on whom it is imposed. Its thrust is to siphon resources from the colonies (and other countries) into the mother country. To restrict manufacturing, to deny the development of local markets, to constrict intercolonial trade, and to make the mother country the port of entry for many goods could hardly benefit the colonists generally.

Perhaps the most fundamental flaw of mercantilism is the view that a nation's wealth can be increased by exporting more in goods and services than is imported. This policy was quite harmful to colonies without providing corresponding benefits to Britain. The British succeeded in a "favorable" balance of trade with the American mainland colonies. The most immediate effect was the gold drain from the colonies to Britain. This tendency was augmented by prohibiting the export of gold from Britain. Moreover, many of the ways by which the colonists might have made up the difference were denied to them by mercantile restrictions.

In consequence, the colonists suffered a shortage of specie. The practical effect was that colonists paid higher prices for goods coming from England than they would have had to do if a free market in gold had existed, because gold was more plentiful in Britain than in America. It is even doubtful that British merchants benefited from this situation as much as might be supposed, for they usually made loans to Americans to enable them to buy their goods. Americans also had their credit in England augmented by such payments as reimbursement for participation in wars (an augmentation at the expense of British taxpayers).

Much of the economic activity within the colonies was an uphill effort to overcome the ill effects of mercantile policies. Probably, the fixing of slavery so extensively can be ascribed in the main to mercantilism. (British policy was opposed to the emancipation of slaves because slaves were frequently collateral for loans.) Planters were driven to expand their production—to the acquisition of more and more slaves—in the often vain hope of balancing their trade. The Triangular Trade by New Englanders, which included the slave trade, was an extended effort to get specie. The paper money emissions which became so common toward the close of the period were efforts to deal with the monetary crisis. Of course, many of the efforts of colonists to find ways to deal with the situation were prohibited before they were well established.

In sum, the break from England was preceded by an impasse attributable to mercantilism. More than a century of wars had been fought in the pursuit of mercantile aims by Britain. These had left a heavy burden of debt which the British people found hard to bear. Thus, the government turned to the colonies as a new source of revenue. But the colonies were hardly in a position to take on the burden. They were already drained of specie, and many colonists were deeply and perpetually in debt to British merchants. To say that they were lightly taxed at home answers nothing as to what the effect of British taxation would be. Mercantile restrictions imposed barriers between Britain and the colonies. An imbalance of trade already existed, with the colonies on the "unfavorable" end of that. Tax payments to Britain could only be made by reducing imports or going deeper in debt to British lenders. When the time came for resisting, colonists made their justifications along different lines than those above, but what they were resisting had been brought on by the mercantile impasse.

7

The First
American Crisis: 1763-66

It may well be that the pivotal event for the onset of American resistance was the coming to the throne of the United Kingdom in 1760 of George III. He was the third of the Hanoverian monarchs of England, the grandson of George II who immediately preceded him, and the great grandson of George I. He was the first of this line of British rulers to be native-born, a fact he thought worth emphasizing. When George III came to the throne, he was in the first blush of manhood, and this promising young man should have been a welcome relief from the rule of his grandfather, who had no high regard for his own abilities. Indeed, the powers of the monarch had declined greatly in the unsure hands of both George I and George II. It was commonly said that ministers were kings during this earlier period, and there can be no doubt that the Whigs had dominated so long that the government was run by factions within a party rather than by political parties.

It became clear rather quickly that George III intended to change much of this. He meant to bring the executive authority into his hands and to direct the course of Parliament as well. George III was a man of strong will—unbendably stubborn when he had set his mind on a course—much courage, and already in grasp of some of the principles of power when he was crowned.

One of his first acts was to displace William Pitt, the Elder, from leadership of the government. Beyond that, he acted to break up the dominance of the Whig party, professing to want members of the cabinet who were the ablest instead of those who belonged to a particular party, but probably moved also to this as a means of loosening Whig rule. His method of dominating Parliament was not particularly subtle: he bought the necessary numbers by handing out sinecures to those who would do his will. He visualized himself as a patriot king who would not only restore some of the glory of monarchy but also instill pride and greatness in the people over whom he ruled. Instead, it was his lot to see the dismemberment of his empire, and the British people determined to limit the power once again of a briefly resurgent monarchy.

This new king's determination to rule as well as to reign affected the colonial situation in two ways particularly. Whig ministers had generally ruled with an eye toward accommodating the Americans rather than using undue force. For example, Pitt arranged to reimburse the colonies for their effort during the French and Indian War rather than insist that they should honor requisitions without hope of return. Over the years, Parliament had permitted the colonies to legislate for themselves—subject to having their acts vetoed, of course—rather than imposing legislation upon them for their internal arrangements. As the new monarch broke up this Whig rule, he appointed officers more concerned with imposing British rule and less concerned with maintaining good trade relations which would benefit British merchants.

Secondly, the new monarch augmented his power by increasing the number of appointive positions. By appointments he rewarded his friends in Parliament and increased the number of people who owed their positions to him. This fact of political life gave George III incentive to maintain larger armies and navies as well as more civilian agents in the colonies. That such actions did not endear the monarch to his colonial subjects did not greatly trouble him during the early years of his rule.

It is difficult to decide exactly when the train of events got under way which led to open resistance in the colonies. The British government adopted a more rigorous enforcement of the navigation laws during the French and Indian War. As already noted, George III came to the throne in 1760. Convention has it that the train of events began in earnest in 1763. But there was one bellwether event which occurred in the colonies before that time. It involved a court case which was argued in 1761 in Massachusetts over the issuance of writs of assistance in that colony. A writ of assistance was a kind of general search warrant without a fixed date of termination which would enable officers to search for merchandise illegally brought into the colonies. Unlike a search warrant, it did not require the naming of the place to be searched or what goods were to be located. Such writs had been issued in 1755, and there were applications for new ones after George III came to the throne.

James Otis took the leadership in opposing the issuance of new writs before the court in the old townhouse in Boston. If Otis had contented himself to argue against the issuance of the writs on the grounds simply that there were few precedents for them in more recent times, the occasion might not have been remembered. But he went much further than this: he proclaimed such writs to be contrary to reason and denounced them as arbitrary and tyrannical by nature. According to John Adams' reconstruction of his speech, he said: "Every one with this writ may be a tyrant; if this commission be legal, a tyrant in a legal manner also may control, imprison, or murder any one within the realm. . . . Every man may reign secure in his petty tyranny, and spread terror and desolation around him."[1] He declared his opposition to them in emotionally charged language: "I will to my dying day oppose with all the powers and faculties God has given me, all such instruments of slavery on the one hand, and villainy on the other, as this writ of assistance is."[2]

James Otis lost this particular case before the court, but he emerged from it as the man who would take the earliest leadership in presenting and arguing the American cause. His local popularity was vouchsafed in the ensuing election when he became representative for Boston in the Massachusetts legislature. For the next three or four years he used his pen as well as his forensic abilities to formulate and expound the rights of Americans and the limits of British rule. Whether he would have continued his early leadership role in the later stages of resistance will never be known, for he was inactivated by bouts with insanity after 1769.

A cluster of events in 1763 does mark a turning point in British and American relations, as has been commonly held. Up to that point, there is no evidence of resistance to British rule, though, of course, there were objections to particular actions. To all outward appearances, Americans generally accepted British rule if it could not be said that they were always contented with it.

In retrospect, historians are apt to see that the stage was already set for independence. Trends were well on their way to fruition which prepared the way for American separation. Americans were very nearly cut loose already from the Church of England which was the religious basis of being English. Colonists had much experience in politics which prepared them for governing themselves. There was widespread sensitivity to any dangers to liberty in actions by the British government. The natural law philosophy was familiar to thinkers, and was at hand to serve as a basis both for breaking from England and erecting new governments. Feudal, mercantile, and religious restrictions were very nearly anachronisms in America already.

Even so, Americans were a long way from being ready for independence in 1763. The above were conditions which might well have continued to exist for a long while without leading to independence. Americans still professed their allegiance to the king, as they would continue to do for more than a decade. Their rights and privileges they still traced to England, and the claims to their property to royal grants. There was as yet neither a sense of unity among the continental colonies nor any factual unity, except for a common allegiance to the British monarch. The conference at Albany in 1754 had shown how little desire there was for common action by the colonists.

Resistance to Britain, then, was provoked by changes in British policies, and these began most notably with a cluster of actions in 1763. Most of what happened in 1763 was not so much the provocation of resistance as the prelude to it. One of the most momentous of the developments of that year was not provocative at all. It was the Treaty of Paris which brought to a conclusion the Seven Year's War. By its terms, Britain got all French territory in Canada and all territory east of the Mississippi river, except New Orleans, belonging to both France and Spain. No longer were the American colonies threatened by European powers with immediately adjacent territories. It was now much easier to think in terms of independence from Britain.

Restrictions on opening up this new territory did provoke many colonists. Pontiac's Rebellion broke out as Indians feared and resisted encroachment by the white man in the interior. The British government attempted to prevent settlement beyond the mountains by the Proclamation of 1763. The crucial part of the Proclamation is found in this prohibition: "that no governor or commander in chief of our other colonies or plantations in America, do presume for the present, and until our further pleasure be known, to grant warrant of survey, or pass patents for any lands beyond the heads or sources of any of the rivers which fall into the Atlantic Ocean from the west or north west. . . ."[3] The effect of this on colonists has been described in this way: "The establishment of the boundary line of 1763 blocked at once the plans of land companies such as the Ohio Company of Virginia which had a grant west of the line, and the schemes of new companies which planned to take up land in the Ohio and Mississippi valleys. The whole region on which men had fastened such high hopes was now reserved to the despised Indians."[4] These restrictions were particularly galling in view of the fact that taxes were shortly to be levied on the colonists to help pay for their defense.

Another symptomatic event occurred in 1763. It is known as the "Parson's Cause." It was a symptom both of the potential for resistance to British impositions and of the limits to that resistance at this time. The "Parson's Cause" was a court case arising out of the payment of the Anglican clergy in Virginia. A Virginia Act of 1748 provided that each such clergyman should have an annual salary of sixteen thousand pounds of tobacco. Confronted with a crop failure in 1758, the Virginia legislature authorized that all debts and taxes payable in tobacco could be paid at the rate of two pence per pound of tobacco, a rate of about one-third the price that tobacco was bringing. The Privy Council in England disallowed the law, and some clergymen sued for damages. The most famous suit was brought by the Reverend James Maury. The court found the law invalid and remanded the case to trial before a jury to determine the amount of damages to be paid.

The case attained its fame because of the efforts of Patrick Henry, who was one of the lawyers opposing Maury. Patrick Henry's arena was politics, and the endeavor in which he excelled was oratory. It took him a while to discover this. He was an undistinguished student. He tried his hand twice at storekeeping, and was a failure both times. His efforts at becoming a farmer met with a like reward. He then studied law briefly, and was admitted to practice at the age of 24. He rapidly acquired a sizable practice, and emerged as a popular political leader and a much sought after lawyer following the "Parson's Cause." His fiery oratory in defense of colonial rights eventually earned him a special niche in history books and a unique position among American heroes.

According to the Reverend Mr. Maury, who was, of course, a biased witness, Patrick Henry "harangued the jury for near an hour" toward the close of the case known as "Parson's Cause." He argued that the Virginia Act of 1758 met all the qualifications of good law, and "that a King, by disallowing Acts of this salutary nature, from being the father of his people, degenerated into a Tyrant and forfeits all right to his subjects' obedience." Moreover, he declared that it was the duty of the clergy of an established church to support law, and not to be going into the courts to challenge it. The jury upheld Mr. Maury's claim, as it was informed by the court it must, and awarded him one penny's damage for his losses. British rule had been technically vindicated, but everyone perceived that Henry had, in fact, won the case. His remarks about the king's becoming a tyrant were greeted with murmurs of "treason,"[5] but neither judge nor jury reproved him. Virginians were used to maneuvers by which the will of British rulers was thwarted. There was nothing new in this. Henry's rhetoric was audacious, however, and the reward he received in public admiration suggests that sentiment was shifting away from ancient loyalties toward new visions.

Occasions for expressing these changing sentiments were not long in coming. In fact, a change in ministries in Britain had occurred before some of the above events which set the stage for provocative action. In April of 1763, George Grenville became Chancellor of the Exchequer and formed around him a new government. Grenville should have been able to deal with Britain's financial problems, if anyone could, for he had long experience in finance. He had served earlier as a lord of the treasury and as treasurer of the navy. Moreover, "Grenville's chief concern was revenue and economy; they were his passion, which he pursued relentlessly. . . . He could not endure the sight of red ink, an unbalanced budget, or waste and extravagance. . . ."[6] King George found him to be a bore with his interminable talk of money, but Grenville was the man given the task of doing something, and do something he did from 1763 to 1765.

George Grenville's ministry was responsible for two major lines of action on the American colonies. One was the tightening of administration and enforcement of the laws. The other was the passage of laws which were aimed at raising revenue from the colonies. An apparently casual action by Parliament in 1763 set the stage for much that followed. In March of that year funds were voted for maintaining a standing army in America. This was handled without much ado, since there was already an army in America in connection with the war. Grenville had a more direct hand in stationing naval vessels in America. He was First Lord of the Admiralty, and had much to do with getting the law passed which effected this. "The law gave naval officers power to act as customs officials. . . . By the autumn of 1763, naval vessels were cruising in American waters from Newfoundland to the West Indies, with their officers and crews on the alert for the profits to be gained from the capture and successful prosecution of illegal traders."[7] A profound change was occurring between Britain and her colonies; the decision to have military force available was a prelude to increased exercise of authority by Britain. This change could be made with little fanfare because it did not differ on the surface from what had just been done during the French and Indian War.

That Grenville meant business should have been clear from his orders to customs officials in 1763. Appointments to major customs posts in the colonies had long been sinecures for Englishmen. Quite often they drew their pay while continuing to reside in Britain. Grenville decreed that henceforth they must reside in America. Many who held such positions resigned rather than to go to live in the colonies, and new officers were appointed in their stead.

Grenville took the lead in getting much new legislation for the colonies in 1764. The key piece of legislation is the one usually referred to as the Sugar Act, though it dealt with a great deal more than sugar. The act lowered the duties on molasses coming into the colonies, prohibited the importation of rum, added items to the enumerated lists, and provided strenuous regulations on shipping for its enforcement. The greatest departure from precedent in it was that it was designed to raise revenue. The preamble reads, in part: "Whereas it is expedient that new provisions and regulations should be established for improving the revenue of this kingdom . . . .: and whereas it is just and necessary, that a revenue be raised, in your Majesty's said dominions in America, for defraying the expences of defending, protecting, and securing the same; we . . . have resolved to give and grant unto your Majesty the several rates and duties herein after mentioned."[8]

Even more galling to many people involved may have been the onerous regulations on shipping from the British West Indies. Captains of vessels had to have affidavits, certificates, definitive listings of goods, and had to post bond. Moreover, the burden of proof that he had in every way complied with the law was placed on the shipper in order to reclaim a vessel after it had been seized by the authorities. The Act read, in part: ". . . if any ship or goods shall be seized for any cause of forfeiture, and any dispute shall arise whether the customs and duties for such goods have been paid, or the same have been lawfully imported or exported, or concerning the growth, product, or manufacture, of such goods . . . , the proof thereof shall lie upon the owner or claimer. . . ."[9] In addition, the act provided mandatory decisions for juries, partially, at least, taking discretion from them. "The result of these provisions was to free customs officers from virtually all responsibility for their actions. . . . Small wonder that the Americans fought back."[10]

The Currency Act of 1764 was yet another attempt of the British government to impose its authority. This act forbade the colonies south of New England to make any further issues of paper money which would be legal tender in any sense. They were now to be at the mercy of a money situation which was artificially tipped in favor of Britain.

The colonists had hardly had time to take in the implications of the Sugar Act when Parliament passed the Stamp Act. It was passed in March of 1765. The Stamp Act required that after November 1, 1765, stamps be used on all legal papers, commercial papers, liquor licenses, land instruments, indentures, cards, dice, pamphlets, newspapers, advertisements, almanacs, academic degrees, and appointments to office. The money collected from the sale of stamps was to go to the British treasury to be used for expenses incurred in America. This act was the most clear-cut departure from tradition yet made by the British government, for it placed a direct tax on the Americans, something that had not been done before.

It was followed in very short order by an indirect taxing measure, an act known as the Quartering Act, passed in May of 1765. The act provided for the quartering of troops in the facilities of colonial governments, in alehouses and inns, and in unoccupied dwellings. So far, so good, but the act also provided that "all such officers and soldiers, so put and placed in such barracks . . . be furnished and supplied there by the persons to be authorized or appointed for that purpose . . . with fire, candles, vinegar, and salt, bedding, utensils for dressing their victuals . . . without paying any thing for the same. That the respective provinces shall pay unto such person or persons all such sum or sums of money so by them paid. . . ."[11] In short, the colonies were to be indirectly taxed for the maintaining of troops in quarters; they might levy such taxes themselves, but they were to be compelled to do so.

However, the fat was already in the fire well before news of the Quartering Act had reached America. Resistance was mounting in America even before the Stamp Act was passed. Some were alarmed by the revenue aims of the Sugar Act, perceiving in them a violation of the principle of taxation without representation. "When it was learned in Boston that the British government intended to collect duties on foreign molasses, the merchants appointed a corresponding committee to consolidate the opposition of the Northern merchants to the Sugar Act and to 'promote a union and coalition of their councils.' "[12] The New York legislature denied the justice of duties placed on the trade of New Yorkers, and declared that it was their right to be free of involuntary taxes.[13]

But it was resistance to the Stamp Act that drew the colonies together in a unity of opposition. Opposition was shaping up even before the act was passed. Nor was Parliament wanting in opponents of the taxing idea. When Charles Townshend asked: "Will these Americans, children planted by our care, nourished up by our indulgence . . . , will they grudge to contribute their mite . . . ?" He was answered in resounding terms in a speech by Sir Isaac Barré:

> They planted by your care? No! Your oppressions planted 'em in America. They fled from your oppression. . . .
> They nourished by your indulgence? They grew up by your neglect of 'em. As soon as you began to care about 'em, that care was exercised in sending persons to rule over 'em. . . .
> They protected by your arms? They have nobly taken up arms in your defence. . . .[14]

This was the famous "Sons of Liberty" speech, for Barré used the phrase in describing the Americans, and it came to be used as the basis of organizations in America. Before the Stamp Act was passed, several colonial legislatures went on record as opposing it. All this was to no avail, the die had been cast in 1764, and Parliament proceeded to the enactment of a direct tax.

Not only was Parliament misinformed as to the probable reception of the act in America, but even colonial agents representing colonies in England had misjudged American sentiment and determination. Several agents accepted commissions as stamp agents, actions which they were to regret. Even the usually prudent Benjamin Franklin caused friends to be appointed stamp agents and expressed himself of the opinion that the wise course would be to abide by the law.[15]

Whether it would have been wise to do so or not, obedience was not the course followed in America. On the contrary, Americans moved from opposition to resistance to outright defiance. Colonial legislatures adopted resolutions against the tax. Virginia led the way under the prodding of Patrick Henry. He charged that the Stamp Act was an act of tyranny and was reported to have declared: "Tarquin and Caesar had each his Brutus, Charles the First his Cromwell, and George the Third—" The Speaker of the House interrupted him to declare that he had spoken "Treason!" With only a brief pause, Henry continued: "—may profit by their example! If *this* be treason, make the most of it."[16] Not all of Henry's resolutions were adopted by the House of Burgesses (though they were all published in newspapers elsewhere), but, of those that were, the following gives the crux of the argument:

> *Resolved.* That the taxation of the people by themselves, or by persons chosen by themselves to represent them, who can only know what taxes the people are able to bear, or the easiest method of raising them, and must themselves be affected by every tax laid on the people, is the only security against a burthensome taxation, and the distinguishing characteristick of British freedom, without which the ancient constitution cannot exist.[17]

Massachusetts sought to go beyond the action of separate resolutions by colonial legislatures to some sort of common action. The assembly of that colony, therefore, sent out a call for a congress. It was fulfilled, at least partially, by the meeting of the Stamp Act Congress in New York in October of 1765. Six legislatures sent delegates, and three other colonies were represented by delegates not so formally chosen. The delegates in Congress assembled affirmed their allegiance to the king and their willing subordination to Parliament when it acted properly. But they resolved that there were limits to this authority, some of which they spelled out:

> That it is inseparably essential to the freedom of a people, and the undoubted right of Englishmen, that no taxes be imposed on them but with their own consent, given personally or by their representatives. . . .

That the only representatives of the people of these colonies are persons chosen therein by themselves, and that no
taxes ever have been or can be constitutionally imposed on
them, but by their respective legislatures.[18]

The most dramatic action, of course, was direct action. The groundwork was laid for direct action by the Committees of Correspondence,
and much of it was done by the Sons of Liberty. The first effort was
to secure the resignation of stamp agents, without whom the stamps
could not readily be distributed. In some colonies, stamp agents resigned when they perceived the temper of the people. In others they
held out for awhile, and were subject to threats, abuse, and humiliation.
The case of Jared Ingersoll of Connecticut who had accepted an appointment as stamp agent while in England as colonial representative shows
the lengths to which crowds went sometimes to secure a resignation.
"They caught Ingersoll at Wethersfield and silently and pointedly led
him under a large tree. They parlayed for hours . . . , with Ingersoll
squirming, arguing and refusing to resign. The crowds . . . grew so
large and threatening that finally Ingersoll read his resignation to the
mob and yielded to the demand that he throw his hat in the air and
cheer for 'Liberty and Property.' "[19]
So successful was this direct effort that on the day that the Stamp
Act was to go in effect there were no stamps available in the mainland
colonies. The question became now whether business would go on as
usual in defiance of the law. If the law were observed, ships would not
sail, courts would not hold sessions, newspapers would not be published, and much of life would come to a standstill. Many newspapers
continued to be published; ships sailed, and some courts carried on business. In short, the colonists operated in defiance of the law.
Parliament was confronted with a crisis in America, one of its own
making, when it convened in December of 1765. However, the king's
speech opening the session acknowledged only that "matters of importance have lately occurred in some of my colonies in America. . . ."[20]
Even so, Parliament had to take some kind of action. It had to take
Draconian measures to achieve enforcement, or it had to back down.
Grenville's ministry had already fallen, and a new government was
organized under the leadership of Rockingham. With the matchless
orator, William Pitt, Earl of Chatham, taking the lead in the debate
for repeal, the House voted 275 to 167 for repeal on February 22, 1766.
The bill was signed into law on March 18. However, Parliament refused
to yield on the principle, for it insisted on passing the Declaratory Act,
which went into effect on the same day that the Stamp Act was repealed.
The Declaratory Act tried to make up in unyielding language for what

had, in fact, been yielded. It declared, in part: "that the King's majesty, by and with the advice and consent of the lords spiritual and temporal, and commons of *Great Britain*, in parliament assembled, had, hath, and of right ought to have, full power and authority to make laws and statutes of sufficient force and validity to bind the colonies . . . in all cases whatsoever."[21]

The theoretical issue was joined, but the crisis had passed—for the moment.

This was the first American crisis. It was the first because for the first time all the colonies were drawn together in action and resistance to Britain. Heretofore, they had been separate, linked only by their common allegiance to Britain; now, they had been linked without that tie in common sentiment and for a common cause. Not only that, but they had seen Britain falter before their resolution and back down.

Several other points need to be made about this crisis. One is that it was provoked by British action. Parliament was the innovator, abandoning precedent to tax the colonies, extending itself to direct taxation, which hardly anyone in America would admit was its right. The colonists were defending; in an important sense, they were conservative, for they were attempting to preserve the rights and privileges they had enjoyed. Another point is that the course on which Parliament was bent was potentially tyrannical. Force was being assembled in America; Parliament was moving to take colonial control of their domestic affairs from them. Thirdly, the colonists based their arguments on the rights of Englishmen and the British constitution. They were not rebelling; they were resisting what they perceived as unconstitutional action.

The colonists drew a line beyond which they said Parliament was not to go. They denounced direct taxes imposed from without, and distinguished between internal and external taxation; the latter some theorists held to be acceptable. Parliamentary leaders learned from this debacle. Never again would they act so directly on America. They would now try by less direct means to accomplish their object. But the Americans had been aroused; henceforth, every act of Parliament would be examined with great care to see if there was in it a potentiality for oppression. Such acts were not long in coming.

8

British Acts
Become Intolerable

The repeal of the Stamp Act in early 1766 did not put an end to resistance in America. It did lower the level of the contest between Britain and America from its crisis proportions by removing the most conspicuous irritant. But repeal of the Stamp Act only whetted the appetite of some Americans for much more thoroughgoing removal of British impositions. As early as April the New York Sons of Liberty were demanding that "Americans should also insist on the removal of all restrictions on trade, the abolition of post offices and admiralty courts, and they should do so 'while the colonies are unanimous.' "[1]

After all, most of the parliamentary acts against which the colonists objected were still on the books, and executive action remained unaltered. Troops were still stationed in America, and naval ships of war were stationed along the coast. The Sugar Act was still in effect. New York merchants sent a petition to Parliament in 1766 complaining bitterly about the effects of trade restrictions upon their commerce. Restraints upon imports and exports of sugar were particularly galling, and their trade was hurt badly by limitations on how wood products could be sold.[2] The Quartering Act still placed requirements on the colonies involved which some of them refused to comply with. The Currency Act restricted the issuance of paper money both upon colonies which had responsibly retired theirs in the past as well as those which had not. And there was the Declaratory Act with its strident claims about the unlimited powers of Parliament.

The colonists employed a variety of tactics in their resistance to British impositions during the decade or so after 1763: some legal, some extra-legal, and others illegal. These tactics ranged from resolutions of legislatures, to petitions to the government in England, to unauthorized conventions and congresses, to boycotts, to demonstrations, all the way to rioting and the intimidation of officials by mobs. The use of some of these latter tactics in recent years has been justified on the grounds that they were employed by our venerated forebears—an excuse whose merits would be dependent upon analogous conditions. It may be of some use to examine the conditions of the resort to violence by some Americans of that earlier time, both for the light it will shed on their situation as well as what it may tell us about the appropriateness of this justification for contemporary violence. By such an examination, too, the issues between the colonists and the British can be sorted out.

What tactics are appropriate is surely dependent on the options available. To understand what options were available to the colonists, one needs to review the political situation.

The colonists did not fully control their governments. Far from it, in most cases. Usually, the governor was appointed from England (the charter colonies of Connecticut and Rhode Island were exceptions), and he quite often received instructions from officials there. No more did the colonists ordinarily choose the members of the governor's council. The assembly was popularly elected, but its actions could be severely circumscribed. It met on call from the governor, could have its acts vetoed by him, and was subject to being dismissed or dissolved by the executive. There were even efforts to control assemblies from England. For example, the New York legislature was suspended for its failure to provide supplies for the troops under the Quartering Act. Therefore, legislatures were greatly hampered when it came to preventing impositions on the colonies. No direct action was open to them ordinarily because of the power of governor and council to negate such action.

Nor was there any established means for intercolonial action; none had ever been set up, and the British were not about to allow any to be legally established during the decade under consideration. At best, only extra-legal means were available for concerted action across the lines of colonies. The means for legal action by the colonists were limited then, not, as is the case usually, the means for some minority to express itself, but for the colonies as a people. This distinction is quite germane both for the justifications of revolution which would be offered in the 1770's and for such justification as there could be for illegal action prior to the revolt.

Now the elected legislatures had gained considerable power during the colonial period, as was shown in an earlier chapter. That power derived mainly from their authority to originate taxes and appropriations. Governors even depended upon the elected legislature for their salaries in most colonies, and all actions requiring moneys awaited legislative action. Governors and other crown officials were dependent upon or subject to the local populace in other ways as well. The force that had ordinarily been at their disposal before the period under discussion had to be exercised by militia and other local persons. Crown officials had to act through courts whose judges might be appointed by governors but whose most basic decisions were made by juries; and they could, themselves, be brought before the courts for mistreating colonists.

In short, a precarious balance of powers had grown up over the years in most colonies. Colonial legislatures were counter-balanced by governors and councils, and the governor's power was limited by the necessity of his relying upon elected legislatures. Action depended upon a considerable measure of co-operation among the branches of government. If they would not act together, many kinds of action could not be taken.

Massive resentment was aroused in the 1760's, then, when Parliament moved to alter these arrangements: by taxing colonists, by making appropriations, by sending standing armies, by setting up admiralty courts without juries, and so on. The thrust of parliamentary action was to eviscerate the independence of elected legislatures. The Quartering Act points this up, for the act required that colonies appropriate supplies for troops within the colony. If a legislature had to act in this fashion, it was hardly independent of Parliament. If Parliament could tax the colonists, it could appropriate moneys to free officials within the colonies from dependence on the legislatures. The fear of this was no phantom, for Parliament was moving in this direction on governor's salaries. Of course, taxation by Parliament raised another basic issue. The Connecticut legislature put the matter in this fashion in 1765:

> That, in the opinion of this House, an act for raising money by duties or taxes differs from other acts of legislation, in that it is always considered as a free gift of the people made by their legal and elected representatives; and that we cannot conceive that the people of Great Britain, or their representatives, have right to dispose of our property.[3]

In fact, Parliament was moving to unbalance the powers within colonies and make the colonies subject to itself. The colonists raised the question from the outset whether Parliament had the authority to do this. This question, in turn, led to an even more basic one: What was the extent of parliamentary authority over America? This was a question for which no definitive answers had ever been given. As Richard Bland of Virginia said in 1766: "It is in vain to search into the civil constitution of *England* for directions in fixing the proper connection between the colonies and the mother-kingdom. . . . The planting of colonies from *Britain* is but of recent date, and nothing relative to such plantation can be collected from the ancient laws of the kingdom. . . ." He argued that "As then we can receive no light from the laws of the kingdom, or from ancient history to direct us in our enquiry, we must have recourse to the law of nature, and those rights of mankind which flow from it."[4] Others sought to base the argument, however, on charter rights.

Colonial spokesmen generally maintained that Parliament could properly regulate relations among the parts of the empire and with other nations. They accepted the sovereignty of the British government over them and did not question—during the early years—that Parliament played a role in changes in the actions of the sovereign. Beyond these general functions, Parliament should not go. The position of Parliament regarding its powers over the colonies was set forth in the Declaratory Act: it could legislate for the colonies in all matters whatsoever.

Who was right? The answer to that question depends on what is right. The majority in both houses of Parliament never proposed to consider the question. They did not doubt that they had the authority to take what actions they would (Where were the limits upon them?), and they did not appear to doubt that when called upon they would have the necessary power to enforce their acts. It was not a matter of what was right (a minority in Parliament disagreed about this), it was only a matter of what was expedient.

The colonial opposition, from the beginning, did tackle the question from the angle of what was right. They believed that Parliament, by right, was limited in what it could do. They believed that the original charters, the British constitution, and, in the final analysis, the laws of nature, set bounds to the authority of Parliament. The colonists should be adjudged to have been right, then. Since Parliament chose to act on the grounds of expediency, it is only fair that they should be judged, in part, on those grounds. It turned out not to have been an expedient course, for by it the American empire, except for Canada, was lost. Since Parliament did not choose to stand on right, the colonist's position as to right can be accepted without diffculty, because it was not contested.[5]

In any case, Parliament and the colonies were on a collision course each time they acted from their opposite premises. Parliament might, and did, find it expedient to back down on particular issues, though not on the general principle. The colonists, on the other hand, since they did not suppose themselves to be acting from expediency, did not back down. Once Parliament no longer found it expedient to back down, the die was cast.

Parliament plunged ahead with new legislation aimed at the colonies in 1767. The leader in formulating this legislation was Charles Townshend, and it became known as the Townshend Acts. For a while after the repeal of the Stamp Act, things began to look better for the colonies. William Pitt formed a cabinet, and he had been quite outspoken on the side of the colonies during the debates over the Stamp Act. In fact, Pitt was far and away the most popular Englishman in America at this time, though truth to tell he had little competition. But Pitt was made the Earl of Chatham, moved into the House of Lords, and was debilitated by illness. The legislative leadership passed to Charles Townshend, chancellor of the exchequer, in 1767.

The act which has drawn the most attention was the one levying import duties on glass, lead, painter's colors, paper, and tea. During the debates over the stamp tax the distinction between internal and external was talked about considerably. Some got the impression that Americans accepted external taxes, but not internal ones. Operating from this premise, Townshend argued that Americans should accept these new duties, since they were levied on imports and would be considered external taxes. The act indicated that it was for the purpose of raising a revenue, that such moneys as were raised would go first to defray costs of governing in America, that what was left would go to the British treasury, and that the duties must be paid in silver. It also authorized the use of writs of assistance to be used in searching for goods on which duties had not been paid and specifically empowered "his Majesty's customs to enter and go into any house, warehouse, shop, cellar, or other place, in the *British* colonies or plantations in *America*, to search for and seize prohibited or uncustomed goods" with writs which courts in America were directed to issue.

Another act, passed at the same time, was the American Board of Customs Act. This established a board of customs for America, to be composed of five commissioners, and to be located at Boston. A little later in the year, an act was passed suspending the New York legislature for not providing troop supplies. In a similar vein, an act in September of 1767 curtailed the power of colonial elected legislatures. Finally, an act passed in July of 1768 extended and spelled out the jurisdictions of vice-admiralty courts in the colonies and increased the number of courts in America from one to four.

Resistance to the Townshend duties, as to the other British actions, was preceded or accompanied by theoretical formulations, formulations which held that British action was in violation of immemorial rights. These theoretical formulations frequently appeared first as a series of anonymous letters in newspapers and then as pamphlets, though the order might be reversed. America had quite a number of men ready to enter the lists with such writings at critical junctures. James Otis, Samuel Adams, Daniel Dulany, and Richard Bland provided some of the early grist for the mills of opposition.

The man who came forward to do duty against the Townshend Acts was John Dickinson, a Marylander born, who was sometimes from Pennsylvania but most regularly from Delaware. He belongs in that select circle of men entitled to be called Founding Fathers. From 1767 to 1775 he was the theoretician of colonial resistance. Though he opposed declaring independence, he headed the committee which produced the Articles of Confederation. He served in the army for a time during the War for Independence and was a delegate to the constitutional convention from Delaware, though leadership in such matters was now in other hands.

Dickinson's position on the Townshend duties was published as a series of letters published weekly in the *Pennsylvania Chronicle and Universal Advertiser* beginning November 30, 1767. These collected letters were called *Letters from a Farmer in Pennsylvania*. New England newspapers began publishing them in December, and before it was over all colonial newspapers except four published them. They were published as a pamphlet in 1768, went through seven American editions, one in Dublin, two in London, and a French translation.[6] A historian sums up their impact in this way: "Immediately, everyone took Dickinson's argument into account: Americans in assemblies, town meetings, and mass meetings adopted resolutions of thanks; British ministers wrung their hands; all the British press commented, and a portion of it applauded; Irish malcontents read avidly; even the dilettantes of Paris salons discussed the Pennsylvania farmer."[7]

For one thing, the tone of the *Letters* was right. Dickinson not only claimed a formal loyalty to the king and the empire but actually cast his argument in terms of the well being of the empire. Though the natural law philosophy underlay much of what he wrote, he did not emphasize natural laws and natural rights so as to distinguish them in a divisive manner from the rights of Britons under the Constitution, as some writers had rushed to do prematurely. His appeal was to tradition, precedent, prudence, self-interest, the desire of liberty, and continuity with the past. And though he bade Americans to resist the Townshend duties, he proposed that they do so in an orderly fashion. First, they should send petitions; if these did not get results, turn to something like a boycott of goods; only when all peaceful means had failed, should other approaches be considered. But he pled with Americans not to give in to a spirit of riotousness. "The cause of *liberty* is a cause of too much dignity to be sullied by turbulence and tumult.

It ought to be maintained in a manner suitable to her nature. Those who engage in it, should breathe a sedate, yet fervent spirit, animating them to actions of prudence, justice, modesty, bravery, humanity and magnanimity."[8]

The great appeal of his work stemmed, of course, from the fact that he shredded the argument for the Townshend duties, showed it to be grounded in sophistry—no better than the case for the Stamp Act, only more subtle—and found the duties violative of the rights of British subjects and potentially confiscatory. As for these duties being acceptable because they were external taxes, he thought the case hardly worth considering. The objection to taxation by Parliament did not hinge upon the distinction between internal and external; it was to taxation as such. Americans accepted, he pointed out, as they had accepted, duties that were for the purpose of regulating trade, but not those levied for the raising of revenue. The latter were clearly taxes, and they involved the taking of property without the consent of the owners. True, incidental revenues might arise from the regulation of trade, but they were a consequence, not the cause of it. No such case could be made for the Townshend duties; they were laid on items which must be obtained from England. Certainly, it was not the aim of the British to inhibit trade in them nor to restrain it. In fact, it was simply a tax, for the colonists were not permitted to obtain the goods elsewhere, and might, if the British chose, be prohibited from manufacturing them. There was ample precedent for this.

Property was no longer secure, Dickinson said, if the principle of parliamentary taxation of the colonies be once accepted. "If the parliament have a right to lay a duty of Four Shillings and Eight-pence on a hundred weight of glass, or a ream of paper, they have a right to lay a duty of any other sum on either. . . . If *they* have any right to tax *us*—then, whether *our own money* shall continue in *our own pockets* or not, depends no longer on *us*, but on *them*. 'There is nothing which' we 'can call our own; or, to use the words of Mr. Locke—WHAT PROPERTY HAVE' WE 'IN THAT, WHICH ANOTHER MAY, BY RIGHT, TAKE, WHEN HE PLEASES, TO HIMSELF?' "[9]

Colonial elected legislatures began to act in 1768. Massachusetts took the lead in February by drawing up a Circular Letter which it sent around to the other colonies. This letter was subsequently endorsed by New Hampshire, Virginia, Maryland, Connecticut, Rhode Island, Georgia, and South Carolina, sometimes by assemblies, and, if they were not sitting, by the Speaker.[10] The British reply came from the Earl of Hillborough in April; it was sent as a circular letter to the governors of all the colonies. He had already written to Governor Bernard of Massachusetts that at the next session of the House of Representatives he "must 'require' " them "to rescind the Circular Letter and declare" their " 'disapprobation of and dissent to that rash and hasty proceeding.' "[11] To the other governors, he declared that his expectation was that their assemblies would not participate in this new effort to arouse resentment to British rule. "But if notwithstanding these expectations and your most earnest endeavors, there should appear in the Assembly of your Province a disposition to receive or give any Countenance to this Seditious Paper [the Massachusetts Circular Letter], it will be your duty to prevent any proceeding upon it, by an immediate Prorogation or Dissolution. . . ."[12] In June, Hillsborough ordered troops to Boston.

It was obvious from these and other instances—the harassment of shippers by customs agents, the increasing of military forces in the colonies, the rejection of petitions—that petitions and resolutions alone would not produce a change in British policy. The colonists, then, moved toward attempting to hit Britain where it would hurt—in trade. Boston took the lead in adopting a non-importation agreement in August of 1768. What they proposed to do, among other things, was to cease almost all imports from Britain. The movement to do this spread through the colonies, though it was rough going. Understandably, importers and shippers were not overly enthusiastic about this, especially those for whom this was a major source of income. Moreover, it needed to be a concerted effort throughout the colonies. If it were not, ports which remained open could put the efforts of the others to naught. Colonists did succeed in closing down the major port cities in America to most British imports in the course of 1769. The best weapon against ports which did not co-operate was to cut off commercial relations with them. This usually brought them into line.

Though non-importation was far from absolute, it did succeed. Imports from Great Britain into the colonies fell from £2,157,218 in 1768 to £1,336,122 in 1769.[13] Some ports did much better than this average. For example, Philadelphia's imports from Britain dropped from £432,000 in 1768 to £200,000 in 1769 to £135,000 in 1770.[14] More importantly, since the object of non-importation was not simply to reduce imports from Britain, the British began to back down once again in the face of determined colonial opposition. In 1769, Parliament moderated its position on the Quartering Act to allow colonies to supply troops on their own initiative.

More success for the colonies was to follow with the coming of a new ministry. Lord North became, in effect, Prime Minister in early 1770, a position which he was to hold until 1782. During these years he served George III as best he could, doing his will during a time when a man of lesser loyalty and fortitude would have sought a less demanding job. He served his king first by acting to reduce tensions in America. In April, the Townshend duties were repealed, except for the tax on tea. Some concessions were also made in the application of the Currency Act.

It was not long before the non-importation agreements began to be abandoned. There was considerable sentiment for continuing them—after all, the tax on tea had not been repealed, nor had other sources of tension been removed—but many of the merchants had had enough of such self-denial. By various maneuvers, they opened up the ports to British goods once again. This course was the more attractive generally because the hasty efforts at increasing domestic manufactures to replace British imports had produced few tangible results.

The colonies were comparatively calm during 1771. Although there had been clashes between British troops and colonists at New York and Boston (the latter leading to the "Boston Massacre") in 1770, these did not expand into any general conflict. Such as remained of the British threat to the colonies was difficult to dramatize; there can hardly be said to be a trend toward oppression if the oppressive measures are being reduced. At any rate, no major figure ventured forth to attempt any dramatization. Even though tea continued to be taxed, the amount of tea imported into the colonies from England increased from the low point for the past several years of 110,000 pounds in 1770 to 362,000 pounds in 1771.[15]

It was, however, the calm before the storm, the clouds for which began to gather in 1772. The first of these was the burning of the revenue ship, the *Gaspée*, by Rhode Islanders in June. The *Gaspée* had been harassing shipping coming into Rhode Island for some time; the captain was particularly obnoxious in his treatment of those on ships stopped for searches. The *Gaspée* ran aground, and while she was in that disabled condition, a party boarded her, drove the crew off and burned the ship. An investigating committee turned up no useful information but its appointment from England stirred resentment. A little later in the year, the British Exchequer took over the payment of the salaries of the governor and judges in Massachusetts. Here was the move that had been long feared: to remove crown officials from reliance on the elected legislature. In November, Boston formed a committee of correspondence which sent statements to other towns in Massachusetts and to all colonial assemblies. Early the next year, the House of Burgesses in Virginia established a committee of correspondence, and most other colonies followed suit.

What stirred the colonists to open resistance once again, however, was the Tea Act in May of 1773. The purported intent of this act was to rescue the East India Company. That company was in dire straits, on the verge of bankruptcy, and sorely in need of a market for its tea. Though imports had picked up in the American market, it is generally believed that most of the tea consumed in America came from the Dutch; by buying such tea the colonists unlawfully evaded the tax on it. The Tea Act was devised to make tea from the East India Company almost irresistible. It enabled that company to sell tea directly in America, relieving it of the necessity of selling it first at auction to merchants in England. "By eliminating the middleman . . . the company was able to sell tea in the colonies cheaper than in England," even though it was still taxed in the colonies. "More significantly, its tea now undersold that of the Dutch smugglers."[16]

The British were about to succeed in doing what John Dickinson indicated to be the danger. They were going to establish a monopoly for a taxed item, something which could not be competitively produced in America, but was very popular. It is likely that had Parliament contented itself with establishing a monopoly it might have got away with it. But the fact that tea was taxed entangled the monopoly question with taxation-without-representation. The objections which had been raised before had now a fresh exemplar; but now Americans were to be seduced into compliance by a lower price.

It did not happen. True, the East India Company caused chests of tea to be loaded on many ships for America, and these put into port at Boston, Philadelphia, New York, and Charleston. The colonists were ready for them; they would not buy or consume the tea, nor would they allow it to be landed if they could help it. The most dramatic opposition occurred at Boston, where Bostonians dressed as Indians boarded the ships and heaved the chests into the water. Patriots prevented tea from being landed in Philadelphia. It was landed and transferred to the customs house at Charleston; there it stayed until war came.

This time Parliament did not back down when confronted by colonial resistance. The majority determined, instead, on a policy of coercion, a policy backed by four acts passed between March 31st and June 2nd of 1774. They are known formally as the Coercive Acts. The force was to be concentrated on Boston and Massachusetts. The Boston Port Act closed the port of Boston to commercial shipping until such time as the East India Company had been compensated for the tea. The Massachusetts Government Act provided that the governor's council would be appointed by the king, not elected as had been the case, that the governor and king would appoint judges, that juries would be chosen by the sheriff, and that town meetings could not be held without the consent of the governor, except for annual election meetings. The Administration of Justice Act was of general effect and provided for the trying of certain officials from the colonies in England, if the governor thought it necessary. The Quartering Act applied generally to the colonies, also; it authorized the quartering of troops in occupied dwellings.

The colonists dubbed them the Intolerable Acts.

9

Prelude to Independence

The issue was joined, and unremittingly pressed, after Parliament passed the Coercive Acts in 1774. George III declared in September of that year that "the die is now cast, the colonies must either submit or triumph. . . ."[1] Young Alexander Hamilton put the matter this way: "What then is the subject of our controversy with the mother country?—It is this, whether we shall preserve that security to our lives and properties, which the law of nature, the genius of the British constitution, and our charters afford us; or whether we shall resign them into the hands of the British House of Commons. . . ."[2] Heretofore, when Britain had been faced by colonial resistance, Parliament had backed down. This time, Parliament held its ground, and the executive prepared to use force. When that happened, a new dimension was added to the issue, the dimension of independence—independence or submission.

Colonial leaders did not rush to formulate the issue in this way. On the contrary, they clung to the connection with Britain, continued to profess their allegiance to the king, and indicated a willingness to negotiate if Britain would attend to their grievances. Indeed, George III had been ruling for sixteen years before independence was declared, specific grievances had gone unresolved for thirteen years, and British troops were encamped against American forces for more than a year. Colonists did sometimes rush to resist particular measures, but they moved very slowly in conceiving of changing their relationship to Britain.

Nor can it be maintained that the colonists moved slowly in grasping the nettle of independence in order simply to manipulate the British into taking aggressive measures which would determine the outcome of the question. The provocation came increasingly without the aid of colonial inducement. Probably, most Americans did not want independence throughout the years of resistance. What is even more certain is that many Americans did not want the quarrel to eventuate in independence and that others who did begin to think of separation were loathe to alienate this goodly number so long as it could be avoided. So far as we can tell, virtually all Americans opposed various of the British measures, with the obvious exception of Crown officials. This near unanimity was sundered by the question of independence. The slowness of the movement for independence to surface can be attributed to the desire to avoid internal divisions as well as, perhaps, the calculation of leaders not to outrun their followers.

The colonists, in any event, did not move swiftly toward deciding for independence; and on the positive side, they employed deliberative bodies when and where they could to make the decisions. Of course, these deliberative bodies were frequently not legal, but they were the nearest thing to it that the colonists had available. From 1774 into 1776 the colonists were frequently denied their legal legislative assemblies; and when these could not meet, other bodies resembling them were assembled.

The main focus of the Coercive Acts was on Boston and Massachusetts. The Boston Port Act which closed the port of Boston until the tea was paid for might conceivably have separated Boston from the rest of Massachusetts, at least for a time. But when other acts followed to alter the government of all of Massachusetts, this potential effect was nullified by Parliament itself. There was a greater probability that Massachusetts would be isolated from the other colonies and that the British might succeed in a policy of divide and conquer. But the colonial leaders were intent on preventing any such policy from succeeding. The Committees of Correspondence were already in existence. Moreover, other colonies had grievances of their own as well as those shared with Massachusetts.

Confronted with the Coercive Acts, some of Boston's leaders wanted to take immediate economic measures against Britain by way of retaliation. However, there was widespread sentiment throughout the colonies for a congress to be held to decide upon what action to take. Providence called for such a congress on May 17, Philadelphia on May 21, and New York City on May 23. The Massachusetts House of Representatives went along with the idea by issuing a call for a congress on June 17. Within colonies, delegates were elected by provincial congresses or county conventions. The First Continental Congress met in September, 1774, in Philadelphia. Twelve colonies sent 56 delegates. Only Georgia did not send delegates, which was not surprising, since that colony was not very populous, its government was not self-supporting, and it was dependent more than others on Great Britain.

But before the Congress assembled, important new formulations of ideas had entered the stream. In July, Thomas Jefferson's *A Summary View of the Rights of British America* appeared, followed in August by James Wilson's *Considerations on . . . the Legislative Authority of . . . Parliament*. While neither of these works necessarily represented colonial opinion, they do indicate the direction in which it was thrusting. The colonists had held firmly to the idea from 1765 on that Parliament could not lay taxes for the raising of a revenue, but they had shifted to a harder and harder position as to what was the authority of Parliament over the colonies. The main objection to the Stamp Act was that it was a direct tax. The major objection to the Townshend Duties was that they aimed to raise a revenue. The Tea Act was opposed at the outset both because it was monopolistic and would raise a revenue. Jefferson of Virginia and Wilson of Pennsylvania went beyond this position to suggest that the legislative assemblies in America were equals of Parliament in law-making and that Parliament really should have no authority over America.

Jefferson's position comes out in part in his criticism of an earlier act of Parliament suspending the legislature of New York. He said, "One free and independent legislature hereby takes upon itself to suspend the powers of another, free and independent as itself. . . ."[3] In a closing impassioned appeal to the king, Jefferson pleaded: "No longer persevere in sacrificing the rights of one part of the empire to the inordinate desires of another, but deal out to all equal and impartial right. Let no act be passed by any one legislature which may infringe on the rights and liberties of another."[4] Through the debates over the years there had been general agreement by colonial spokesmen that it was necessary for Parliament to regulate commerce with other nations. That is, Americans were still very much under the influence of mercantilist assumptions. Jefferson, however, appeared to see no need for such regulation; rather than a benefit to the colonies the regulations interfered with the natural course of trade and set the stage for tyranny. For example, he says: "That the exercise of a free trade with all parts of the world, possessed by the American colonists as of natural right . . . , was next the object of unjust encroachment. . . ." Their "rights of free commerce fell once more the victim to arbitrary power. . . . History has informed us that bodies of men as well as individuals are susceptible to the spirit of tyranny. A view of these acts of Parliament for regulation, as it has been affectedly called, of the American trade . . . would undeniably evince the truth of this observation."[5] In short, the colonies did not need parliamentary regulation of their trade but should rather see it as a usurpation of their rights and an instrument of tyranny.

103

James Wilson's argument is mainly that the only political connection of the colonies was with the king. To support this view, he reviews American history:

> Those who launched into the unknown deep, in quest of new countries and habitations, still considered themselves as subjects of the English monarchs, and behaved suitably to that character; but it nowhere appears, that they still considered themselves as represented in an English parliament extended over them. They took possession of the country in the *king's* name: they treated, or made war with the Indians by *his* authority: they held the lands under *his* grants, and paid *him* the rents reserved upon them: they established governments under the sanction of *his* prerogative, or by virtue of *his* charters. . . .[6]

The principle toward which Wilson was moving is one which eventually came to be known as the dominion theory of empire, a theory in which each province had its own government but continued to have allegiance to the English monarch. John Adams argued this case more explicitly in the *Novanglus Letters*, which appeared after the First Continental Congress had dissolved itself.[7]

The First Continental Congress had a relatively brief session from September 26 to October 22 of 1774. It dealt with four major points during that time. The first of these was the Suffolk Resolves which were presented by Massachusetts delegates and when confirmed were formal advice from the Congress to that colony. The Resolves declared the Coercive Acts unconstitutional, advised Massachusetts to form its own government until such time as the acts were repealed, recommended that the people of that colony arm themselves and form a militia, and called upon them to adopt economic sanctions against Britain. This was, indeed, a strong stand against British action, and it is not too much to label it defiance.

The Congress next dealt with the Galloway Plan of Union. It was the work of Joseph Galloway of Pennsylvania, and is usually considered to have been conservative in character. Be that as it may, the Plan was intended not only to provide a general government for the colonies but to do so within the general frame of royal and parliamentary authority in the British empire. The Plan was defeated, but there is little reason to suppose that had it been adopted anything would have come of it.

The Declaration and Resolves was the major policy position adopted by the Congress. It set forth the rights of the colonies, enumerated the abuses of recent years, delineated, once again, the limits of parliamentary authority, and called for economic sanctions. A considerable debate occurred within committee as to whether they should found their argument for rights on natural law or not.[8] The issue almost certainly was not over whether there is natural law and natural right but over the impact of referring to them on the colonial relationship to Great Britain. Those determined to preserve the connection with Britain wanted to hold on to the idea of their tracing their rights to Britain. Once the claim went to the laws of nature the basis for making a definitive break would be laid. The outcome, however, was that the Congress confirmed both sources for their rights. The preamble to the ringing statement of rights reads:

> That the inhabitants of the English colonies in North America, by the immutable laws of nature, the principles of the English Constitution, and the several charters or compacts, have the following rights [among others]:
> That they are entitled to life, liberty, and property, and they have never ceded to any sovereign power whatever, a right to dispose of either without their consent.
> That our ancestors, who first settled these colonies, were at the time of their emigration from the mother country, entitled to all the rights, liberties, and immunities of free and natural-born subjects within the realm of England.
> That by such emigration they by no means forfeited, surrendered, or lost any of those rights. . . .[9]

The line of action they were to undertake was provided for by the establishment of a Continental Association. The men gathered at the Congress hoped to get British policy altered by the use of economic sanctions. They adopted a program of non-importation, non-consumption, and non-exportation from, of, and to Britain, the non-exportation to be put into effect later than the others. Enforcement was to be carried out in this way. "In the first place, the people were asked to pledge themselves not to buy British merchandise—the Nonconsumption Agreement—thus leaving ill-disposed merchants no market for their proscribed wares. Secondly, the enforcement of the Associated was entrusted to local committees. . . ."[10] Economic sanctions are, of course, a two-edged sword: they hurt the imposers as well as those on whom they are imposed, though not necessarily in equal degree. In any case, they were probably the most nearly peaceful means open to the colonists to attempt to inflict damage on the British. In the colonies there was much sentiment that whatever they did without would be good for them, in any case.

Whatever the merits of economic sanctions in general, they did not lead to a peaceful resolution of the dispute between the colonies and England. The great majority of those in power in England favored the use of force now to bring the colonists to terms. Colonial petitions, declarations, and resolutions were rejected with alacrity by Parliament. Colonial agents in London were refused in their request to appear before the House of Commons on behalf of a petition from America by a vote of 218-68. Petitions fron London and Bristol merchants were denied an effective hearing by a vote of 250-89. William Pitt, now Earl of Chatham, offered a resolution for the withdrawal of troops from Boston; it was defeated by the Lords temporal and spiritual, 68-18. Charles James Fox's effort to get the ministry censured by the House for its American policies was defeated 304-105.[11] On February 2, 1775, Lord North, the king's chief minister, declared that some of the colonies were in a state of rebellion and that more troops should be sent to America.[12]

Since the two sides were now set on a collision course, it was only a matter of time until the contest would erupt into open hostilities. On February 9, Parliament officially declared Massachusetts to be in a state of rebellion. On February 26, British troops attempted but failed to seize colonial military supplies at Salem. Late in the month Lord North succeeded in getting what was billed as a conciliatory plan through Parliament. It permitted the colonies the option of taxing themselves instead of having the tax imposed by Parliament for meeting imperial expenses. The concession hardly interested the colonies. On March 22 Edmund Burke, longtime friend of America in Parliament, made his famous speech calling for reconciliation with America. It did not sway Parliament, but the next day Patrick Henry addressed his fellow Virginians in a speech of a different temper which may have helped to sway a continent. Had it been heard by all colonials in the version with which later Americans are familiar, it would surely have aroused the passions of many of them for action. Henry grew weary of the vain efforts of those seeking peace by some strategem or other. To those of this temper, he cried:

> Gentlemen may cry peace, peace—but there is no peace. The war is actually begun! The next gale that sweeps from the North will bring to our ears the clash of resounding arms! Our brethren are already in the field! Why stand we here idle? What is it that gentlemen wish? What would they have? Is life so dear or peace so sweet as to be purchased at the price of slavery? Forbid it, Almighty God—I know not what course others may take; but as for me, give me liberty or give me death!

No more were Lord North and the king determined upon peace. On March 30, Parliament passed the New England Restraining Act, which barred the North Atlantic fisheries to New Englanders and prohibited any trade between these colonies and anyone else except in Britain and the British West Indies. The next month these provisions were extended to several of the colonies south of New England. On April 14 General Gage got his orders to use force to break up the rebellion in New England. He acted with dispatch by sending troops to Concord on April 19 under orders to seize a munitions depot there. These troops were met by colonials at Lexington, someone fired ("the shot heard round the world," Thomas Paine said), and a small battle took place. It was enlarged during the course of the day, as riflemen gathered from all sides and threatened to destroy the British forces at one point. Reinforcements arrived, however, and the British were able to return to Boston. Seventy-three British troops were killed during the day, and a lesser number of colonials. Fighting on a war-like scale had taken place; the resolution of the British and the Americans would now be tried by arms.

Less than a month after Lexington and Concord a Second Continental Congress assembled at Philadelphia (May 10). The First Congress had voted its own dissolution, but they provided that a new congress should meet if the disputes had not been settled. So it was that a new body was assembled that would attempt over the next half dozen years to guide the affairs of what was not yet the United States. Among the members of the Second Continental Congress were some of the most talented men ever to grace the American scene, men whose names will live as long as the founding of the Republic is remembered. From Massachusetts came John and Samuel Adams along with John Hancock who was elected to preside over the congress, from Pennsylvania came Benjamin Franklin, Robert Morris, and James Wilson, among others, from Connecticut came Roger Sherman and Oliver Wolcott, from Virginia came George Washington, Richard Henry Lee, and Thomas Jefferson, and so on through the roll call of the signers of Declaration of Independence, as well as many who had left the Congress by that time. Some of the most talented followed other pursuits for the states during the war so that during some of the most trying days it was not so lustrous a body. But at its inception it contained most of the men who would play the leading roles in guiding America to independence.

Congress was confronted with the task of what to do about the fighting from the moment it met. New Englanders had taken matters in hand partially already, and on the same day that Congress met in Philadelphia Ethan Allen and Benedict Arnold led a force of colonials in taking Fort Ticonderoga on Lake Champlain. And on June 17 the

Battle of Bunker Hill took place as a result of a British decision to drive the Americans from a redoubt on Breed's Hill. This battle pitted a British army against a colonial army, and though the British drove the Americans from their positions they did so at the expense of heavy casualties.

Before the Battle of Bunker Hill, however, Congress had acted to take charge of the fighting. George Washington was appointed commander-in-chief of the armed forces of the colonies; he left straightway to take charge of the forces in Massachusetts, which he accomplished on July 3. George Washington had gained considerable military experience in the French and Indian War. He had sided with the colonies from the outset, and while he was never strident in his resistance he was already beginning to show that firmness which was to become his hallmark. A very important consideration at the moment of his selection, of course, was that he was from Virginia, the most populous of the colonies; and the New Englanders could see that it was essential to bring other colonies to their support. The choice of Washington was unanimous, and through all the difficult years and wrangling between Washington and Congress, that body never really faltered in its support of him. Washington chose not to take a salary for his contribution but only to have his expenses paid.

Though feeling was running high in America against Britain, there were those in Congress who believed that they would be remiss in their duty if they did not make yet another effort to achieve reconciliation. John Dickinson took the leadership in drawing up and getting through Congress on July 5, 1775 what is known as the Olive Branch Petition to the king. The members assembled declared themselves "Attached to your Majesty's person, family, and government, with all devotion that principle and affection can inspire. . . ." This being the case, "We, therefore, beseech your Majesty, that your royal authority and influence may be graciously interprosed to procure us relief from our afflicting fears and jealousies. . . ."[13] Recognizing the realities, however, Congress on the next day adopted declarations drawn by Jefferson and Dickinson which explained the occasion for their taking up arms.

Congress adjourned on August 2 to await developments. They were not long in coming, for George III proclaimed the colonies to be in open rebellion on August 23. Benedict Arnold led an expedition to Canada in the fall, with the permission of General Washington. In October, Congress authorized a navy, followed by the opening up of correspondence with other nations in November, with the idea of gaining friends. In November, the colonies received word that the king had refused to receive the Olive Branch Petition. The House of Commons then defeated a motion to make the Petition the basis of reconciliation by a vote of 83 to 33. Late in 1775 a royal proclamation was issued closing the colonies to all commerce after March 1, 1776.

That all these things had occurred and that the colonists still could not bring themselves to declare for independence indicates how reluctantly they took that step. By the winter of 1775-1776, some goodly number had already decided for independence; but many had not. This was a most difficult decision to make, much harder than merely deciding for resistance. Those who took this step must forswear ancient allegiances, must commit the most heinous of crimes (or so they had been taught) by becoming traitors, must hazard their lives and fortunes upon the uncertain outcome of a war, must almost certainly divide the country, and might well let loose domestic disorder on a large scale. Prudent men must ever ponder carefully their course before taking such an irrevocable step. Arguments were made in public for and against independence even as men wrestled inwardly with the difficult question. If men of those times had used such terms as "conservative" and "liberal," which they did not, they might well have debated the question of which was the conservative position. From one point of view, it would have been conservative to have continued old allegiances and connections. But from another angle, Britain was the innovator, and the colonists had insisted all along that they were contending for the ancient constitution and the old order and harmony that had prevailed. Indeed, the father of conservatism, Edmund Burke, saw the justice of their contention though, of course, he could not advise the colonists to become independent.

Probably, much of the waiting was in the hope that England would take some action that would sway the most reluctant toward independence. While this never happened, as time went on, and Britain committed more and more acts, more did decide for independence.

But it was the little book, *Common Sense*, published by Thomas Paine in January of 1776 which did so much to galvanize American opinion in favor of independence. Within three months, 120,000 copies of it were in circulation. George Washington said that it "worked a powerful change in the minds of many men," and the testimony of other contemporaries as well as historians confirms this judgment.

That this little pamphlet should have had such currency and impact must surely be attributed to the fact that it encapsulated an idea whose time had come rather than to the character of its author. Few would have predicted before 1776 that Thomas Paine would have the niche in history which he gained. He was born in Norfolk, England, the son of a staymaker. He had not done well as a government clerk, as a husband, or as manager of his own financial affairs. Benjamin Franklin encouraged him to come to America in 1774, which he did, to be made editor of the *Pennsylvania Magazine*. Somehow he grasped the tendency of the currents in the new land and was able to render them into language which moved his lately acquired fellow countrymen, the phrases of which still ring with power after two centuries.

Paine took as his task in *Common Sense* the convincing of Americans that the time had come for independence. He sought to convince them that the time was right, that they could succeed, and that their fears of the consequences of independence should be seen in contrast with the certainties of ruin if they did not follow the indicated course.

The body of the work begins in a peculiar way; it is theoretical and apparently remote from his object. He iterates the distinction between government and society, a distinction which, he says, people frequently do not take care in making. Society, he points out, is natural in origin; it arises out of the need of man for his fellows. Government, by contrast, is a construct, albeit a necessary one. The point was quite germane, however. Paine was commending to a people that they cast off the government over them. If government and society can be distinguished one from the other, they can be separated. To rend society might be ruinous, but to cast off a government which was not performing its allotted function would only provide the opportunity for something much better.

Much of Paine's rhetoric was aimed at monarchy in general and in particular. The colonists, many of them, had shifted in their thinking to the point where they were willing to acknowledge their allegiance only to the king. This was the remaining cord to be severed. Of the institution of monarchy, Paine said:

> Government by kings was first introduced into the world by the heathens, from whom the children of Israel copied the custom. It was the most prosperous invention the devil ever set on foot for the promotion of idolatry. The heathens paid divine honors to their deceased kings, and the Christian world has improved on the plan by doing the same to their living ones. How impious is the title of sacred majesty applied to a worm, who in the midst of his splendor is crumbling into dust![14]

Of English monarchy, he had even more scathing things to say. Where did the line originate?

> A French bastard landing with an armed banditti and establishing himself king of England against the consent of the natives is in plain terms a very paltry, rascally original. It cer-

tainly has no divinity in it. However, it is needless to spend much time in exposing the folly of hereditary right; if there are any so weak as to believe it, let them promiscuously worship the ass and lion, and welcome. I shall neither copy their humility nor disturb their devotion.[15]

George III was disposed of as the "royal brute of Britain," and a long line of monarchs disparaged as hardly worthy of mention. But the whole subject of monarchs soon palls on him: "Of more worth is one honest man to society, and in the sight of God, than all the crowned ruffians that ever lived."[16]

Paine deals with another difficult point for Americans. England is the mother country, or so it has been claimed. He denies the allegation. Europe is the origin of America, he says, in what may be one of the weakest of his arguments. But, in any case, Britain did not mother America; the inhabitants of the New World were driven from her shores and, in contrast even to the behavior of brutes, she was making war on them. Moreover, there is no reason in an island attempting to govern a continent.

Above all, Paine held up for examination the past record under Britain and contrasted it with the vision of what America should and could be. This should move men to an early separation.

> O ye that love mankind! Ye that dare oppose not only the tyranny but the tyrant, stand forth! Every spot of the Old World is overrun with oppression. Freedom has been hunted round the globe. Asia and Africa have long expelled her. Europe regards her like a stranger, and England has given her warning to depart. O! receive the fugitive, and prepare in time an asylum for mankind.[17]

It took little more to tip the scales for independence. In May of 1776 Congress learned that the king had succeeded in hiring German (generally referred to as Hessian) troops to send against them. On June 7, Richard Henry Lee introduced a resolution to the effect that the colonies were now independent of Britain. On June 11, Congress appointed a committee to draw up a declaration. The painful decision was all but made.

10

The
Declaration of Independence

The Declaration of Independence is a peculiar, unusual, and in many ways, unique document in the modern world. Of revolutions there has been a surfeit, and more, in the last two hundred years. And accompanying them have been pronouncements, directives, statements, proclamations, and declarations enough for a good start on papering the walls of the Pentagon. Of all such documents, however, one stands out and looms above the rest—the Declaration of Independence. Not only has it been revered usually by the people of the United States, provided the grist for innumerable orations, been memorized—in part—by school children; it also has been almost endlessly quoted in reproach of actual American ways and has been looked to by peoples of other lands as a standard. Supreme Court justices have appealed to it, would-be revolutionaries have claimed its rhetoric, while those of a conservative bent have sought their principles within it. For most of the history of the United States only one national holiday—Thanksgiving—has ranked with the 4th of July, the day set aside for celebrating the signing of the Declaration of Independence.

It is somewhat strange and a matter for wonder that this document among all those of an era rich with elegant statements should have attained its unique position. John Adams thought that the second day of July would be celebrated, for it was on that day that the resolution for independence was adopted. Moreover, he later declared of the Declaration that "There is not an idea in it, but what had been hackneyed in Congress for two years before."[1] That portion of the document to which people usually refer is exceedingly brief, comprising, at most, two paragraphs, the first of which is only a sentence in length. The remainder of the document is of historical interest only. Moreover, the Declaration is not now, and never has been, a part of the fundamental law of the United States. It lies outside the structure of law which is made up of constitutions, statutes, and the common law. There are, of course, reasons for its position, and they will come out in an analysis of the document and discussion of its background and extension.

There are three dimensions of the Declaration of Independence which should be carefully considered for a clear understanding of it. The first is the contemporary context within which it was written, adopted, proclaimed, and served its purpose. However much it may have come to belong to the ages, the Declaration had a definite purpose and a particular role at the time. The second dimension is its past. The words and phrases are given their meaning not only within the contemporary rhetoric but also from historical doctrines and beliefs. Too, the later applicability of anything said is conditioned by the context of a then past history. The third dimension is its future. What men have made of the document, frequently out of context and with no attention to the concepts which give it any continuing validity, tells us something of the reason for its importance.

The story of the composition and adoption of the Declaration is fairly simple. Richard Henry Lee's resolution for independence, introduced on June 7, 1776, was not immediately adopted. On June 10, Congress decided to delay further discussion of it until July 1, for many delegates awaited instructions, or changes in instructions, from their legislatures before acting affirmatively for independence. Lee's simple and straightforward resolution would have been adequate for the formal declaring of independence. But America badly needed aid from foreign powers if the appeal to arms was to be successful. Thomas Paine had suggested in *Common Sense* that some sort of manifesto be published in order to gain friends with other nations: "Were a manifesto to be published and dispatched to foreign courts, setting forth the miseries we have endured and the peaceable methods which we have ineffectually used for redress; declaring at the same time that . . . we had been driven to the necessity of breaking off all connections . . .—such a memorial would produce more good effects to this continent than if a ship were freighted with petitions to Britain."[2] This was apparently the origin of the idea for a declaration. Therefore, following the determination to delay adopting Lee's resolution, Congress appointed a committee to produce such a document. The committee was composed of Benjamin Franklin, John Adams, Robert Livingston, Thomas Jefferson, and Roger Sherman.

Thomas Jefferson was assigned the task of producing a draft of the proposed declaration. Had John Dickinson been favorably disposed toward independence at this juncture, the task would probably have been his. Jefferson had only lately acquired a considerable reputation as a writer with his *Summary View of the Rights of British America*. In any case, his selection turned out to have been one of the happiest decisions ever made by a committee. Some minor changes were suggested by Franklin and Adams, and these were incorporated in the document. Congress also made a few alterations.[3] But the finished work was substantially what Jefferson had presented to the committee. Much of the honor which has fallen to the Declaration should be credited to Jefferson's felicity of style, graceful turns of phrase, and the evocative power of words appropriately juxtaposed.

Congress acted quickly once the Lee resolution came before it again on July 1. The next day it was approved unanimously by 12 colonies, though the New York delegation abstained. And then—on the July 4 date which was to be celebrated by posterity—Congress approved the Declaration of Independence.

The stated purpose of the Declaration was to declare to "mankind" the "causes which impel them to the separation." It was addressed, then, to the world at large. It can be conveniently divided into three parts for purposes of discussion: the first is a theoretical justification of revolution and independence; the second is an enumeration of the abuses suffered at the hands of the British; and the third is the formal declaring of independence.

The theoretical justification of revolution is contained in the first two paragraphs, which are also the most often quoted parts of the Declaration. Interspersed through these paragraphs runs a litany of phrases which have become etched in the minds of Americans: "Laws of nature and of Nature's God," "truths to be self-evident," "all men are created equal," "endowed by their Creator," "unalienable Rights," and "Life, Liberty and the pursuit of Happiness." The ideas may have been hackneyed, as John Adams said, but the phrases in which Jefferson caught them elevated them above the trite and ordinary to the sublimity of enduring poetry.

Yet, ideas are dangerous, as every tyrant knows and even parents of small children suspect; and there is no more dangerous context for setting forth thoughts than the one for which these were written. The Declaration not only declares independence but also proclaims revolt —revolution. Sages may debate as long as they will whether the American revolution was indeed a revolution—and the question is important in some of the later meanings of the word—but there can be no doubt that it was a revolution in the root sense of the word. That is, it was a revolt against and a casting off of the governmental authority which had been exercised over the colonies. Not only that, but it was *successful*—the basic distinction between a revolution and a rebellion. Nothing more dangerous to the peace and safety of a people can be imagined than a revolution: the former authority is cast off, whether law and order will be maintained is gravely in doubt, and man's bent to destruction is likely to be loosed from the ultimate means of confining it.

The point of emphasizing the danger of revolution is to enter a warning: the opening paragraphs of the Declaration of Independence are not something to be casually trotted out on any and all occasions. They are a theoretical justification of revolution, and those who intend less than revolution may well take care in how they refer to them. But the point is also to note the qualifying conditions of the document as to what justifies revolt: "Prudence, indeed will dictate that Governments long established should not be changed for light and transient causes; and accordingly all experience hath shewn, that mankind are more disposed to suffer, while evils are sufferable, than to right themselves by abolishing the forms to which they are accustomed."

The case for revolution, as Jefferson presented it, can be summarized in this way. The Creator has endowed men with certain rights. Governments exist for the purpose of securing these rights to those under them. When a government rather than performing these ends primarily begins destroying them, and indicates by a long term trend that it cannot be brought back to its purpose, "it is the Right of the People to alter or abolish it. . . ." This is the nub of the argument.

There is much that is left out of the simple statement of the doctrine of the right of revolution contained in the Declaration of Independence. There was no need to spell it out on this occasion, and many of the restrictions are implicit. The oppressions must afflict the people generally; they must, therefore, be by a power alien to the generality of the people. And the right to revolt belongs, at the least, only to a majority, probably only to a consensus, and, ideally, to the people generally. This is to say that *a minority does not have a right to revolution*. The whole idea of a minority having such a right is shot through with contradictions. The minority could only effect this "right" by overcoming the majority. If a minority had a "right" to alter or abolish a government and to erect another in its stead, it would be a "right" to impose its will on a majority.

Do minorities not have rights, then? Assuredly, they do, or so Jefferson and many of his contemporaries thought. All men have rights; but the recourse to revolution belongs only to the preponderance of the people. But suppose a minority (or, for that matter, a combination of several minorities) is oppressed and persecuted, what recourse do the members have? The Founders believed that the members of a minority have rights as individuals which should be protected in the system along with the rights of those who happen to belong to the

116

majority or consensus. For example, they have the right to persuade others of the justice of their cause—that is, to become the majority. Freedom of speech and of the press are devices for assuring the opportunity of exercising the right of persuasion. But suppose all fails within the system to relieve the oppression? What is the ultimate recourse of a minority? The ultimate recourse of an oppressed minority is migration. The right to migrate for a minority is the corollary of the right to revolution for a majority.

The right of revolution is metaphysical, not existential (and none may logically claim such a right who have not a metaphysics on which to found their case). No government can, in practice, admit the right of its people to revolt against it at any time. The moment such a right is acknowledged effectively, the government abdicates its former power and another government takes its place. No governmental system can be contrived which provides for the right of revolution (though, interestingly, the right of migration can be established). The matter is as clear as it can be when it is seen that the right of revolution involves the right to take up arms against the government. A government ceases to be *the* government when men take up arms against it with impunity. The United States government can decree that the 4th of July is a national holiday—Independence Day—, and celebrations can be held in which the first two paragraphs of the Declaration of Independence are read, but the United States Constitution could not, and does not, incorporate within it the right of revolution. (It does, however, provide for turning out of office some of those who govern, at stated intervals, but the discussion of this can wait.) That is to say, again, the right of revolution is metaphysical, not existential, an explanation of which follows.

The right of revolution has its being prior to, outside of, and beyond government. Jefferson was making his case within a tradition whose groundwork was laid long before. The Declaration of Independence had a past, then, which needs to be a little explored. The two main traditions appealed to are theism and natural law. The rights alluded to are said to be derived from "the Laws of Nature and of Nature's God," and ones with which "they are endowed by their Creator." If there were only history and present existence, no right to revolution could be established, for no government that ever did or does exist could or would accord it. The appeal to right, in this sense, requires an appeal to right that existed before history. It is an appeal to that which and He who was before governments came into being. Although our language has no tense for it, it is an appeal to the timeless and the enduring, to that which has no tense.

In this timeless sphere, Jefferson tells us, "all men are created equal," and are endowed by their Creator "with certain unalienable Rights, that among these are Life, Liberty, and the pursuit of Happiness." This has been, no doubt, the most troublesome passage in the Declaration. What can it mean that all men are created equal? The most immediate meaning, within the time context, is that Americans are equals of Englishmen. They had been contending for this since the dispute between the two had occurred. Americans had claimed that they had the same right to tax themselves as Englishmen, the same right to legislate, and eventually they claimed the same trading privileges. It was the failure of the British government to accord them equal rights which had provoked the dispute. The justification for revolt now became the fact that they had been deprived of their rights. This needs further discussion in terms of what men were to make of the phrase later. Before going into that, one other matter from the past needs to be considered.

The justification for revolt by the colonies was tied up with the institution of monarchy. Whether or not they would have their grievances redressed depended in considerable measure upon the will of the king. Hereditary monarchy had long posed a problem in political theory, at least for Western thinkers. Suppose the monarch were a tyrant? Suppose he imposed his will, in an arbitrary and despotic fashion, over the people? It had long been held, by some, that it was the right of the people to kill a tyrant. However attractive the idea might have been to some Americans, they never seriously considered it. And for very good reason: it would not have settled the issues in contention. But the fact that they were ruled by a monarch gave the colonists a justification for revolution that is denied to those who live under elective executives.

Returning to the matter of equality, it should be stated that the phrase "all men are created equal" had and has a much broader potential of application than to the simple proposition of the equality of Englishmen and Americans. Its meaning is fairly clear in the context: all men have an equal claim to certain natural rights. More, the case is implicit for equality before the law, that is, that the law shall deal with acts and not classes of people. Nor is there any reason to doubt that Jefferson believed this principle applied to blacks as well as whites, and that there should only be free men, not slaves.

Later in American history, some have read the Declaration of Independence into an idealistic framework. It is from this angle that some would see the Declaration as calling for continuing revolution and as a dream for America that is yet to be realized. Such notions separate the doctrines almost entirely from the context of ideas behind them as

118

well as the temporal context in which they were written. Continual revolution is a nonsensical notion; within this context, at least, it could only mean a continual warfare over who is to govern. Jefferson based his argument on metaphysical propositions, not idealistic ones. The equality upon which he bases his position is one that has always been, not one that might someday be achieved. True, he declares that the purpose of government is to secure men their rights. It is surely true, also, that governments have most frequently not done this well. The point may be too abstruse to be readily grasped, but Jefferson was not saying that an ideal government would establish this ideal equality; he was saying that a government performing its *appropriate* function would do so. Of course, the phrases do not touch upon equality within society at all; they apply to equality before the law.

The theoretical justification of revolution contained in the first two paragraphs tells us only that there can occur situations in which a people may be justified in revolting against the authority over them. This is the case, we are told, when the government has consistently abandoned its role of protecting the people in their rights and become the persistent violator of them. It is the burden of the body of the Declaration to show that the British government had done this to America.

The case is summed up in the next to last sentence of the second paragraph: "The history of the present King of Great Britain is a history of repeated injuries and usurpations, all having in direct object the establishment of an absolute Tyranny over these States." It should be noted here that all the acts are blamed upon the monarch. There was, of course, a reason for doing this as a tactic. Loyalty to the king was the tie that Americans had clung to the longest. It was the one which now must be disavowed and broken if independence was to be achieved. Some purport to see in this blaming of all the acts of the government upon the king disingenuousness by Jefferson and those who concurred in his formulations. The charge has little merit; the tactic is fully justified in British constitutional theory. By that theory, the acts of ministers are acts of the king. Even the acts of Parliament are acts of the Crown-in-Parliament. Moreover, the king had neither disallowed nor disavowed the acts in question, which he might have done. If there was disingenuousness to be charged, it should be about the fact that they had delayed so long in laying upon the king the blame for what was happening. Colonists had, for a decade, blamed Parliament and ministers for what was happening. But this, too, is understandable; it was a means of resisting without revolt. Now the case could be stated bluntly, and the blame could be placed where it justly rested, in the final analysis.

In any case, the British government was indicted for its acts by

119

a listing of them in the Declaration, acts charged to George III. Even a truncated version shows how weighty and damaging was the case against him:

> He has refused his Assent to Laws. . . .
>
> He has forbidden his Governors to pass Laws. . . .
>
> He has refused to pass other Laws for the accomodation of large districts of people. . . .
>
> He has called together legislative bodies at places unusual, uncomfortable, and distant from the depository of their Public Records. . . .
>
> He has dissolved Representative Houses repeatedly. . . .
>
> He has refused for a long time, after such dissolutions, to cause others to be elected. . . .
>
> He has endeavoured to prevent the population of these States. . . .
>
> He has obstructed the Administration of Justice. . . .
>
> He has made Judges dependent on his Will alone. . . .
>
> He has erected a multitude of New Offices, and sent hither swarms of Officers to harrass our People, and eat out their substance.
>
> He has kept among us, in times of peace, Standing Armies without the Consent of our Legislatures.
>
> He has affected to render the Military independent of and superior to the Civil Power.
>
> He has combined with others to subject us to a jurisdiction foreign to our constitution. . . .
>
> For quartering large bodies of armed troops among us.
>
> For protecting them . . . from Punishment. . . .
>
> For cutting off our Trade with all parts of the world.
>
> For imposing Taxes on us without our Consent.
>
> For depriving us, in many cases, of the benefits of Trial by Jury.
>
> For transporting us beyond Seas to be tried for pretended offences.
>
> For abolishing the free System of English Laws in a neighbouring Province, establishing therein an Arbitrary government, and enlarging its Boundaries. . . .
>
> For taking away our Charters. . . .
>
> For suspending our own Legislatures, and declaring themselves invested with Power to legislate for us in all cases whatsoever.

He has abdicated Government here, by declaring us out of his Protection and waging War against us.

He has plundered our seas, ravaged our Coasts, burnt our towns, and destroyed the Lives of our people.

He is at this time transporting large Armies of foreign Mercenaries to compleat the works of death, desolation, and tyranny. . . .

He has constrained our fellow Citizens taken Captive on the high Seas to bear Arms against their Country. . . .

He has excited domestic insurrections amongst us. . . .

A case can be made, of course, that there is some hyperbole amongst the charges listed. Some of the acts were done only against selected colonies. One or two of them may have been mere potentiality. Some of the charges are repeated in slightly different formulations. Yet every one of them has substance behind it. The nature of the Declaration was such that an act done against one of the colonies could properly be considered as done against all of them. A jury charged with establishing the facts alleged in the indictment almost certainly would have found Britain guilty of all, or almost all, of the charges brought, after reviewing the mass of evidence that could have been assembled.

The Declaration of Independence was not suddenly sprung upon Britain and the world. The Americans had not suffered abuse in silence, only to lash out in a fit of anger without warning. As Jefferson said: "In every stage of these Oppressions We have Petitioned for Redress in the most humble terms: Our repeated Petitions have been answered only by repeated injury." Not only had appeals been made to the king but also to the British people, or, as the Declaration says, "to our British brethren." But "They too have been deaf to the voice of justice and consanguinity."

But one course lay open to the Americans, then, and they were taking it. The final paragraph declares the independence of the states from Great Britain. The phrases of the concluding paragraph are, if anything, more felicitous than those of the opening paragraphs. The rhetoric, once again, rises above anything remotely petty or trivial to state the case for the ages. There is an appeal "to the Supreme Judge of the world for the rectitude of our intentions," and "in the Name, and by Authority of the good People of these Colonies." They "solemnly publish and declare" that they are "Absolved from all Allegiance to the British Crown," and that they are "Free and Independent States." "And for the support of this Declaration, with a firm reliance on the Protection of Divine Providence, we mutually pledge to each other our Lives, our Fortunes and our sacred Honor."

The Declaration of Independence has been celebrated but not because it contains a theoretical justification of revolution or because it indicted George III for the wrongs done the colonies. Americans have no more generally venerated revolution as a good than they have clung to an enmity with the British people. The message of the Declaration is that revolution is a thing to be avoided so far as can be done, and entered upon only under dire necessity. The results of revolution are too unpredictable to warrant its encouragement; the destruction it portends too likely for the casual contemplation of it as a means to good ends. Revolution is negative and destructive. Far from being a thing of great value, it is a devaluation of the political coin of the realm.

The Declaration of Independence has been celebrated for good and sufficient reasons, reasons other than those connected with revolution. It has been celebrated, of course, because it marks the beginning of independence. It marks, too, the inception—the birth—of a nation, though it probably had not been conceived at the time. It was surely almost accidental that the very name by which this nation was to be called—the United States of America—appeared in the Declaration. It was only the statement of a hoped-for condition—"the united States of America"—when it was written.

The Declaration contains, too, a principled statement of the great purpose for which governments exist—to protect the people in the enjoyment of their rights. The first two paragraphs of the Declaration may be read and re-read—as they have been over the years—not as a justification or call for revolution but as a reminder of the good and proper ends of government to a people who have in their hands the control of the government over them. It contains, too, in its main body a list of abuses to which governments are prone. These United States had a goodly beginning, in spite of the revolution which was made. The good beginning was because of the great principles which were raised up before the people in the Declaration of Independence.

11

The War for Independence

It was one thing to declare independence; it was another to acquire it. It was one thing to rebel against British rule; it was another to bring off a successful revolution. It was one thing to make war; it was another to win it. It was one thing to deny the old authority; it was another to establish a new rule. The pledge which closes the Declaration was one to be taken seriously; those who signed it committed their "Lives," their "Fortunes," and their "sacred Honor." True, those who gathered around to sign the document engaged in some bravado. John Hancock scrawled his name large enough that the king could read it without his spectacles. When reproached with the fact that there were enough people by the same name in his state to assure him virtual anonymity, Charles Carroll from Maryland added "of Carrollton" to his signature, noting that there was only one man who would fit that description. But the task that lay ahead required endurance and tenacity to match the decisiveness just exercised.

The difficulties confronting the Patriots—for so those who favored independence have been most commonly called—were numerous and resistant to resolution. One such difficulty is frequently ignored by revolutionists, though failure to deal effectively with it thwarts the purposes for revolt; for the American colonists it was to see that the revolt against England did not turn into a revolt against all authority. The usual course of revolution is for a breakdown of authority to follow the repudiation of the old authority. When this happens, there ensues an often brutal contest for power, accompanied by the disintegration of society, bloodletting, and the development of well-nigh irreconcilable divisions among the people. Power is usually consolidated once again and order restored by an autocratic rule. The object for the original revolt, however noble, is commonly lost from sight as the yearning for order supersedes the quest for the good society.

The deepest source of the disintegrative impact of revolution no doubt lies in the human condition itself. What man is there who would not like a fresh start, who would not like to be free of his debts, who would not like to be relieved of the tangle of duties and obligations in which he finds himself, who would not relish the opportunity for starting over. Revolution appears to offer such an inviting prospect. As he made his way home from the First Continental Congress, John Adams encountered a man fired by emotions such as these. The man said: "Oh! Mr. Adams, what great things have you and your colleagues done for us! We can never be grateful enough to you. There are no courts of justice now in this province, and I hope there never will be another."[1]

John Adams understood that this was not a laudable opinion, and there were many others who intended to prevent the dissolution that would accompany the domination of events by men holding such opinions. The Americans were generally successful in avoiding many of the pitfalls of revolution. But, by the refusing to arouse the populace by holding forth visions of beatitude that would follow from their efforts, they also forfeited fanatical zeal in their followers. The American Patriots had quite limited means for achieving their limited ends.

A more obvious difficulty at the time was posed by the Loyalists —those who remained loyal to the king and to England. So long as the colonies retained their connection with Britain, most Americans joined in the opposition to British policies during the period of rising discontent. They sometimes differed over tactics and as to the correct theoretical position on the constitution. But once the decision for independence was made, some goodly number of people retained their loyalty to Britain. These threatened to turn the war into a domestic civil war as well as a war against Britain.

How many Loyalists there were was in doubt at the time and has remained so ever since. Those prosecuting the war in Britain wanted to believe that Americans in general retained their loyalty, especially that the sober and substantial inhabitants did. Hence, they were favorably disposed to exaggerated accounts of their numbers. Such a view made sense of the idea of subduing the "rebels," for after such a conquest Britain still might rule America if a substantial portion of the population was loyal. Moreover, British armies were continually being encouraged to come to this or that province on the grounds that Loyalists would turn out to support them in great number. The extent of loyalism has been revived as an important historical question in the twentieth century by those attempting to make a Marxist or class-struggle interpretation of American origins. These historians have resurrected what was once the British view for reasons quite different than those that would have interested King George III. On this class-struggle interpretation, men of wealth and position in America were usually Loyalists, and the thrust for revolt came from the lower classes.

This interpretation is not substantiated by the facts. A modern historian describes the social status of the Loyalists in this way: "Some came from quasi-aristocratic families, like the Fenwicks of South Carolina, and others were the humblest folk. They were rich, like Joseph Galloway of Pennsylvania, and they were poor; they were large landowners, and they were middling and small men of property; they stood behind counters, and they possessed hands unwrinkled by trade or toil. . . . Truth to tell, the Loyalists were of every station and every occupation."[2] He goes on to point out that Anglican clergymen and other officials dependent upon Britain for appointment or livelihood were likely to remain loyal. He also notes that some men of conspicuous wealth were among the Loyalists,[3] a point that is offset by the fact that there were prosperous men among the Patriots as well.

Textbook lore has it that the population was divided in this fashion: one-third Patriots, one-third Loyalists, and one-third neutrals. About the only thing to commend this estimate is that it is a formula easily remembered by undergraduates for test purposes. Since no census was ever taken to determine the number of Loyalists and Patriots, most evidence of numbers is indirect. The most critical of such evidence indicates that the Patriots generally preponderated over the Loyalists. Loyalists were able to achieve military successes only in conjunction with British armies. They could not even hold territory gained by the British. Once the main army moved on, Patriot militia usually swarmed over the Loyalists. The following estimate of Loyalist strength may be very near the mark: "In New England they may have been scarcely a tenth of the population; in the South a quarter or a third; but in the Middle colonies including New York perhaps nearly a half."[4]

There were, then, Loyalists in considerable number in America after the Declaration of Independence. They did not, however, succeed in turning the conflict into a fullfledged civil war. They were a threat to internal security; they offered encouragement to Britain to continue the war; they hampered the mustering of the resources of the states; and they attempted to undermine the war effort. It is not surprising, then, that the Patriots dealt with them ferociously when they encountered them in battle or that they were subject to persecution when they were discovered.

The leaders of the revolt had difficulty enough without civil war. They had to lead by way of makeshift governments during most of the war. The colonial governments were no more, once independence was declared. Indeed, they had already been replaced with provincial congresses or legislatures before that event in most states. They subsisted for some time without formal constitutions, and their exercise of authority smacked of extra-legality, to put the best face on it. Though the states were faced with the crisis of prosecuting a war, they were under the necessity of moving carefully in order to carry as many people with them as possible. The states were hardly united, and their war effort was plagued by the fact that each state tended to go its own way. The only union government which existed from 1775 into 1781 was that provided by the Second Continental Congress. It had no constitution, nor any authority except that which derived from the states. It was not a government in the usual sense of the word, though it attempted to perform the diplomatic and military functions of one.

The most perplexing difficulties, however, were military and financial. To confront the most powerful navy in the world, the states had only a few ships that could be called warships; most of the damage they were able to do against the British was done by privateers which depended upon speed rather than armor. The armies should be called occasional rather than regular or standing. True, Congress authorized a Continental Army, made requisitions on the states for men and supplies, appointed generals, and undertook the direction of campaigns. There was a Continental Army from the time of its formation until the end of the war; but at times—usually in winter—it dwindled to the point that it more nearly resembled a party than an army. When some region was threatened, the army could be fleshed out with numerous increments of militia. The British did not usually conduct winter campaigns, so that an occasional army was nearly enough—*for defensive purposes*.

The Continental forces, during most of the war, however, were not sufficient to go on the offensive. The army frequently lacked most of the things which make an army: discipline, effective officers for smaller units, uniforms, blankets, tents, firewood, food, adequate shot and powder, sufficient muskets or rifles and bayonets, and continuity. The initial enlistments were for one year only: only long enough, as Washington observed, for them to absorb some training and come under discipline before their officers had to begin to treat them with great deference in the hope that they would re-enlist. The militia were undependable and unpredictable in combat in the open field; they were of greatest use when they outnumbered the enemy.

Financing was so ineptly managed and the consequences were so important both to the conduct of the war and the founding of the Republic that it will receive treatment in a separate chapter.

It is appropriate to focus attention on the difficulties confronting

126

the Americans in the War for Independence. It enables us to see high-lighted the sacrifices, bravery, and tenacity of those who did persevere to victory. But it is appropriate also to note that the Patriots had advantages as well as difficulties. Americans were fighting, usually, on their own soil. They had the potentiality of supplying many of their wants at home. They did not have to conquer Britain, only to drive her forces from the states. They had much greater prospects of gaining friends among European nations than did Britain, for Britain's successes in the Seven Year's War had been at the expense of other major powers. The American Patriots had a cause, too, which much outranked that of their enemy. They were fighting for liberty and independence; the best that the British could do was appeal to monarchy, empire, and tradition, and their case for tradition was flawed by the innovations which had provoked colonial resistance.

Even the method of assembling and maintaining armies was more appropriate than is often appreciated. It is true, of course, that the army should have been better fed, clothed, shod, munitioned, and housed. A strong case can be made, too, that if Patriot commanders had had larger numbers of seasoned and disciplined troops they might well have won decisive victories long before they did. But it is quite possible that an army composed of men with long-term enlistments in resplendent uniforms, who were extensions of the wills of their officers and who had garnered a series of brilliant victories, would have endangered American liberty. Many thoughtful Americans feared just the sort of army wanted by any man confronted with the military tasks before him. Congress was loathe to encourage long enlistments. They feared a standing army, as might be expected of men of British descent. Americans were conscious not only of British history but of Roman history, and of the threat posed by successful generals. America did avoid the shoal of military dictatorship following the revolution, and a plausible reason why is that there was no army with which anyone inclined to such exploits could be confident of accomplishing them.

The Americans had another advantage, too; they had George Washington as commander-in-chief. Whether he was a great tactician or not is a question that can be left to military historians. But there should be no doubt that he had that peculiar combination of qualities of a man to whom others turn in difficult situations. He was dignified, tenacious, farsighted, disciplined, correct, and a gentleman. His personal bravery was of the sort that is called fearless among soldiers and sometimes foolhardy for a general. More than once he rallied his troops by exposing himself to enemy bullets. A lesser man than he would have committed and lost several armies, if he could have assembled that many. Washington was sorely tempted to risk his army to rescue and

127

redeem his reputation. Yet he resisted this temptation time and again, believing that it was more important to keep an army in the field than hazard the American cause on the chance of gaining personal glory. He said after being driven from Long Island: "We should on all occasions avoid a general action, or put anything to the risk, unless compelled by a necessity into which we ought never to be drawn."[5] He persevered, persevered when beset by critics in Congress and the states, by the shortages and inadequacies of his army, by superior armies, by a war of attrition in the later years, and by mutiny of some of his forces. He had not only to direct his armies against enemy forces that frequently outnumbered his, were better equipped, better disciplined, and better supported but also to keep up a continual correspondence with Congress and with state officials to gain support and to get men and supplies. Small wonder that he often longed to return to Mt. Vernon and pursue his own affairs. Yet he persevered for more than eight years, from 1775 to 1783.

There were, of course, other generals and officers whose leadership and ability contributed to the American cause. Among them would be listed: Benedict Arnold (until his betrayal), Henry Knox, Anthony Wayne, Nathanael Greene, and Daniel Morgan. The Continental Army benefited much, too, from foreign volunteers, notably, Lafayette, de Kalb, and von Steuben. And there were private soldiers, whose names do not adorn the pages of books, but who endured untold misery to remain with the Continental Army and provide the troops without which generals are of no account.

On paper, the British were so far superior to the Americans that no contest might have been expected. They had the most powerful navy in the world. They had an established government, the recognition of foreign powers, centralized taxation, established credit, a much larger population on which to draw, much greater productive capacity, and an existing and disciplined army, though it was small. They hired thousands of Germans to supplement their own forces. Moreover, Loyalists in America might support them.

But the task of the British was much more complex and difficult than that of the Americans. Armies had to be transported across 3,000 miles of ocean in unpredictable sailing ships. Not only that, but the army and navy had generally to be supplied from home, and this transport was frequently exposed to Patriot privateers along the thousands of miles of coast line of the American continent. Once their armies left the shelter of the supporting navies and moved inland, they were among a generally hostile population which rallied against them, as Generals Burgoyne and Cornwallis were to learn to their sorrow. They were always short of transport for inland maneuvers, and George Washington saw to it that very little fell into their hands. If America was divided at home, so were the British, though it did not tell much for the first couple of years.

British strategy was threefold: to isolate the continent from the rest of the world by blockade, to divide and conquer America, and to destroy Washington's army. The policy of divide and conquer had many facets: rally the Loyalists to the cause, separate the regions from one another, capture the major seaports, and so on. Patriot strategy was, above all, to keep an army in the field, and, hopefully, to drive the British from the continent. The British aimed to keep down the atrocities so as not to turn more of the American population against them; in this they were frequently thwarted by armies which plundered and raped wherever they went. Washington's armies were under strict orders not to plunder, but they did engage in confiscations to gain stores and supplies.

Hostilities broke out in Massachusetts, of course, in April of 1775, more than a year before the declaring of independence. For the remainder of the year and into the next, the bulk of the British forces were concentrated at Boston and environs. This force was under siege and cut off on land by Patriots.

The first major battle of the war took place June 17, 1775. It has gone down in history as the Battle of Bunker Hill, though, in fact, it was a battle over Breed's Hill. The Americans, some 1,200 strong, built a redoubt on Breed's Hill, which the British attacked with 2,200 men against a slightly reinforced American force. The British took the hill, but at a cost of 1,000 casualties, two and a half times the losses by the Patriots. General Gage observed that he could ill afford another victory like that. Shortly afterward, Washington assumed command of the Patriot forces, and a stalemate ensued for the next several months.

The scene of action shifted elsewhere. For some time, Benedict Arnold, and others, had been promoting the idea of an expedition into Canada. It was hoped that such an undertaking would bring the Canadians in on the side of the states, would remove a haven from British forces who could from that vantage point launch an attack against the states, and would show to the British the determination of America. The plan was the more attractive because Canada was lightly defended. Congress was reluctant to authorize the expedition because there was still hope of reconciliation. Even so, permission was given for it finally.

Two armies were launched into Canada in late 1775. The main army which set out by way of Lake Champlain was initially under the command of General Philip Schuyler, but he fell ill and was replaced by the much more energetic Richard Montgomery. This army met with a series of successes by taking Forts Chambly and St. John's, followed by Montreal. The way to Quebec, the historic key to dominance of Canada, now lay open.

Meanwhile, the second army under the command of Benedict Arnold was making its way toward Quebec by a more easterly route. Arnold set out up the Kennebec river through Maine along a route the difficulties of which were only hazily grasped at the start. Arnold and his men braved rapids, unsuspected waterfalls, long overland portages, and some of the most miserable weather ever recorded to reach their destination. "So great were the hardships that officers of the two rear divisions turned back with 350 men. But the rest plunged on through a forbidding wilderness, overcoming almost incredible obstacles. Some of them became lost; some died; all who could, struggled forward. . . . After a month of desperate effort, 600 scarecrows of men straggled into a camp on the headwaters of the Chaudière."[6] This was in early November; they reached Quebec a few days later.

On December 2, 1775, Montgomery's army joined forces with Arnold outside Quebec. Although they now had superiority in numbers over the British, they were unable to take advantage of it because Sir Guy Carleton chose to defend the city from behind its walls rather than come out into the open. An assault upon the city on December 31 failed. General Montgomery was able to get a small force within the walls, but he was killed, and Arnold's men who were supposed to make a rendezvous with Montgomery's were turned back after Arnold, who was wounded, relinquished the command. For several months, Americans continued to lay Quebec under siege, but to no avail. Superior British forces eventually arrived; though American reinforcements were also sent to Canada, they were driven out in 1776.

Early in the year of 1776, Washington succeeded in placing cannon on Dorchester Heights overlooking the British positions around Boston. Sir William Howe, now in command of the British army, judged his position to be too exposed, and in March the British abandoned Boston. Howe withdrew by sea to Halifax to await reinforcements. Meanwhile, Washington moved his army to New York in the expectation of a British attack there. It came in August. Howe drove Washington's army from Long Island, from Manhattan, and then from White Plains. It then became a near rout as the British under the field command of Cornwallis followed Washington in a retreat through New Jersey. Washington managed to halt the British advance at the Delaware River in early December. He had gathered all the boats in the vicinity to transport his army across the river; once he had the boats on the other side, he kept them there.

In any case, Howe did not follow up his advantage. He went into

130

winter quarters in New York City, leaving much of his army spread out over New Jersey. For the Continentals, it had been a year of defeats and withdrawals. On the heels of the Canadian losses had come the ousting of Washington's army from New York. The British were now within a few miles from the capitol at Philadelphia. Washington had only the remnant of an army to oppose the military and naval might of Britain.

Howe could retire to the comforts of New York; he had victories enough to sustain him through the winter. No such pleasant option was open to Washington who was faced with the imminent dissolution of his army and, the way things were going, no prospects of another one. If the British would not attack, he must. Under the cover of darkness on Christmas night he crossed the Delaware with his army to attack the Hessian army at Trenton at daybreak. The Germans surrendered shortly after the attack began. A few days later, Washington engineered another victory at Princeton. From his base at Morristown, Washington continued to drive the British from their positions. The extent and impact of the continuation of this campaign is spelled out by Samuel Eliot Morison: "In a campaign lasting only three weeks, at a time of year when gentlemen were not supposed to fight, the military genius of America's greatest gentleman, and the fortitude of some five thousand of his men, had undone everything Howe accomplished, recovered the Jersies, and saved the American cause."[7]

In 1777, the British launched their great offensive aimed at dividing America and destroying the Patriot ability to resist. At the beginning of the year, the massive force of British arms was centered in New York City. Another large army was in Canada. It was placed under the tactical command of General John Burgoyne. General Howe conceived initially of the grand strategy of attacking north from New York to make a junction with an attacking force from Canada. Such a victory along the line of Lake Champlain, Lake George, and the Hudson could have cut off New England from the rest of the states. However, Howe changed his mind, decided to attack Philadelphia instead, and put to sea with that destination in mind. He did leave behind an army, of sorts, under Sir Henry Clinton, but it was insufficient to perform both its tasks of occupation and conducting a major offensive campaign.

For a good portion of the summer, Howe's destination was a mystery to Washington. The fleet was delayed first by an extended calm and then by contrary winds. Upon hearing that the fleet had been sighted to the south, Washington took the main body of his army to the vicinity of Philadelphia, leaving Burgoyne to the mercy of the New England militia, as he said. Washington tried to block Howe's advance with a smaller army at Brandywine Creek in early September, but was defeated and driven off. Howe moved on to the occupation of Philadelphia, which Congress had lately abandoned in haste. Washington's attack early in October on the main British force at Germantown failed to dislodge it. He withdrew his army to Valley Forge after this defeat.

Burgoyne had about 8,000 men at his disposal, including Loyalists and Indians. A detachment under Baron St. Leger was dispatched through the Mohawk valley from Oswego toward Albany. This detachment was dispersed by troops under Benedict Arnold. Burgoyne proceeded southward at a leisurely pace, one not entirely of his own choosing, since his path was frequently blocked by trees newly felled by Patriots. Meanwhile, militia began to assemble around a core of Continentals whose task was to stop Burgoyne. Eventually, so many militia had gathered to augment the Continentals under the command of General Horatio Gates that Burgoyne was outnumbered two to one. His supply route was cut by Patriots. Burgoyne's hope of being relieved from New York City did not materialize; Clinton made only a foray up the river, stopping well short of Albany. Burgoyne was cut off, surrounded; he surrendered his army intact at Saratoga on October 17, 1777. Gates was credited with the victory, but men such as John Stark and Benedict Arnold led the aggressive actions which bottled up Burgoyne.

Saratoga was the first great American victory. Trenton and Princeton had been important battles for keeping up morale, but they had been won at the expense of contingents of British forces. Burgoyne surrendered one of the major armies in America at Saratoga. There had been much sympathy among Frenchmen for the American cause from the beginning. America had sent emissaries even before declaring independence. By 1777, Congress had sent to France the best known American at the time and America's premier diplomat, Benjamin Franklin. An alliance was drawn up between France and the states in February 1778, and shortly thereafter France was drawn into the war.

Not only did Saratoga bring France to the side of the American Patriots, but it showed to any of the British willing to learn the immensity of the task that lay before them. Contemporaries thought General Howe was much too cautious, even lazy and indifferent, if not a secret sympathizer with the Patriots. Historians of a later date have belabored him for unimaginative tactics. Yet Howe was the only commanding general who ever put Washington's army to rout and administered successive defeats. But to those who would see, Burgoyne's defeat showed what could well happen to any British general who committed his forces beyond naval support. Far from finding numerous Loyalists in the hinterland, Burgoyne found the countryside swarming with militia waiting to demonstrate the marksmanship of the backwoods. Nor would the con-

132

tinent succumb to the capture of this or that eastern port city, even if one was the capital. America had no central city; it was a land of farmers mainly who knew not the dependence, common in Europe, on a single city. There was no Rome to fall in America.

It is reasonable to conjecture that the American Patriots should have won the war in 1778. They now had an ally who could challenge the British fleet and overmatch the British army. The Americans had shown that they could defeat a British army. Britain was not in dire straits, but even the government was no longer so determined to win. Lord North got a bill through Parliament in February 1778 aimed at reconciliation with America. A peace commission was dispatched a little later which was authorized to offer Americans just about everything they had asked for short of independence. A command crisis developed in the British forces in 1778. Burgoyne returned home on parole and in disgrace. The Howe brothers resigned command of the army and navy in America. General Howe may have been cautious, but Henry Clinton, who replaced him, was inept. Surely, all it would have taken to drive the British from America would have been a decisive mustering of American strength.

This was not to be the case, however. Perhaps a better omen than Saratoga for the immediate future was Valley Forge. The war was to drag on for the better part of five more years, and the condition of the Continental army at Valley Forge in the winter of 1777-1778 tells us why, at least in part. One of Washington's biographers has described conditions this way:

> Thus, at the beginning of 1778, the Army was witnessing one of the strangest of races, a contest between the axes of the men building huts and the harsh wear-and-tear on the remaining garments of those who still had sufficient clothing to permit outdoor duty. . . . Although hospital huts were built early and in what was believed to be sufficient number, they soon were overcrowded with miserable men who died fast or, if they survived, received little attention. In spite of all exertion, it was the middle of January when the last of the troops were under roof. Even then they did not always have straw to take the chill from the earthen floor of their huts. Thousands had no bed covering.

> Food, of course, was the absolute essential—and food, more than even clothing or blankets or straw, was lacking at Valley Forge. . . . "Fire cakes" frequently were all the half-naked men had to eat in their overcrowded, smoky huts. Early in the New Year most of the regiments had to be told the Com-

missary could issue no provisions because it had none, none whatsoever. . . .

These were desperate hours. Washington continued to watch and to warn. "A prospect now opens," he said February 17, "of absolute want such as will make it impossible to keep the Army much longer from dissolution. . . ."[8]

Indeed, the army did seem to be on the verge of dissolution. "In December 1777, for example, over two thousand men went home. Hundreds of officers tendered their resignations; on one day alone, fifty threw up their commissions."[9] Nor are these resignations and desertions to be wondered at when the hardships of the army are contrasted with the relatively good life of civilians. It is generally believed that about the only people in America suffering privation were in the army. One historian says, "Civilians declined to forgo their pleasures merely because the army was in want; at a ball at Lancaster, Pennsylvania, in January 1778, over one hundred ladies and gentlemen gathered in all their finery to enjoy a 'cold collation with wine, punch, sweet cakes . . . , music, dancing, singing . . . ,' which lasted until four o'clock in the morning."[10] These revels were taking place only a short distance from Valley Forge.

The incongruities here account for the American impotence. The reason for their existence needs now to be explained.

12

The Scourge of Inflation

A theft of greater magnitude and still more ruinous, is the making of paper money; it is greater because in this money there is absolutely no real value; it is more ruinous, because, by its gradual depreciation during all the time of its existence, it produces the effect which would be produced by an infinity of successive deteriorations of the coins. All these iniquities are founded on the false idea that money is but a sign.

—Count Destutt de Tracy

Men at ease and in comfortable circumstances must find it difficult to comprehend the sufferings of the Patriot armies during the War for Independence. These armies had to suffer, in addition to those tribulations incident to war, from lack of clothing, blankets, sufficient food, drink, transport, and many other of the necessities of life. Yet it is the judgment of the generality of historians that most of this deprivation was unnecessary and unwarranted. There was food aplenty in the states, and there was at least the potentiality of enough clothing. It may be added that there were enough men of the right age to have constituted overwhelming forces against those the British actually sent to America, and there was a potentiality for manufacturing adequate munitions for the war. (For example: "In 1775 the Union produced 30,000 tons of crude iron—one seventh of the world's total output.")[1] It is quite probable that the war could have been brought to a successful conclusion long before it was had these resources been devoted to the effort in sufficient amounts. They were not.

The main reason why men and materials were not brought to focus adequately on the war effort was the method used to finance the war.

The successful prosecution of a war—any war—requires that a sufficient amount of energy and resources be diverted from other uses in order to accomplish the end of winning the war. To acquire the necessary goods and services, government enters the market. (This is not to deny that a government may acquire services, and sometimes goods, voluntarily from those who are actuated by principle or other motives. To the extent that this is the case, neither force nor the market may have come into play in the acquisition. But neither the War for Independence, nor any other known to this writer, were fought primarily with such resources.) Government may enter the marketplace in such a way as to take advantage of the services offered in a market, or it may intervene in the market in such ways as to make that instrument virtually useless for its purposes. The market is a place where voluntary exchanges are made, where goods and services are sold to the highest bidder. When government enters the marketplace it becomes a bidder among bidders for the supply of goods and services available. What the government acquires there, others are denied, or vice versa.

Before government can become a bidder in the market it must acquire goods and services, or their equivalent, for making exchanges. This necessity poses what is the most enduring problem of government: the government, as government, is not a producer of goods nor provider of services, and has none of these to offer in exchange. Before it can operate in the market, then, government must acquire these, or their equivalent, from those who own or produce them. In effect, government must take goods and services from those who provide and produce them. For this to be done equitably and justly, experience indicates that this appropriation should be spread over and apportioned among the producing citizenry.

Money has afforded a means for apportioning taxes and a way for government to enter the marketplace for trading without interfering destructively with the function of the market. In short, money can enable a government to use the marketplace as a major source of goods and services which it needs, particularly in war. For this to happen, however, government must respect the nature and character of money. Money is a medium of exchange, i.e., it is that through which are made exchanges of goods for goods, services for services, or any other combinations of these. What a given unit of money will command in goods and services in the marketplace is a ratio between the quantity of money and quantity of goods and services, as modified by the strength of the desires of all who have any of these in their possession or wish to acquire them. To put the matter concretely, if a bushel of wheat brings one dollar this means that the quantity of money is such, the quantity of

136

wheat is such, the desire for wheat is such, and the desire for money is such, that one dollar is the price that will effect an exchange. If the quantity of money is increased, and all else remains the same, the price of wheat may be expected to rise in proportion to the increase of money. A money tax enables the government to reduce the supply of money available to private bidders, and thus to become an effective bidder for its needs in the market.

It is theoretically clear, then, what the consequences would be if the government attempted to get its needs by simply increasing the money supply. It would reduce the quantity of goods and services a given unit of money would command. But why could the government not do this as a means of taxation, thus avoiding the onerous necessity of a direct appropriation of money? Of course, it could do this. Thomas Paine declared that this is just what the Congress did during the War for Independence. It would have cost ten or twelve million pounds sterling, he estimated, to have financed the war by ordinary taxation; "and as while this money was issuing, and likewise depreciating down to nothing, there were none, or few valuable taxes paid; consequently the event to the public was the same, whether they sunk ten or twelve millions of expended money, by depreciation, or paid ten or twelve millions by taxation, . . . And therefore . . . [the] debt, has now no existence; it having been paid by everybody consenting, to reduce as his own expense, from the value of the bills continually passing among themselves, a sum, equal to nearly what the expense of the war was for five years."[2] Thomas Paine was, as usual, an adept pleader of special causes, but he was no scholar, and certainly not an economic historian. His statement that everybody consented is simply not true, and he ignores both the ruinous train of consequences following upon the inflation and the question of whether or not it was effective in its object of providing for the armed forces.

It is not necessary, however, to explore the theoretical impact of the inflation further; it unfolds in the story of the financing of the war. The Congress and the states did attempt to finance the war effort primarily by the issuance of paper money. Congress issued what is known as Continental currency. The notes did not bear interest, as such currency sometimes did, but they were supposed to be redeemed by the states at a later date. Just how much was issued from the first issue in 1775 until an entirely new currency was issued in 1780 is in doubt. The estimates range from $191,552,380[3] to $242,100,176[4]. It is commonly believed today to have been over $200 million[5]. Even if an exact figure could be agreed upon, however, we would still not know how much of the currency was in circulation, for it was extensively counterfeited. There were domestic counterfeiters; and the British government, as a matter of policy, attempted to destroy the currency by introducing counterfeit money.[6]

All accounts agree, however, that Congress issued more and more of the currency over the years through 1779. A recent estimate of the sums issued goes as follows:[7]

1775	$ 6,000,000
1776	19,000,000
1777	13,000,000
1778	63,500,300
1779	90,052,380

This process of issuing more and more set in early. The initial issue was to have been for $2 million, but before it had been accomplished Congress authorized another $1 million.[8] Before the end of the year $3 million more was issued.[9] This despite the fact that Congress had intended only one issue at the beginning. And, there were those who attempted to prevent the escalation. Benjamin Franklin said: "After the first emission I proposed that we should stop, strike no more, but borrow on interest those we had issued. This was not then approved of, and more bills were issued."[10]

The process of issuing more and more of the currency and raising the amounts of single issues is easily explained. Once the money had been issued, it fell into private hands in return for goods and services. The government no longer had access to the currency. Congress then made further issues in order to have money to spend. The more it issued, the less the money was worth; larger and larger issues were made in the attempt to get the results that could be obtained by smaller issues earlier. Reliance on paper money has—for these reasons, and more complex ones where there are combinations of taxation and fiat money financing—a pyramiding effect.

Why did the government not recover the money in some way? In general, this could have been done either by taxation or by borrowing, or some combination of these methods. The government did not retrieve the money for about the same reason it was issued in the first place, namely, to avoid taxes and because the credit of the Congress was not good. Before examining into the question of taxation and borrowing, however, one justification offered for issuing paper money needs to be explored.

Curtis Nettels, a present-day historian, describes the justification for a Continental currency this way: "The Union as a whole suffered from an acute shortage of hard money; all the coin in circulation in 1775

would not have paid a year's expenses of the Continental Army." Some
men at the time of the revolution held that a certain indeterminate
amount of money is necessary to facilitate commerce. They thought that
money could be issued up to the point of meeting the need without
depreciating, but that once the point of sufficiency had been passed,
the currency would begin to decline in value. It may not be an adequate
reply to Professor Nettels to say that Congress could have issued $10
trillion in paper money and it would not have been enough to pay "a
year's expenses of the Continental Army," but the statement is correct.
The only way I can make sense of the earlier idea is to suppose they
believed that price is something inhering in the item offered for sale
rather than being determined by supply and demand. Some clarity may
be brought to the subject by distinguishing between money and currency. Money may be anything which serves as a medium through
which some transactions are made. Currency is that which serves generally in an area to effect transactions. All currency is money, but not
all money is currency. Money becomes currency in one of two ways:
either because it is wanted by traders and is in sufficient supply to effect
transactions, or because it has been made legal tender by some government. The only purpose for making a money legal tender is to force
it into currency when it would not be the currency on its own merits.
The very fact that Congress relied upon tender laws and used even
harsher measures to give their bills currency should dispose of the argument that they were issued because of a shortage of hard money.

The real reason for the Continental currency issues, then, was that
Congress and the states were attempting to finance the war without
levying taxes directly. They are entitled to some sympathy for the difficult situation in which they were trying to function, but no amount
of sympathy alters the consequences of actions. Congress had no authority to levy taxes. With equal validity, it can be said that Congress had
no authority to issue money. The truth of the matter is that Congress
had as little and as much power as it could manage to exercise during
the period under consideration. It had no constitution, hence, no constitutional limits on what it could do. Its members, however, were
delegates from the states. It may well be that had Congress attempted
to levy taxes it would have been repudiated by the states or by the
people. At any rate, Congress did not even attempt to levy taxes. It
was not that the members could see no need for taxes. Congress
declared, on many occasions, that the states should levy taxes. Elaborate
schedules were devised for apportioning the costs of the war among the
states. Solemn proclamations were issued urging the states to tax. For
example, in 1777 Congress admonished the states to "raise by taxation
in the course of the ensuing year, and remit to the treasury such sums

of money as they think will be most proper in the present situation of the inhabitants. . . ."[11]

All this was of little avail. The states were not much more inclined to levy taxes to pay for the war than Congress was. One historian sums the matter up in this way: "Before 1780, most of the states shrank from collecting taxes for any purpose. Massachusetts did not vote any levy in 1776, and in 1778 resorted to a lottery to raise $2,000,000. Virginia waited until 1781 before making a serious attempt to obtain revenue from taxes. The performances of the other states were not much better."[12] There are several reasons for this state of affairs. For one, the hold of the state governments over the citizenry was sometimes precarious, particularly in states where Loyalists were numerous. Extensive taxation might have jeopardized the tenuous attachment which many had for their state governments. For another, the objection to taxation without representation by the British must have turned into a more general objection to taxation. This appears from the difficulty of collecting the taxes that were levied. "In Pennsylvania, for example, from 1778 to 1781, less than half the taxes assessed were collected; it was not uncommon for citizens to slam the door in the tax-collector's face—and get away with it."[13] But, above all, legislators were currying favor with their constituents by avoiding taxation. Sumner said that the "governors of the States could not urge taxation and zeal upon the legislatures without a painful and unpopular contest. The members of a legislature who laid taxes must expect to return to their constituents to face grumbling and popular dissatisfaction."[14]

Instead of taxing to retire the Continental currency, the states issued large amounts of paper money themselves. "The emission of all the states exceeded $200,000,000. Virginia led the way, followed by North Carolina; then came South Carolina. Georgia, Delaware, and New Jersey exercised the most restraint."[15]

A minor stream that added to this flood of paper currency issued by Congress and the states was provided by domestic loans. Loan office certificates and certificates of indebtedness were issued to the extent of $20 million.[16] The loan office certificates circulated generally, one writer notes, "effecting essentially the same consequences as would have attended the issue of an equal quantity of paper money."[17]

Successive interventions were made in the market, interventions which followed logically from the use of fiat money to finance the war. The first of these interventions was to make the paper legal tender so that it would circulate as money. The specific actions to do this were by the states. For example, the Council of Safety of Pennsylvania declared in 1776 that anyone who refused to accept the Continental currency would forfeit whatever he refused to sell and be subject to a pen-

140

alty besides—all this for a first offense—, and be banished from the state for a second offense.[18] In the same year, Rhode Island made both state and Continental notes legal tender. In addition to providing penalties for not accepting this paper, that state prohibited the buying of specie with paper or differentiating in prices of goods when offered gold or silver instead of paper.[19]

Sometimes even more drastic measures were authorized to make people take the paper money. When he was in command of forces at Philadelphia, General Putnam made this announcement: "In future, should any of the inhabitants be so lost to public virtue and the welfare of their country, as to presume to refuse the currency of the American states in payment for any commodities they may have for sale, the goods shall be forfeited, and the person or persons so refusing, committed to close confinement."[20] In a similar fashion, George Washington was authorized to take goods from those who refused the Continental currency and to arrest and confine them.[21]

With such Draconian measures to support it, the Continental paper money did circulate. But the more of it that was issued, the more it depreciated. The most noticeable effect of this to the public was a general rise in prices. (Prices of particular goods and services rise and fall as demand and supply fluctuate even if the amount of money in circulation remains stable. And, given blockades and the kinds of demands incident to war, some prices would have risen inevitably during these years. However, the price increases were not only general but some of them are rises in Continental currency in relation to what they could be bought for in specie, which indicates that it was the currency which occasioned some of the increases.) Some of the state governments intervened in the market further by attempting to fix prices. As frequently happens, the legislators sought to control the effect—the rise in prices—rather than the cause—the increase in the money supply. Congress recommended that regional conventions be held to set prices for particular areas. The New England and Middle states held such conventions, but the Southern states south of Maryland steered clear of price controls. After a convention had agreed upon the general features of prices, it was up to the individual states to enforce the tariffs. The following is a description of penalties adopted by Rhode Island in 1777:

> The penalty of demanding more than the tariff price was set at the value of the article,—half to the State, and half to the informer. Any one who refused for his commodities the tariff price, and afterward sold them for any other goods, was to forfeit the value thereof, half to the State, and half to the informer. If complaint was made that articles necessary for the

141

army or navy were withheld by monopolizers, the State officers and Judges or any two Justices of the Peace might issue a warrant to impress and seize the same, breaking open buildings. The goods were to be appraised by two indifferent men at prices not to exceed those of the tariff. Anybody who contracted to receive for labour or goods more than the tariff rates was to be counted an enemy of the country, and fined twenty shillings for every article sold of the price of twenty shillings or under, and a sum equal to the value of the article, if it was worth more than that.[22]

The price controls, where they were at all effective, resulted in shortages. John Eliot wrote from Boston in June of 1777: "We are all starving here, since this plaguy addition to the regulating bill. People will not bring in provision, and we cannot procure the common necessaries of life. What we shall do I know not."[23] What they did, of course, is what people ever do: evade the regulations, barter, blackmarket, produce a money that will purchase goods, and find a variety of means to perpetuate the market, however inadequate they are compared to the opportunities in a free market.

By 1778, the armed forces were finding it increasingly difficult to acquire goods with paper money. "Though paper money was taken, with more or less reluctance, in return for most things, some services were rendered only upon promises of receiving specie."[24] George Washington wrote in 1779 that "a wagon load of money will scarcely purchase a wagon load of provisions."[25] The country was in the grip of a runaway inflation. Every man of intelligence knew that the root cause was the increase of the money supply (much as this is known in our day), yet there was not the will to deal effectively with it.

To get supplies and transport, the army had to resort to its equivalent of barter, i.e., impressment and requisition from the surrounding populace. There had been some impressment, particularly of transport, from the beginning of the war; but by the time of the Yorktown campaign in 1781 this method seems to have been relied upon almost exclusively.[26] There was more and more of this done before 1781, however. By the latter part of 1779, supplies in general were being requisitioned. On December 11, 1779, Congress "voted requisitions on the States for specific supplies of flour and Indian corn. December 14, they established a system of requisitions and contributions of this kind, Maryland alone voting no. February 25, 1780, an elaborate apportionment of requisitions for such supplies was made. . . . Each State was called upon for the staples which it produced."[27]

The most drastic impact of inflation is that it tends to disintegrate and divide society, to turn employee against employer, the governed against the governors, the creditor against the debtor, the producer against the consumer, the populace against speculators, and so forth. Inflation tends to reverse the rules of economic behavior: where once it was prudent to save money, it becomes expedient to spend it; where once it was good business to supply consumers with durable goods, it becomes profitable to delay the sale; where once creditors were those who were better off, it now becomes good business to borrow money and repay it with a currency that is less valuable than when the loan was made. The solid citizen who is cautious and prudent can do well over the years by hard work, careful investments, and saving, when the money supply is stable. His prosperity may well be described as virtue rewarded. Inflation sets the stage for wealth to be gained in a different fashion: by borrowing, by holding on to goods for the inevitable higher prices, and by attending closely to the swift changes in the value of the money. Such means of gaining riches are widely resented, particularly during a war.

Men contemporary with events frequently described the consequences of the inflation as well as could be done. Josiah Quincy wrote these words to General Washington:

> I am firmly of the opinion, and think it entirely defensible, that there never was a paper pound, a paper dollar, or a paper promise of any kind, that ever yet obtained a general currency, but by force or fraud, generally by both. That the army has been grossly cheated; that creditors have been infamously defrauded; that the widows and fatherless have been oppressively wronged and beggared; that the gray hairs of the aged and the innocent, for want of their just dues have gone down with sorrow to their graves, in consequence of our disgraceful depreciated paper currency. . . .[28]

By 1778, John Adams could say that "every man who had money due to him at the commencement of this war, has been already taxed three-fourth parts of that money. . . . And every man who owed money at the beginning of the war, has put three-fourth parts of it in his pockets as clear gain. The war, therefore, is immoderately gainful to some, and ruinous to others."[29]

A historian who lived through that period has written:

> The aged who had retired from the scenes of active business, to enjoy the fruits of their industry, found their substance melting away to a mere pittance, insufficient for their support.

143

The widow who lived comfortably on the bequests of a deceased husband, experienced a frustration of all his well-meant tenderness. The laws of the country interposed, and compelled her to receive a shilling, where a pound was her due. The blooming virgin who had grown up with an unquestionable title to a liberal patrimony, was legally stripped of every thing but her personal charms and virtues. The hapless orphan, instead of receiving from the hands of an executor, a competency to set out in business, was obliged to give a final discharge on the payment of 6d. in the pound. In many instances, the earnings of a long life of care and diligence were, in the space of a few years, reduced to a trifling sum. . . .

That the helpless part of the community were legislatively deprived of their property, was among the lesser evils which resulted from the legal tender of the depreciated bills of credit. The iniquity of the laws estranged the minds of many of the citizens from the habits and love of justice. The nature of obligations was so far changed, that he was reckoned the honest man, who from principle delayed to pay his debts. The mounds which government had erected, to secure the observance of honesty in the commercial intercourse of man with man, were broken down. Truth, honor, and justice were swept away by the overflowing deluge of legal iniquity. . . .[30]

George Washington wrote: "Speculation, peculation, engrossing, forestalling, with all concomitants, afford too many melancholy proofs of the decay of public virtue. . . ." And a writer to a New Jersey paper assessed the blame for this: "I do not say that the abundance of money is the only cause of the decay of virtue or increase of vice, but I say it is a very principal cause, it operates more this way than any other, yea, than all other causes put together."[31]

The inflation contributed much to the loss of confidence in the Congress, the state governments, and the very cause they were committed to at the time. The idea was advanced, when the first issues of paper money were made, that its becoming currency would help to tie people to the cause of independence. Since the fate of the money—its eventual redemption—would depend upon the success of the revolt, those who came into possession of it would be committed to victory. So it might have been, I suppose, if the Congress had been content with one or two issues, if the states had refrained from issues, and if the governments had then turned to direct taxation. But the effect of issuing more and more was not only to reduce the value of the money but also to undermine confidence in the governments which issued it.

In fact, people began to suspect rather quickly that Congress would eventually repudiate its paper. To counter this fear, time and time again Congress reiterated the determination to redeem it and denounced those who said that it would be otherwise. In 1778, Congress adopted the following resolution: "Whereas a report hath circulated in divers parts of America, that Congress would not redeem the bills of credit issued by them to defray the expenses of the war, but would suffer them to sink in the hands of the holder, whereby the value of the said bills hath, in the opinion of many of the good people of these States, depreciated; and lest the silence of Congress might give strength to the said report; resolved that the said report is false and derogatory to the honor of Congress."[32] One writer notes that "as paper money depreciated more and more, the pledges of Congress in respect to its redemption were more frequent and intense in form of expression."[33]

Congress resolved in September 1779 to issue paper money only to the total of $200 million. "Upon this mountain of paper," a modern historian has written, "Congress resolved to make its final stand. . . . But . . . the defiant proclamation of September 1779 proved the signal for another sharp selling wave in Continental money. By January 1780, the army was paying for supplies twice what it had paid in September 1779; and by March 1780, prices had risen four times above the level of September 1779."[34]

At that point, Congress began the outright repudiation of its paper, though the culmination was to come later. In March of 1780, Congress devalued the currency by proclaiming that it should now trade at forty to one of gold or silver. To finance this exchange, new paper money was to be issued to be redeemed by the states by taxation. An elaborate plan was contrived for the retiring of the old currency and replacing it with the new. The plan did not work. There was no reason why it should. If the new money was more valuable than the old, it would not circulate, according to Gresham's Law, assuming the old money was still legal tender. In fact, the new money quickly fell to the same value as the old,[35] and the whole became virtually worthless by 1781. In March of 1781, Congress abandoned the acceptance of its own paper money as legal tender. It was now to be accepted only on a sliding scale that was supposed to represent its depreciation. Thereafter, it depreciated so rapidly that it shortly ceased to circulate at all.[36] Specie came out of hiding and replaced paper money as the currency of the land.

145

All these untoward events might be accepted as the cost of the war, but only if the currency had enabled the Congress to bring the resources of the country to bear on the war effort. That, however, was emphatically not the case. On the contrary, the paper money plus the absence of significant taxation tended to disperse the resources of the country and the energies of the people. Congress and the states were continually short of money, whereas the populace had an abundance. In consequence, the production, transport, trading, and provision of goods and services were concentrated on the civilian population, and the armed forces received short shrift.

In the later stages of the war, as already noted, the army had to abandon the use of the paper money substantially and turn to direct methods to get goods and services. This was not only an inconvenient and inefficient method of gathering material but also made people resent the army. For example, here are reports of the situation in Virginia in 1781—at a time when a major British army was concentrated there and Washington was about to win his greatest victory. An agent sent to impress transport reported: "I have been much perplexed, for after having impressed them, the owners of some, by themselves or others, have taken, in the nighttime, a wheel or something to render them useless; and I don't recollect any law to punish them, if it could be proved." The Quartermaster wrote to the war office: "Let me entreat, sir, that something may be done to draw the people with their means of transportation into the service willingly. I find them so opposed to every measure that is oppressive that it is almost impossible to effect anything of consequence that way. Many of the teamsters upon the late occasion have deserted with their wagons after throwing their loads out at improper places. . . ."[37]

Nor were taxes in kind a way to get goods where they were wanted. General Washington wrote to the President of Pennsylvania in 1782: "A great proportion of the specific articles have been wasted after the people have furnished them, and the transportation alone of what has reached the army has in numberless instances cost more than the value of the articles themselves."[38] It is not difficult to explain why this was so. The commodities had been taken without reference to a particular need, had been stored where no army might appear, except by accident, and were often spoiled when they were wanted. By contrast with this poor form of barter, the market is an efficient and felicitous device when acceptable money is in circulation; the market tends to make the goods available where and when they are wanted, and money is flexible: it can call forth a variety of goods.

The American cause was not lost as a result of the inflation. It was won despite the inflation. But victory was almost certainly delayed for several years; much suffering resulted; and the people's confidence had been sorely tried. Indeed, we have not finished yet in this work with the consequences of the inflation, for they followed into the Confederation period. But the lessons of the experience were not lost on the leaders of that generation. In time, they were used to try to prevent a recurrence of the mistakes. Unfortunately, we cannot report that these lessons are still remembered to the seventh generation.

13

The American Triumph

That the Americans were eventually triumphant in the War for Independence is a matter of record. The triumph was military, diplomatic, and big with portent for the future of republics. That the triumph could have come earlier, could have been more decisive, and could have involved the United States in fewer entanglements, is speculation. George Washington thought that the victory could have come much sooner. In his circular letter to the governors of the states in 1783, he declared that if he had sufficient space he "could demonstrate to every mind open to conviction, that in less time, and with much less expense than has been incurred, the war might have been brought to the same happy conclusion, if the resources of the continent could have been properly drawn forth. . . ."[1] Speculation is not history of course, but it does sometimes help to shed light on history. The prolongation of the war due to the failure to muster American resources effectively brought in its train a host of consequences, some of which entangled America with European powers at just that time when they were effecting their independence of England.

The scope of the war was greatly broadened from 1778 onward. It spread and extended over much of the North American continent. There was extensive fighting in the Ohio valley, in Georgia and the Carolinas (fighting which involved Loyalists on a considerable scale, and heightened domestic animosities), in western New York, as well as elsewhere. Those who follow only George Washington's army during the course of the war lose sight of the vast amount of territory being contended for. The war became, also, a world war before it was over. France entered the fray against Britain in 1778, Spain in 1779, and Holland in 1780, though the last two were not allied with the United States.

In addition, there was a naval League of Armed Neutrality of other European powers organized against Britain.

American diplomats went to Europe seeking allies, munitions, and, above all, loans, to bolster sagging finances. European monarchs were hardly devoted to the idea of the rise of a republic in America or its independence (though some Frenchmen were); most of them did have axes to grind with Britain. Moreover, there was territory they would like to acquire or protect, and trade they would like to gain for their ships and ports. The aborning United States was caught up to some extent in the cross currents of the conflicting interests of European powers. Some Americans—notably Silas Deane, Arthur Lee, Benjamin Franklin, John Adams, and John Jay—experienced the machinations of European diplomats at first hand, an experience which confirmed most of them in their beliefs about the corruption of the Old World. However, America came out of all this much better than might have been expected.

Despite the French alliance and the portending entry of other European powers into the conflict, the American military position did not generally improve for some while. British strategy did change from what it had been up to 1778. During the early part of the war, Britain had focused the major military effort on the Middle States and their seaport cities. This approach was largely abandoned after Saratoga. Though the British continued to hold New York City and to concentrate the major army there, as things turned out this was a defensive position from 1778 until the end of the war.

British strategists at home pushed for the concentration of offensive measures in the South. Having failed in their efforts to conquer America by attacking at the points of the concentration of strength, they advocated attacking at the weakest point. This strategy had much to commend it. After all, the key to the effective control over much of what had been English America was Virginia. Virginia was the most populous of the states, the oldest of the colonies, the one in which the Anglican religion had been longest established, the producer of much that was most wanted by British merchants for world trade, and the hub of the Southern wheel. If Britain could control Virginia and the lower South, plus Canada, it might still dominate the vast eastern Mississippi valley region. Virginia already laid claim to much of the territory west of the Alleghenies; the conquest of Virginia might vouchsafe it to Britain. The approach to Virginia might be made from the lower South which was the weakest link in the colonial chain. Georgia was the least populous of the states, and a considerable portion of the population of South Carolina was slave. North Carolina was known to have an important Loyalist contingent.

150

Savannah fell to British forces in December of 1778, and early the next year they took over the rest of Georgia and installed a Loyal government. But the British stationed in Georgia had little success during the next year with their forays into South Carolina; the force sent there was not adequate to such a campaign. Early in 1780, however, General Clinton, who had been reluctant to undertake the Southern campaign, finally did so; he was able to take Charleston May 12, 1780 with a vastly superior military and naval force. Clinton returned to New York, entrusting the Southern campaign now to Lord Cornwallis. Cornwallis was probably the ablest field commander the British ever had in America. He was daring, courageous, beloved of his men, could win battles when the odds were against him by audacious tactics, and did win many battles. In fact, he won most of the battles and lost the war.

For the remainder of 1780, Cornwallis see-sawed back and forth between South and North Carolina with his army. Virtually the whole Patriot army in that region had been surrendered at Charleston, necessitating the assembly of a new force in the deep South. Congress sent General Horatio Gates, the victorious commander at Saratoga, southward with a core of Continentals to do the job. As it turned out, his victory at Saratoga had given Gates a much greater reputation than he deserved. Cornwallis routed his army at Camden in August; Gates fled the scene of battle on the fastest horse he could command, and was sixty miles away before he considered it safe to stop. His army was scattered, and his reputation was ruined.

Nathanael Greene assumed command of the Patriot forces in the Carolinas late in the year, and he proved worthy of the calling. He was as successful at maneuvering as his mentor, George Washington, but Cornwallis did not tarry overlong to test his talents. Instead, Cornwallis moved northward into Virginia in 1781, while Greene drove southward into South Carolina. In the course of the year he was so successful against British posts that they held only Charleston by the end of the year. Indeed, a pattern emerged in the South similar to the one elsewhere on the continent. The British frequently won the pitched battles, but once the main army moved on, the post left behind soon fell to Patriot forces.

During the late spring and into the summer of 1781 Cornwallis rampaged across Virginia with a much larger army than the Americans could muster in that state. When the American forces were increased, Cornwallis decided to establish a base accessible to the sea. He decided upon Yorktown which is located on the peninsula between the York and James rivers. He set up camp there in early August.

Virginians had for some time been pleading with Washington to come with his army to save his home state. However, Washington was confronting the largest British army in America in New York; victory over it would most likely be decisive; he wanted only the help of the French fleet to undertake it, and the French fleet was rarely available to him. However, he determined upon concentrating his effort against Cornwallis at Yorktown when the French agreed to aid him. Washington's Continentals were now reinforced by a major French army under the command of the Comte de Rochambeau. Washington took pains to tie Clinton's army down in New York both by leaving a sizable detachment behind and by getting misleading information to him.

The attacking army usually has a plan which, if it works, should bring victory, much as each play by the offense in football is conceived to make a touchdown—if it works. In battle, the aim is to bring such force to bear at selected points that it may be expected to break up the opposing army. Timing and coordination are the requisite conditions and are the most difficult to achieve. Washington's plan depended upon much greater coordination of a variety of elements than would commonly be involved. He had to move an army several hundred miles, most of them going over land. His heavy artillery was dispatched by sea, but its arrival was dependent on the dispersal of the British navy. The French navy had to be available at the right time or Cornwallis might be reinforced or his army transported elsewhere.

For once, all went well for the combined American and French undertaking. Clinton kept his army in New York; Admiral de Grasse, the French naval commander, turned up with the fleet at the right time, and lured the British navy out to sea after having successfully engaged it in action. Cornwallis stayed where he was, cut off by sea from retreat. The Continentals and the French were joined by the militia to make a formidably superior force under Washington. Cornwallis did not deign to attempt daring maneuvers to break out in these circumstances; after only a brief try against the forces, which did not even bring most of his army into play, he surrendered his army intact. The memorable date was October 19, 1781.

Yorktown was the great victory of the American War for Independence. It had all, or almost all, of the right ingredients. Washington was in command of the victorious; after so many years of perseverance in the face of the odds, his hour had come. That Cornwallis should have been the British commander defeated was as it should be, too, for no other British commander had routed so many American armies. Even the surrender was dramatically conducted, though Cornwallis sent a subaltern to do the dishonors. With the French lined up on one side and the Americans on the other, the British marched between them to the tune of "The World Turned Upside Down" to the place where they laid down their arms. The British turned their eyes toward the

French, as if in contempt of the Americans. They were roundly jeered by the Americans who waited to do so, wisely, until the British had thrown down their arms. Thus ended the last great battle of the war.

There had been and were to be American victories elsewhere, some with great portent for the future, though none so dramatic or decisive for victory in the war as that at Yorktown. Neither the British nor Americans had entirely neglected the western and southern frontiers. The British attempted to dominate the land beyond the mountains largely with the aid of the Indians. However, in 1778 and 1779 George Rogers Clark of Virginia broke the back of this dominance. Of Clark's victory at Vincennes in 1779, a military historian has said: "His march across flooded Illinois may not compare for hardship with Arnold's long journey through the Maine wilderness in 1775, yet the issue was happier, the victory complete and significant. British power in the West was broken, and despite the failure to take Detroit, Clark helped make it possible for the vast area to be included within the boundaries of the United States of America at the peace treaty."[2] Less grand in its dimensions but equally important for a smaller area, Georgia was reconquered by the Patriots in 1782, the culmination of a long series of exploits by General Anthony Wayne.

Much went on during the War for Independence besides military and naval battles, of course. Nor was the American triumph, in the final analysis, simply a military triumph. What Americans would do with their independence was surely more important than whether they would have it. One thing Americans were determined not to have for very long was arbitrary government. They thought that the way to avoid this was to have a written constitution. When Richard Henry Lee made a motion for independence in the Second Continental Congress in June of 1776, he included with his resolution a proposal that some plan of confederation be devised. Such a plan to be acceptable, of course, would have to be of the nature of a constitution. A committee was appointed to attend to this even before independence had been formally declared. A few days after the adoption of the Declaration, the committee presented what were called Articles of Confederation to the Congress. They were drafted, in the main, by John Dickinson.

Congress did not move with such dispatch to approve them, however, nor the states to their ratification. Some debate was wedged in from time to time between the more pressing items of business which confronted the Congress. The Articles of Confederation were finally adopted by Congress in 1777 and sent along in due course for the states to ratify. Most of the states acted within the next fourteen months, but Maryland withheld ratification for several years. The main issue was western lands, particularly the extensive claims of Virginia beyond the

153

mountains. Virginia would have been huge in comparison with the other states if it had consisted only of the present states of Virginia, West Virginia, and Kentucky, which it did; but that parent state laid claim to vast territory in the Ohio valley as well. Agreements of the states involved to yield up their western claims brought Maryland into the fold on March 1, 1781.

On the occasion, the *Pennsylvania Packet* editorialized in this jubilant fashion:

> This great event, which will confound our enemies, fortify us against their arts of seduction, and frustrate their plans of division, was announced to the public at twelve o'clock under the discharge of the artillery on the land, and the cannon of the shipping in the Delaware. The bells were rung, and every manifestation of joy shown on the occasion. . . .[3]

Truth to tell, however, it had taken more than half as long to get the Articles adopted as they would serve as the foundation for a union.

The Articles of Confederation were born of the necessity for the states to unite in order to carry on war against Britain and were given their content by the reaction to the increasing use of British power which occasioned the war. While men recognized the need for united action against a common enemy they were most reluctant to locate much power in a central government—or, if Madison was right in his later analysis, even to establish such a government.

There was considerable ambiguity as to the status of the states and of the union from the outset. That ambiguity was a product both of history and the desires of the people. On the one hand, the colonies had never been united with one another before 1776—except by their allegiance to the king of England, which tended to separate them from one another rather than to link them together. On the other hand, they acted together both in their resistance to British impositions and eventually in separating from England. There was no point in time when the states were independent and sovereign on their own. As John Fiske said: "It is . . . clear that in the very act of severing their connection with England these commonwealths entered into some sort of union which was incompatible with their absolute sovereignty taken severally."[4]

Yet, the term "state" was early used to apply to most of them, and the name has stuck (in general usage even when the "state" involved is actually styled a "commonwealth"). The most common meaning attached to "state" in political theory and usage is this: "the body politic as organized for supreme civil rule and government." A "state" is also usually referred to as sovereign and independent.

The Articles of Confederation did attempt to clear up any confusion in status; the question was formally resolved in favor of state sovereignty. The union established under the Articles was styled a confederation. In common usage, a confederation is an alliance or league among sovereign states. The articles appeared to affirm that this was to be the case. Article II says, "Each State retains its sovereignty, freedom and independence, and every power, jurisdiction and right, which is not by this confederation expressly delegated to the United States, in Congress assembled." What is implied here is a division of powers: some to be retained and exercised by the states individually, others to be conferred upon the confederation to be exercised jointly. But once such powers were conferred, the states would lose their absolute sovereignty. Could some plan not be devised whereby the states could retain their sovereignty individually, yet act together in common concerns? The Articles of Confederation attempted to do this.

What was tried was to make the Congress continually and completely dependent upon the states. Congress was denied the power of taxation, nor did it have any enforcement machinery of its own, i.e., it had neither constabulary nor courts. Moreover, the representatives to the Congress were to be chosen by or under the direction of the state legislatures. Each state was to have only one vote in the Congress, though a state might have from two to seven delegates. Care was taken that the members of Congress did not gain personal power. This was guarded against by having members subject to recall by the states at any time and prohibiting that any person serve more than three years in any six year period. The picture that emerges from this is of the states resolutely clinging to their power.

With the above restrictions upon it, Congress was ostensibly granted extensive authority. It was empowered to make war and peace, send and receive ambassadors and ministers, emit bills of credit, borrow money, make treaties and alliances, establish a post office, settle various kinds of disputes arising among the states, appoint high ranking military and all naval officers, fix the value of coins, regulate weights and measures, and manage Indian affairs where a state was not directly involved. Further to cement the union, the Articles provided that each state was to give full faith and credit to the acts of the others and that citizens of any state could move from state to state.

The Articles also limited state power in a variety of ways. States were prohibited to carry on diplomatic relations with other countries or enter into treaties or alliances with them without the consent of Congress. In a similar fashion, states were forbidden to form alliances or confederations with one another. States were limited in the military or naval forces they could have and restricted in their war-making powers to defensive action.

Although the Articles of Confederation were soon to be adjudged inadequate to the needs of union—and a further critique of them is made in a subsequent chapter—, they are nonetheless important for reasons in addition to the fact that they served briefly as a basis of governing the United States. First of all, the Articles were the first United States constitution. They were influential in the drawing of the constitution of 1787; some of the language was taken verbatim into the later document. They provided for a limited government with specified powers, probably the most important principle of the Constitution. And, the Articles attempted to divide and separate powers among two different levels of government, a principle which the later document incorporated much more effectively. The Articles of Confederation signify the triumph of limited constitutional government in America, even though they were a groping toward and a demonstrably insufficient realization of it.

The greatest achievement under the Articles of Confederation was the Treaty of Paris of 1783. By its terms the thirteen states not only attained their independence but also acquired an empire beyond the mountains. The acquisition of this vast domain was probably the greatest diplomatic triumph in American history. That a people who had won so few battles, who had such a weak central government, who had never managed to bring many of their resources to bear in the prosecution of the war effort, who were so dependent on the aid of other countries, should have such success at the peace table requires a little explanation.

The American success was helped by the precarious situation of the English. Britain wanted an end to the war, but her leaders were eager to prevent gains by European powers. Lord North's government fell in early 1782 in the most humiliating manner. A motion carried to make it a crime to advance the notion that the colonies could be restored by war. Lord North was replaced by the Earl of Rockingham, "the old Whig and repealer of the Stamp Act," who "was recalled to preside over a government committed to the abandonment of the former American colonies in revolt and to the liquidation of the world war in progress."[5] He died shortly, and was replaced by Lord Shelburne who was, if anything, more favorably disposed to the Americans than Rockingham.

France had already renounced any claim to any territory on the continent of North America in the Franco-American Alliance of 1778. Even so, France was not eager to see Canada become a part of the

156

United States. Moreover, France was allied with Spain and was, in this way, entangled with Spanish territorial ambitions. As if this were not enough, Congress instructed its peace commission to follow the guidance of the French in the treaty making.

It was left to the peace commission either to utilize to American advantage the animosities, jealousies, and rivalries of European powers or to have American ambitions subordinated to them. It was in the hands, then, of Benjamin Franklin, John Jay, and John Adams. A hostess thinking in terms of compatible guests probably would not have invited these three at the same time. Jay and Adams could get along well enough together. Both men were distrustful of European diplomats; they considered them corrupt and devious. Jay's recent experiences in Spain had fortified him in this opinion. John Adams was a Yankee—an American—, and proud of it. Truly one of the great men among the Founders, Adams' greatness was circumscribed by a temperament which tended to alienate others and a physique more suited to a mortician than a statesman. It was his fate to labor ever in the shade of men whose most lauded attainments he would hardly have considered worthy of his least efforts. He lacked Franklin's resiliency, Washington's commanding presence, Hamilton's dynamic drive, and Jefferson's knack for illuminating philosophical positions with unforgettable prose. Yet, great man he was, his constancy to the American cause was as enduring as Washington's, and his sacrifices for it were rarely exceeded. What he lacked as a diplomat he made up for with his commitment to his country. Benjamin Franklin was well, Benjamin Franklin: diplomat par excellence, homely economist, scientist and inventor, and international *bon vivant*. A good diplomat is one who yields everything to the other party except the substance for which they are contending. For much of his life Franklin had devoted himself to the austere task of learning to get his way by subterfuge. His years in Paris were a fitting epitome to a long life. These three matched and overmatched the best Europe could send against them.

Even before negotiations got under way, informal French and Spanish proposals had been brought to Jay's attention which would have turned the territory south of the Ohio over to Spain and allowed Britain to keep the territory north of the Ohio. "If this French proposal, which so pleased the Spaniards, had been adopted, the United States would not have secured from Great Britain title to the region now composing the present states of Ohio, Indiana, Illinois, Michigan, Wisconsin, and Minnesota, and would have lost to Spain the western part of Kentucky and Tennessee, Mississippi, and part of Louisiana, along with most of Alabama."[6] In view of the fact that Spain wanted Gibraltar from Britain and Britain wanted to hold on to Florida, the above dispositions might have been made if all interested parties had gathered around a table to negotiate or if France had been allowed the role of arbitrator.

This did not happen. The Americans ignored the instructions of Congress to defer to France, negotiated a settlement with Britain, and saw to it that this settlement was subsequently made a part of the overall treaty. They were faithful to the terms of alliance with France, for this was not a separate peace, but they undoubtedly exceeded the bounds Congress had set for them.

In the treaty, the United States got all the territory west to the Mississippi river, south to the 31st parallel, and north to a line bisecting the Great Lakes, or south of Canada. The British also conceded that the people of the United States could use the North Atlantic fisheries. The independence of the states was affirmed, hostilities were to cease, and Britain agreed to remove her armed forces from the United States "with all convenient speed."

There were some concessions made by the United States. Both sides agreed that creditors of either country should have no obstacles put in the way of collecting debts owed them by citizens of the other. Most of the creditors involved were British. Congress was to recommend to the states that the rights and property of Loyalists be restored, and the treaty provided that the persecution of Loyalists should end. Britain and the United States agreed to the free navigation of the Mississippi, but Spain, the other country with territory on it, did not join in the agreement.

The Treaty of Paris was truly an American triumph. George Washington described its portent in these words: "The citizens of America, placed in the most enviable condition, as the sole lords and proprietors of a vast tract of continent, comprehending all the various soils and climates of the world, and abounding with all the necessaries and conveniences of life, are now, by the late satisfactory pacification, acknowledged to be possessed of absolute freedom and independence."[7] Some decades ago, an American historian declared: "On the part of the Americans the treaty of Paris was one of the most brilliant triumphs in the whole history of modern diplomacy."[8] A more recent diplomatic historian has seconded this opinion: "The greatest victory in the annals of American diplomacy was won at the outset by Franklin, Jay, and Adams."[9]

The greatest triumph of all, however, requires an appreciation of what might have been but was not to stand out in relief. The most critical moment for the success of the American Revolution almost certainly came in 1783. It was at about the time of the British withdrawal of forces from the east coast. The Continental army, what remained of it in camps along with what might have been summoned again into serv-

158

ice, was now the only considerable force in the United States. This was the moment for a military *coup d'état*, if there was to be one, the moment when the American Revolution might have followed the course of so many others. Nor was the provocation lacking. The military had been sorely neglected during the long years of war. Now that the victory had been won, the army was invited to disband and its members return home without being paid what had so long been promised.

George Washington was almost certainly the key to what would and did happen at this critical juncture. His prestige had grown during the years of his command, until at the end of the war he was the pre-eminent American. His critics had harmed only themselves; they were chipping at granite with teaspoons. He was approached more than once with the idea that he take over the country. There is no evidence that he ever seriously contemplated such a course. On the contrary, he rebuked those who hinted at such things, and persisted in doing his duty as he saw it. His duty as he saw it was, having finished his military task to lay down his sword, following the path he had ever trod of subordination to the civil authorities, and return to his peaceful pursuits at Mount Vernon. His every utterance confirmed, too, that in this case duty was happily joined to his heart's desire, for he longed for the leisure to pursue his private affairs. Moreover, the manner in which he conducted himself in his resignation and retirement should leave no reasonable doubt as to his sincerity. A little retelling of some of the events of his last months of service will underscore the point.

Two events of early 1783 indicate that there was danger of a military revolt. The first of these is the one known as the Newburgh Address, which was a letter sent around to Washington's officers exhorting them to take matters into their own hands to get what they thought they deserved. Washington ordered his officers assembled and to be presided over by General Horatio Gates who, it is believed, had a hand in the Address. When they were assembled, Washington came into the room and asked to be allowed to say a few words to them. He told them that he knew well how much they had suffered and could sympathize with their wish to be rewarded. But he bade them to keep their faith in and with Congress. He had with him a letter from a member of Congress which he thought might help to restore their faith if he read from it. But when he opened it up to read, he had difficulty making out some of the words. He took out his eyeglasses and put them on—he had not worn them in public before—, and looking up from the letter, he said: "I have grown gray in your service, and now find myself growing blind." It is said that the eyes of those gathered round filled with tears, for they knew how sturdily he had borne so much for so many years. It was hardly necessary for him to finish what he had to say.

Once Washington withdrew, the officers adopted a resolution affirming their confidence in Congress and declared that they rejected "with disdain the infamous proposals contained in a late anonymous address to them."[10] Of less potential for mischief was an event in June, though it does show what might have been. Fewer than a hundred soldiers of the Pennsylvania Line regiment descended on Congress at Philadelphia and threatened them in such a way that Congress retired to hold its deliberations at Princeton. Washington sent troops to put down this little uprising in Pennsylvania.

The last major contingent of British forces departed from New York City in early December of 1783. Just prior to their taking leave the Continental troops moved into the city to see that everything went off in an orderly way. It was an occasion for great rejoicing as the Continentals marched in, for the British had occupied the city for more than seven years. A spectator wrote: "We had been accustomed for a long time to military display in all the finish and finery of garrison life; the troops just leaving us were as if equipped for show, and with their scarlet uniforms and burnished arms, made a brilliant display; the troops that marched in, on the contrary, were ill-clad and weather beaten, and made a forlorn appearance; but then they were *our* troops, and as I looked at them and thought upon all they had done and suffered for us, my heart and eyes were full, and I admired and gloried in them the more, because they were weather beaten and forlorn."[11]

The time had at last come for George Washington to take leave of the army he had served for eight and a half years. He notified the officers that he would bid them farewell at Fraunces' Tavern at noon of the day of departure. All who could make it gathered there. It was a moving occasion. Washington was so filled with emotion that he could hardly speak. "With a heart full of love and gratitude," he said, "I now take my leave of you. I most devoutly wish that your later days may be as prosperous and happy as your former ones have been glorious and honorable." So saying, he asked that each of them would come by to shake his hand, since he feared he would not be able to make it around to them. General Henry Knox, who had served him faithfully for so many years, came first; Washington was so overcome that a handshake would not do. He embraced him as both of them wept. "Once done, this had of course to be done with all from Steuben to the youngest officer. With streaming eyes, they came to him, received the embrace, and passed on."[12]

Washington hoped to make it home to Virginia by Christmas when he set out from New York. But there were many festive occasions to be attended along the way, and he had business to do first. He journeyed to Philadelphia to turn in his accounts. Then he went on to Annapolis to resign his commission before Congress.

This he did just after twelve o'clock on December 23rd. The galleries were packed for the occasion, though many members of Congress were absent at this time. As the ceremony began, Washington's biographer says that "a hush of high expectance prevailed." Washington began his address: "Mr. President: The great events on which my resignation depended having at length taken place; I have now the honor of offering my sincere Congratulations to Congress and of presenting myself before them to surrender into their hands the trust committed to me, and to claim the indulgence of retiring from the service of my country."[13]

> It was a solemn and affecting spectacle. . . . The spectators all wept, and there was hardly a member of Congress who did not drop tears. The General's hand which held the address shook as he read it. When he spoke of the officers who had composed his family, and recommended those who had continued in it to the present moment to the favorable notice of Congress he was obliged to support the paper with both hands. But when he commended the interests of his dearest country to almighty God . . . his voice faltered and sunk, and the whole house felt his agitations.

When Washington regained his composure, he concluded strongly:

> Having now finished the work assigned me I retire from the great theatre of action, and bidding an affectionate farewell to this august body under whose orders I have so long acted I here offer my commission and take my leave of all the employments of public life.[14]

As soon as the ceremony was over, Washington set out for Mount Vernon, and by hard riding was able to make it home to spend Christmas day with his wife and grandchildren. The American Cincinnatus had returned to his plow.

14

Freeing the Individual

Scribes are quite often merciless tyrants in dealing with characters out of the past, spearing them with an assortment of verbs and freezing them in predetermined categories with their adjectives, much as a butterfly collector does with his helpless insects. There is no surer way to shatter the integrity of an individual or to distort a historical epoch than by the indiscriminate use of categories. No man of wit is likely to believe that a category comprehends him, even when it is well chosen. But when categories drawn from other times and places are imposed upon men and events which are foreign to them, the result can only be to confuse the subject under discussion.

Some twentieth century historians have done just this to American history of the late eighteenth century. They have called Americans of the time by names, some of which were unknown to them and others which they would have disavowed; they have labeled them as revolutionaries or reactionaries, democrats or aristocrats, nationalists or state's righters, liberals or conservatives, and other such categories. They have tried to thrust the events into revolutionary and "social" revolutionary categories, categories drawn from other revolutions and other circumstances. It is a journalistic habit into which many historians have fallen to attribute an absoluteness to the views and thrusts of men which violates both what they intend and ultimately do. Debates, even great historical debates, can be quite misleading. Men often advance positions with more certainty than they feel, appear to be unalterable in their determination, yet may shortly yield to the other side with good humor when they have lost. Some historians appear to have no difficulty whatever in discovering men's motives, but the fact is that we are not privy to their motives.

The subject to be treated below is the reforms and innovations made by Americans mostly in the decade after the declaring of independence. The above prelude was deemed necessary because the writer both wishes to make known the fact that he is familiar with the crosscurrents of interpretation of these years by twentieth century historians and to disavow many of the categories that have been used. After the Americans broke from England they made some changes; they sometimes differed among themselves as to what the direction of change should be; but there is no need to question their motives or their basis. Above all, there is no need to push this one into that category and that one into this, with the category being excessively large for the matter at issue and much too confining for the man over any period of time. More rubbish has been written about the class positions and interests of the men of these times than any other in American history, so far as I can make out. The present writer has neither the space nor inclination to spend energy upon trying to refute what has not even been well established.

What is established is that some changes were made during these years. The main thrust of these changes is the freeing of the individual: freeing him from foreign domination, from various government compulsions, from class prescriptions, and for greater control of his own affairs. And, in conjunction with these, there was an effort to erect safeguards around him that would protect him in the exercise of his rights. The thrust to do these things was made along several different paths, and each of these is worth some attention.

A primary aim of the Americans was independence. They wanted to be independent of England, of course; that was what the war was fought about. Many Americans had come to believe that they could only have the requisite control of their affairs by separating from the mother country. This was achieved, of course, by terms of the Treaty of Paris. But Americans longed also to be independent of European entanglements. Time after time, during the colonial period, Americans had been drawn into wars that originated in Europe but spread to the New World. Americans wanted to be free of the dynastic quarrels, the imperial ambitions, and the trade wars which rended Europe and shook much of the rest of the world. To many Americans, Europe was the symbol and embodiment of corruption, decadence, and foreclosed opportunity. To be independent of Europe was, in the final analysis, to be free to follow courses which had not yet, at any rate, proven to be so laden with disaster.

Independence did not mean, nor should it be taken to connote, the rejection of either the English or European heritage. Indeed, there was little irrational rejection of either heritage that comes to mind. Though Americans rejected European aristocracy they did not, for that

164

reason, change names of places in this country derived from aristocrats.

Perhaps, the most extensive thrust of this period was to free the individual from government compulsion. Libertarian sentiment had been maturing for some considerable while in America; it was fostered both by legal trends and religious and other intellectual developments. Once the break from England came, Americans used the occasion to cut away a body of restraints no longer in accord with their outlook.

Religious liberty was widely secured within a decade or so of the break from England. Much of it came by way of the disestablishment of churches. The establishment most readily dispensed with was that of the Church of England. While the Church of England was established throughout the South as well as in New York, it was not very popular; many of its clergy remained loyal to England, and adherents of it were outnumbered by dissenters in most states. Its disestablishment was made even easier because it was a national church; membership in it was tied to loyalty to the king of England. The Church of England was everywhere speedily disestablished. But these actions were not simply prompted by convenience, for there was increasing belief in religious liberty. Several states had no established churches: namely, New Jersey, Rhode Island, Pennsylvania, and Delaware. But they used the opportunity afforded by independence to remove or reduce restrictions. Some of the disabilities of Roman Catholics were cut away.

The established Congregational church was maintained for several decades longer in Massachusetts, Connecticut, and New Hampshire. There was, however, some liberalization in these states. The Massachusetts constitution of 1780 affirmed that every man had the right to worship in his own way, that no church should be subordinated to any other, and that tax moneys could be used to support ministers other than Congregationalists. However, church attendance was required still, and ministers were supported from taxes.[1] "New Hampshire followed in the steps of Massachusetts, but Connecticut held out much longer against what its citizens regarded as the forces of iniquity. They allowed dissenters to escape payment of taxes to the established church if they presented the clerk of the local church with a certificate of church attendance signed by an officer of the dissenter's own church."[2]

The constitutions of New Jersey, Georgia, North and South Carolina, Delaware, and Pennsylvania "explicitly provided that no man should be obliged to pay any church rate or attend any religious service save according to his own free and unhampered will."[3] But Virginia made the greatest effort to assure religious liberty. This might have been a reaction to the fact that Virginia had the longest establishment and one of the most rigorous. Thomas Jefferson, James Madison, and George Mason were leading advocates of religious liberty, but they did not succeed in getting their ideas into law until 1786. This was done by the Virginia Statute of Religious Freedom, which proclaimed religious liberty a natural right. An impressive preface states the case:

> Whereas, Almighty God hath created the mind free; that all attempts to influence it by temporal punishments or burthens, or by civil incapacitations, tend only to beget habits of hypocrisy and meanness, and are a departure from the plan of the Holy author of our religion . . .

The legally effective portion of the statute reads this way:

> That no man shall be compelled to frequent or support any religious worship, place, or ministry whatsoever, nor shall be enforced, restrained, molested, or burthened in his body or goods, nor shall otherwise suffer on account of his religious opinions or belief; but that all men shall be free to profess, and by argument to maintain, their opinion in matters of religion, and that the same shall in no wise diminish, enlarge, or affect their civil capacities.[4]

This was what Americans were to come to think of as religious liberty in the course of time.

The movement for freeing the slaves reached a peak in the 1780's which it would not soon attain again. Even before the break from England, the slave trade was acquiring a bad reputation in America, but such efforts as were made to restrict it were negated by the mother country. Fiske says, "The success of the American Revolution made it possible for the different states to take measures for the gradual abolition of slavery and the immediate abolition of the foreign slave-trade."[5] Nor was sentiment against slavery restricted to states in which there were few slaves. Some of the outstanding leaders from the South during this period, most of them slaveholders, spoke out against slavery. Henry Laurens, a leader in South Carolina, wrote in 1776: "You know my Dear Sir. I abhor slavery . . .—in former days there was no combatting the prejudices of Men supported by Interest, the day I hope is approaching when from principles of gratitude as well [as] justice every Man will strive to be foremost in shewing his readiness to comply with the Golden Rule. . . ."[6] Thomas Jefferson argued in his *Notes on the State of Virginia* that slavery had a bad influence on the manners and morals of the white people as well as devastating effects on the Negroes. He longed for and hoped to see the day when all slaves would be emancipated. He warned his countrymen of the impending impact on them

166

if this were not done: "And can the liberties of a nation be thought secure when we have removed their only firm basis, a conviction in the minds of the people that these liberties are the gift of God? That they are not to be violated but with his wrath? Indeed I tremble for my country," he said, "when I reflect that God is just: that his justice cannot sleep forever. . . ."[7]

Some states began to act almost as soon as the opportunity arose. In 1776, Delaware prohibited the importation of slaves and removed all restraints on their manumission. Virginia stopped slave imports in 1778; Maryland adopted a similar measure in 1783. Both states now allowed manumission at the behest of the owner. In 1780, Pennsylvania not only prohibited further importation of slaves but also provided that after that date all children born of slaves should be free. Similar enactments were made in the early 1780's in New Hampshire, Connecticut, and Rhode Island. In Massachusetts, the supreme court decided that on the basis of the constitution of 1780 slavery was abolished in that province. Even North Carolina moved to discourage the slave trade in 1786 by taxing heavily such slaves as were imported after that time. In order to protect free Negroes, Virginia made it a crime punishable by death for anyone found guilty of selling a freed Negro into slavery.[8]

How far sentiment against slavery had gone may well be best indicated by the Northwest Ordinance (1787), an act of all the states, as it were, in Congress assembled. The act provided: "There shall be neither slavery nor involuntary servitude in the said territory, otherwise than in the punishment of crimes, whereof the party shall have been duly convicted. . . ." This article was passed, according to one of its proponents, without opposition.[9]

The bills of rights drawn and adopted in the various states contained provisions intended to assure individual liberties. These bills of rights were usually drawn and adopted along with constitutions but were frequently separate documents. They were usually cast in the language of natural rights theory. For example, Article I of the Massachusetts Declaration of Rights states:

> All men are born free and equal, and have certain natural, essential, and unalienable rights; among which may be reckoned the right of enjoying and defending their lives and liberties; that of acquiring, possessing, and protecting property; in fine, that of seeking and obtaining their safety and happiness.[10]

Virginia was the first state to draw both a constitution and a bill of rights. Actually, Virginia's Bill of Rights was adopted June 12, 1776, while the would-be state was still a colony. It was the work primarily of George Mason, was circulated among the states, and became a model for such instruments.

The Virginia Bill of Rights guaranteed trial by jury in both criminal and civil cases, prohibited excessive bail and fines, declared general warrants to be oppressive, and acknowledged freedom of the press. The protections of a person accused of a crime were spelled out:

> That in all capital or criminal prosecutions a man hath a right to demand the cause and nature of his accusation, to be confronted with the accusers and witnesses, to call for evidence in his favour, and to a speedy trial by an impartial jury of his vicinage, without whose unanimous consent he cannot be found guilty, nor can he be compelled to give evidence against himself; that no man may be deprived of his liberty, except by the law of the land or the judgment of his peers.

The only specific protection of property, other than the provision for jury trial in civil cases, was the requirement that men "cannot be taxed or deprived of their property for public uses, without their own consent, or that of their representives so elected. . . ."[11]

The Massachusetts Declaration of Rights of 1780, the work mainly of John Adams, was considerably more thorough. In regard to property, it said: "No part of the property of any individual can, with justice, be taken from him, or applied to public uses, without his consent, or that of the representative body of the people. . . . And whenever the public exigencies require that the property of any individual should be appropriated to public uses, he shall receive a reasonable compensation therefor."[12] Other rights were alluded to besides those mentioned in the Virginia Bill: freedom from unreasonable searches, the right to bear arms, the right of peaceful assembly, the prohibition of ex post facto laws, the prohibition of attainders by the legislature, as well as most of those covered in Virginia.

The Northwest Ordinance sums up, in Article II, what may well be considered a consensus of the protections of the rights of the people most needed:

> The inhabitants of the said territory shall always be entitled to the benefits of the writs of *habeas corpus*, and of the trial by jury; of a proportionate representation of the people in the legislature, and judicial proceedings according to the course of the common law. All persons shall be bailable, unless for capital offences, where the proof shall be evident, or the

presumption great. All fines shall be moderate; and no cruel or unusual punishments shall be inflicted. No man shall be deprived of his liberty or property, but by the judgment of his peers, or the law of the land, and should the public exigencies make it necessary, for the common preservation, to take any person's property, or to demand his particular services, full compensation shall be made for the same. And, in the just preservation of rights and property, it is understood and declared, that no law ought ever to be made to have force in the said territory, that shall in any manner whatever, interfere or affect private contracts, or engagements, *bona fide*, and without fraud previously formed.[13]

Some recent writers have claimed that the Founders distinguished between "human rights" and property rights in favor of "human rights." It should be clear from the above that no such distinction can be discerned, nor has the present writer ever seen a quotation from the original that could reasonably be construed to show that the Founders made any such distinction.

Property was, however, freed from various feudal restraints during this period and made more fully the possession of the individual holding title to it. The most general encumbrance on property ownership was the quitrent—a periodical payment due to king or proprietor on land, a payment that originated in the late Middle Ages as money payments displaced personal servitude. Such claims were speedily extinguished following the break from England, and land thereafter was held in "fee simple." Such royal prerogatives as the right of the monarch to white pines on private land were, of course, nullified. States abolished entail, also, a move which enhanced the authority of the owner to dispose of his lands, since entailed estates could not be broken up.

With the Declaration of Independence, the whole edifice of mercantilism as imposed from England was swept away. One history describes the impact of this as follows: "As a result of the American Revolution, freedom of enterprise, that is, the equal opportunity of any individual to engage in any economic activity he chooses in order to amass wealth, and to hold onto his wealth or dispose of it as he pleases, became a living reality in America to a greater degree than before."[14]

Another sort of innovation may be described as anti-class in its character. Fixed classes are supported and maintained by government where they exist. Americans of this period wanted to remove government support of classes and prevent the growth of special privileges by which classes are shaped. Some of the actions already described were, in part, anti-class measures. For example, the established Church of England was hierarchical and, in England particularly, a major support of class arrangements. Its disestablishment in America struck at the root of government support of class structures. Entailment was a means of perpetuating great estates, just as quitrents were devices for maintaining aristocracies. Other actions were taken that were even more pointedly aimed at removing government from its role as class perpetuator.

One of these was the abolition of primogeniture. Primogeniture was the rule that the estate of one who died without a will should go either whole or in large part to the eldest son. States abolished this rule and adopted the practice of dividing the estate equally among the children when the father died intestate. The tendency of this was for great estates to be broken up from time to time.

Various sorts of provisions were made in state constitutions to prevent the growth of aristocratic privileges. For example, the Virginia Bill of Rights had this provision:

> That no man or set of men, are entitled to exclusive or separate emoluments or privileges from the community, but in consideration of publick services; which, not being descendible, neither ought the offices of magistrate, legislator or judge to be hereditary.[15]

The Massachusetts Declaration held:

> No man, nor corporation, or association of men, have any other title to obtain advantages, or particular and exclusive privileges, distinct from those of the community, than what arises from the consideration of services rendered to the public; and this title being in nature neither hereditary, nor transmissible to children, or descendants, or relations by blood; the idea of a man born a magistrate, lawgiver, or judge, is absurd and unnatural.[16]

The animus against titles of nobility found expression sometimes. So strong was the animus against hereditary positions that the Society of the Cincinnati, a voluntary association of officers who had served in the War for Independence, found it expedient to abandon the rule that membership could be inherited to allay the indignation against them. Frequent elections and restrictions on the amount of time one could serve in office were efforts to prevent the emergence of a ruling class, at least in part.

The kind of equality sought by prohibitions against governmentally fostered classes was equality before the law. So far as any other equality

170

was concerned, American opinion of that time accepted differences in wealth and social station as inevitable and desirable results of differences in ability and effort. Undoubtedly, there were those in that day who would have liked to have some portions of the wealth and estates of others—who coveted what was not theirs—as there are in any day, but they were either inarticulate or ashamed to profess their views. Some historians have made much ado about the confiscation and sale of Loyalist estates during the war. This is treated as if it were a redistributionist scheme, and there is an attempt to give factual support to this notion by pointing out that large estates were sometimes broken up before they were offered for sale. This did sometimes happen, but it does not follow that it was done with any motive of equalizing holdings. Small parcels attract more bidders than large ones; hence, the price attained for large estates was likely to be increased by dividing them up. Moreover, large estates were sometimes formed or added to by buying several parcels.[17]

There were some general changes in governments during this period, changes in degree from what they had been under British rule. The main tendency was to make the state governments more dependent upon the popular will than they had been during the colonial period. The new state constitutions required that all state officers either be chosen by the electorate or appointed by those who had.

The main impetus behind making governments depend more closely on the electorate was a profound fear of government. This suspicion was most clearly shown in a distrust of governors and courts, those parts of the government that had not been popularly chosen during the colonial period. The colonists feared the legislatures, too, or so the limitations on them would indicate, but out of their colonial experience, they feared them less than the other branches. In point of fact, Americans relied rather heavily on a narrow and provincial colonial experience in making their first constitutions. Probably, Massachusetts and New York should be excepted from these strictures.

The office of governor—or whatever the executive might be called, for some states abandoned briefly that colonial title—was stripped of much of the power and most of the independence enjoyed by colonial chief executives. Colonial governors had usually possessed an absolute veto over legislation. The new executives were stripped of the veto power in all but two of the states—Massachusetts and New York—and in these the power was somewhat weakened. In all the states but New York the legislatures or the constitutions governed the assembling and dispersal of the legislative branch. In eight of the states, the chief executive was elected by the legislature, and he was made, thereby, greatly dependent upon it. His tenure of office was usually quite brief. In nine states, it was only 12 months, and nowhere was it for a longer period

171

than three years. To prevent the growth of personal power in the hands of the governor, most state constitutions limited the number of terms he could serve in a given period.[18]

The courts generally were made more dependent on legislatures than they had been formerly. The Pennsylvania constitution described the relationship this way: "The judges of the supreme court of judicature shall have fixed salaries, be commissioned for seven years only, though capable of reappointment at the end of that term, but removable for misbehavior at any time by the general assembly. . . ."[19] Even so, the principle of separation of powers generally prevailed between the courts and the legislature more fully than between governors and legislatures.

The legislatures were subject to frequent elections, a device for making them closely dependent upon the electorate. In ten of the states the lower house was subject to annual elections; in two states their terms were only for six months. The members of the upper house usually had somewhat longer terms, but one state did not even have an upper house.[20] Even so, the powers of the legislatures were quite extensive. Thomas Jefferson complained that in Virginia:

> All the powers of government, legislative, executive, and judiciary, result to the legislative body. . . . An *elective despotism* was not the government we fought for, but one which should not only be founded on free principles, but in which the powers of government should be so divided and balanced among several bodies of magistracy, as that no one could transcend their legal limits, without being effectually checked and restrained by the others.[21]

What had been generally done was this: Americans in establishing their state governments had sought to check them by the electorate rather than by an internal balance of powers. The people could, however, use their influence to abet arbitrary government as well as to check it.

There was also some extension of the franchise during this period. Particularly, several legislatures were reapportioned to give inhabitants in the back country a more nearly proportionate voice in government. One trend, in this connection, was the movement of state capitals inland from the coast to make them more accessible to the back country.

Most of these were changes of degree rather than of kind. To call them revolutionary, as some twentieth century historians have, is a distortion of what happened and a stretching of the meaning of revolution beyond reasonable confines. Insofar as they were changes from what had prevailed, they were culminations of trends long afoot. Americans had been tending toward religious liberty in practice long before they established it in fundamental law. They had been evading, so far as they could, quitrents, primogeniture, and entail. Their new governmental structures embodied much of what they had been contending with the British for. Bills of rights, bicameral legislatures, and weak executives, were built on the British model. The assault on special privilege did run contrary to recent British practice to some extent, but it was quite in accord with what Americans had been doing almost since they had reached the New World. If in their early enthusiasms in government building they did not attend to a broader experience than their colonial one, this did not make their acts revolutionary, only precipitate. They were clear enough that they wanted to protect the individual from government in the enjoyment of his rights; they did not at first realize how much more this took than felicitously phrased declarations. Weak governments do not make liberty and property secure; that is the office of powerful governments internally restrained. Many Americans were to learn this lesson, and rather quickly. But just as their first experiments were not revolutionary in character, no more were their later alterations a counter-revolution.

15

The Critical Period

Americans established weak governments after they separated from England. Indeed, the governments were weakest at the points requiring greatest strength, namely, in the conduct of relations with foreign powers and in the executive branch. It is easy to understand and sympathize with their reasons for establishing weak governments. Government, any government, has the potential for tyranny. Its monopoly of the use of force within its jurisdictions tends to make those under it impotent in conflict with it. Men are drawn to it by the opportunity it offers for the exercise of power, and the likelihood of the abuse of power is almost as certain as death and taxes. Why not, then, guard against these potentialities becoming actualities by keeping government weak? Let the power reside mainly in the people, and make those in government come hat in hand frequently asking for what they need. Why not, indeed?

Because, in the first place, the attractiveness of a weak government to the law-abiding is based largely on illusion, the illusion that weak is synonymous with limited and restrained. It is not; it is synonymous with impotent, frail, and lack of power to perform allotted functions. Government maintains peace by having the respect of the decent, holding the irrational in awe, and intimidating the lawless. A weak government is more likely to be arbitrary, capricious, and even despotic than a strong one, for the uncertain status of its ability to use force leads to unpredictable usages. The weakness of Congress set the stage for its inflationary policies. The weakness of state governments resulted in arbitrary practices for raising supplies for the army during the war. A weak government is prone to preying on the weak—those who most need its protection—and this penchant is probably aggravated by popular governments which are continuously seeking popular support. The treatment of Loyalists by the state governments during and after

175

the war is probably a case in point. Above all, weak governments invite challenges to their authority which, when brought forth, result in war or revolution. How critical the situation was in America in the mid 1780's is and will remain in doubt, but the portent of crisis follows necessarily from the condition of the governments.

That the state governments were weak as well as the Congress is revealed by analysis. Governors were made nearly impotent by their dependence on the legislatures. Legislatures had considerable power of making laws, but they were not charged with executing them. The Congress established by the Articles of Confederation had little power at all. It was charged with major responsibilities, yet it had no independent executive, no courts of its own, nor any direct sources of revenue. Moreover, the members of Congress were made so dependent upon state legislatures for their tenure that they were most reluctant to act.

The bane of republics is a lack of continuity of government because the government changes hands so often. Each election may bring a new set of rulers. Monarchy does not suffer much from this defect, but it has others which disqualified it for Americans. The constitution makers of the revolutionary period aggravated the discontinuity attendant upon republics. Not only did constitutions frequently call for annual elections but also there were sometimes limitations on how frequently within a period an individual could serve. Members of Congress had no assurance of continuation from one session to the next or even that they might not be recalled during a session, and they were prohibited to serve more than a portion of a given period. It was difficult, in these circumstances, for the governments to have even that continuity which they can have in republics. It is true, of course, that it was virtually impossible for one man to gain much power, but it was equally difficult for him to exercise governmental authority.

The greatest weakness of governing power was in conducting relations with foreign countries. The responsibility devolved upon the Congress for carrying on these relations, but that body did not have the power to compel the acceptance of its decisions. It had no courts dependent upon it with authority to act upon the people. There was talk that Congress might use force upon states, but such a measure would have been war. The states had more powerful governments than did the Confederation, but they lacked authority to conduct foreign relations.

By their grants of power to their governments, it is clear that Americans did not sufficiently appreciate the necessity for some government exercising the powers that the British had during the colonial period. A good case could be made that this was true regarding trade restrictions, but the failure to empower a government to deal effectively with foreign nations was like burning down the barn to get rid of the rats if what they opposed was mercantile regulations.

That Congress was almost impotent in dealing with other nations does not have to be concluded from theory alone; history affords examples enough. Nowhere was the weakness clearer than in relations with England. John Adams became minister to the Court of St. James in 1785. He hoped to obtain a commercial treaty with Britain that would open British colonial ports to American ships. But he found the government there unwilling to make any concessions, almost contemptuous of the usefulness of any agreement with the Confederation, and well satisfied with commercial relations as they stood. Instead of being able to make new agreements, Adams found himself occupied with questions surrounding the terms of and compliance with the Treaty of Paris of 1783.

The British reproached the United States through Adams for not complying with the terms of the treaty. The treaty required Congress to recommend to the states that the rights of Loyalists be restored. (This had been a concession by the United States, since the British were not committed to nor did they make reparations for damages done by their armies or Loyalists in the United states.) Congress did, indeed, make such a recommendation to the states, but some of the states were more inclined to further retaliation, and none of them was favorably disposed to full restitution for Loyalists. Technically, Congress had complied with the terms of the treaty, but the failure of the states to heed their recommendation pointed up the weakness of the Confederation. The treaty also specified that the states would not hamper or impede the collection of debts by British citizens. One history says: "There is no doubt that this article was violated both in letter and spirit. Virginia, where the debts were heaviest. . . , led the way in passing laws hampering the recovery of British debts."[1] Congress was, of course, powerless to do anything about the state recalcitrance.

American compliance with the treaty was made the more pressing, because the British used it as an excuse for failure to comply in the Old Northwest. They had several military posts on the American side of the Great Lakes. Contrary to the treaty provisions, they did not evacuate them; instead, a secret order to hold them indefinitely went out in 1784. Though the posts themselves were peripheral, they provided bases for the British to exercise influence on Indians in American territory and for carrying on a lucrative fur trade.[2] This increased the difficulty of making white settlements in the area and, thus, of the sale of lands by the Confederation.

Difficulties with Spain were, if anything, more pressing than those with Britain. Trading privileges were not at issue, for Spain had opened up her most important colonial ports to America. The major issues were the location of the boundaries between the United States and Spanish territory to the south and west, and navigation and use of the Mississippi and ports on it. The difficulty arose out of differences in claims and designs on the old Southwest between the United States and Spain. Spain had lately reacquired Florida, which included at that time a West Florida extending all the way to the Mississippi. Spain continued its historic claim to the vast territory west of the Mississippi. These territories gave Spain control over the gateway to the Gulf of Mexico. The fact that Britain had ceded territory to the United States did not greatly impress the Spanish, particularly when these same British were clinging to their own posts to the north in defiance of the treaty.

In 1784, Spain concluded treaties with Indians within the territory of the United States. Moreover, Spain held onto a military post at Natchez which had been acquired during the war but which was now within the treaty territory of the United States. Spain also made private agreements with Americans for the use of the Mississippi ports and was working to undermine the allegiance of those west of the Applachians to the United States. It was the position of both Britain and the United States that navigation of the Mississippi River was free to all, but Spain did not recognize this position. Nor would Spain grant the right of deposit of goods in New Orleans—a right essential to the effective use of the Mississippi—to the United States.

Of course, use of the Mississippi was an absolute requirement for the commercial development of the trans-Allegheny region of America. The expense of transporting freight from the west to the east overland was prohibitive; only lightweight cargo of very high value could even be considered worth transporting in this fashion. Even so, settlers poured into this area in increasing numbers in the 1780's from the older states despite the fact that, as matters stood, they must either switch their allegiance to Spain or be denied the opportunity of developing the country. John Jay conducted negotiations over a considerable period with the Spanish diplomat, Diego de Gardoqui, but the United States had little to offer and the Spanish little to fear from the continuation of the deadlock. Jay saw scant hope for settling the dispute favorably to the United States by negotiation and was entirely unenthusiastic about a recourse to arms. "For," he said in 1786, "unblessed with an efficient government, destitute of funds, and without publick credit, either at home or abroad, we should be obliged to wait in patience for better days, or plunge into an unpopular and dangerous war with very little prospect of terminating it by a peace, either advantageous or glorious."[3]

Not all the difficulties of the Confederation were with European countries; those people commonly called the Barbary Pirates along the African coast of the Mediterranean disrupted trade in a particularly distressing way. Several Moslem principalities, or whatever they should be called, had long preyed on shipping in the Mediterranean. Countries who wished to avoid their depredations were expected to pay bribes. Once the Americans cut themselves loose from British protection, they were exposed to these pirates. Algeria went to war with the United States, or so rumor had it, seized two American ships, and enslaved their crews. The enslaved Americans "were forced to carry timber and rocks on long hauls over rough mountainous roads."[4] Congress offered to ransom the sailors, but the amount they could and did offer was too small. A "diplomat" from another principality approached the United States with the proposition that the harassment of shipping would cease if tribute in sufficient amount were paid. As things stood, however, the United States could neither afford to pay tribute nor assemble the necessary force to suppress the pirates.[5]

Many of the Confederation's troubles can be traced to financial difficulties. These were frequently tied in and contributed to the ineffectiveness in dealing with foreign nations. A country that had repudiated its currency at the outset and whose diplomats had to go cup in hand, as it were, to other nations seeking funds was hardly in a good bargaining position. There were, of course, domestic as well as foreign consequences of the financial shambles of the Confederation.

The methods used to finance the war had left not only a debt (despite the repudiation of the currency) but also a legacy of consequences which many do not ascribe to the inflation. Inflation through the year of 1780 was followed by a drastic deflation. There is no mystery about the cause of the deflation; when the tender laws were removed the Continental paper ceased to circulate as money. Much the same thing happened to the paper money that had been issued by the states during the war. Specie replaced paper as currency, but there was much less of it than there had been of the other. Prices then had to be adjusted downward to make trade feasible in the new currency. The supply of currency was further depleted when trade with Britain was resumed, for the United States had an unfavorable balance. Americans still showed a marked preference for British goods and large quantities of them were imported, but the British did not buy goods of nearly the same value from Americans. There had long been an imbalance between the two, but it was worse now because the British would not allow Americans to make up the difference by carrying goods to British possessions. "The result was that within a year or two after the war . . . there was a dearth of both paper money and hard money."[6]

A drastic deflation produces, or *is*, what is most commonly called a depression. The deflation itself can be correctly described as a healthy corrective to the inflation that preceded it, a return to sound values from the grotesquely inflated situation that disrupted the market. Depressions, on the other hand, are universally deplored, at least in our time. Nor is this so strange, for although prices can be adjusted to the monetary situation, the same can hardly be accomplished regarding obligations contracted during the inflation. Prices fall, money is hard to acquire, yet debts remain to be paid. As one historian writing about these times said: "Hard is the lot of one who, burdened with taxes and debts and destitute of cash, is beset by falling prices of the things he makes and sells."[7]

Historians differ as to the extent, depth, and impact of the depression of the 1780's. Some hold that it deepened and worsened in the latter part of the decade.[8] One historian, at least, cites considerable evidence that economic conditions were greatly improving after 1785.[9] For example Benjamin Franklin wrote in 1786: "America never was in higher prosperity, her produce abundant and bearing a good price, her working people all employed and well paid, and all property in lands and houses of more than treble the value it bore before the war; and our commerce being no longer the monopoly of British merchants, we are furnished with all the foreign commodities we need, at much more reasonable rates than heretofore."[10] George Washington wrote in a similar vein in 1787: "In the old states, which were the theatres of hostility, it is wonderful to see how soon the ravages of war are repaired. Houses are rebuilt, fields enclosed, stocks of cattle which were destroyed are replaced, and many a desolated territory assumes again the cheerful appearance of cultivation."[11]

The truth seems to be that some people were in distress, and some were prosperous. That is not an earthshaking conclusion, because much the same can be said at any time. But those not doing well at this time were frequently hurt in one way or another by the legacy from the war. Those who had gone into debt to buy real property on long terms during the inflation were undoubtedly often hard put to pay off in the much scarcer money that was now being used. For example, in Worcester County, Massachusetts, over 2,000 suits were taken to court for recovery of debt in one year.[12] Americans had to adjust not only to a reduced money supply but also to a new trading situation after the break from England. To many, the new situation provided new opportunities, but others tried to cling to and make a go of the old relations (particularly was this true of trade with England). The states were generally deeply in debt from the war, and some of them attempted to retire their obligations by levying taxes. This could be particularly hard on those who owed debts for their land and had to pay high property taxes as well.

180

These facts are relevant to a mounting crisis in the United States because they were the occasion for pressures on the governments to do something about them. Some of the functions people were accustomed to have government perform were either not being performed or were irregularly performed. Americans not only had a legacy of mercantilism but also one of monetary manipulations. Debts, taxes, and trade regulations plagued the new governments. There was not even a standard currency throughout the United States.

When the Continental and state currencies were repudiated, people used coins primarily for a medium of exchange. There were few minted in America during this period, so that foreign coins circulated mostly: "English, French, Spanish, and German coins, of various and uncertain value, passed from hand to hand. Beside the ninepences and four-pence-ha'-pennies, there were bits and half-bits, pistareens, picayunes, and fips. Of gold pieces there were the johannes, or joe, the doubloon, the moidore, and pistole, with English and French guineas, carolins, ducats, and chequins."[13] In addition to the difficulty of calculating the respective value of each of these coins, there was the complication that coins were frequently worn or clipped. A man who accepted one of the latter at full value might have it discounted when he tried to use it. Americans did not have *a* medium of exchange; they had media through which exchanges of money for money were almost as precarious as exchanges in goods and they were using coins whose sovereigns could not regulate and over whom Americans had no control.

There was hardly any reason, however, for the citizenry to have any confidence in the monetary actions of the Congress, nor, for that matter, of the legislatures of the states. Not only had the Confederation repudiated its currency, but the debts which it still recognized were poorly serviced. The total debt of the United States at the end of the war, foreign and domestic, was about $35,000,000. Far from being retired, it continued to grow. By way of requisitions from the states, Congress received $2,457,987.25 in the period from November 1, 1781 to January 1, 1786. This was barely enough to pay current expenses for the government.[14] Robert Morris sent along this comment when he resigned as head of the treasury in 1783: "To increase our debts while the prospect of paying them diminishes, does not consist with my ideas of integrity. I must, therefore, quit a situation which becomes utterly insupportable."[15] Those who succeeded him may have had less integrity than he professed, but they were hardly better supplied with money.

It was commonly held that the greatest deficiencies of Congress under the Confederation were the lack of the power to tax and the inability to regulate trade. There should be no doubt that the lack of the power to tax made Congress almost impotent to perform the functions

181

allotted to it. As to trade, Congress was almost powerless either to regulate or to prevent the states from doing so. Whether trade needed
regulating was debatable, but if it did, a strong case could be made
against the states doing it. Indeed, some states undertook to set up
tariffs and to discriminate against ships of other lands, particularly those
of England. But it was exceedingly difficult for states to set rates which
would accomplish even those dubious advantages supposed to follow
from them. If the tariffs were too high, in comparison with those of
surrounding states, goods might come into the state from ports of entry
located in other states. If imported goods were finally consumed in
another state from the one imposing the tariff, the state was actually
levying taxes on citizens of other states.

The regulation of trade by the states worked against a common market for all the United States and threatened to turn some states against
others. John Fiske described the situation this way:

> Meanwhile, the different states, with their different tariff
> and tonnage acts, began to make commercial war upon one
> another. No sooner had the other three New England states
> virtually closed their ports to British shipping than Connecticut
> threw hers wide open, an act which she followed by laying
> duties upon imports from Massachusetts. Pennsylvania dis-
> criminated against Delaware, and New Jersey, pillaged at once
> by both her greater neighbours, was compared to a cask tapped
> at both ends.[16]

Trade discriminations sometimes lead to war. Not only was there the
possibility that one American state might go to war against its neighbor
but also that discriminations against or by foreign countries might lead
some country to go to war against a state. In such a case, the United
States would be drawn into the war, for the authority to make war was
vested in Congress. To say the least, the situation was anomalous.

It is strange, but true, that the events which finally provoked
Americans to do something about the union did not directly involve
the Congress and its ineffectiveness. Perhaps it is not so strange on
reflection, for Congress rarely did anything. The failure to act may be
indictable, but I think it would be hard to get a jury to convict. Congress
presented a low silhouette to its critics. True, it repudiated its currency,
could not pay its debts, could not force the states to meet their quotas,
could not protect its citizens abroad, and did not do most of the things
it was authorized to do with much energy. But, then, it seldom gave
offense, and people spread over a vast land were more used to opposing
government action than seeking it. It is most probable that if some crisis

182

had swept Congress away it would have gone with a whimper rather than a bang. In our day, we have seen exile governments seeking a country to govern; the United States was an exile country awaiting a government.

It was trouble in New England in 1786-87 that aroused fears which prompted men to action. Paper money, taxes, and debts were the occasion of challenges to some state governments. Most states were under pressure to make paper money issues. Seven had done so by 1788 but, as might be expected, there was considerable opposition to such actions. Rhode Island not only issued paper money but revived harsh methods to try to make it circulate. Faced with fleeing creditors and merchants abandoning the state, the "legislature passed an act declaring that anyone refusing to take the money at face value would be fined £100 for a first offense and would have to pay a similar fine and lose his rights as a citizen for a second."[17] When the act was challenged, the court declared its opinion that the act was unconstitutional. The judges were called before the legislature, interrogated, and some of them dismisssed. Rhode Island's government was viewed with contempt by many Americans.

Rhode Islanders would probably have been left to suffer the disadvantages of their own government or get out—the latter was becoming an attractive option—but it was not easy to take so sanguine a view of events in Massachusetts. There was widespread dissatisfaction with the foreclosures on farms and imprisonment for debts. Some of the discontented wanted a moratorium on the collection of debts and/or paper money to be issued. Taxes were also levied in such a fashion as to arouse resistance to their collection. The discontent may have been agitated by British agents; certainly, money was made available for the discontented to use to take action, though who was behind this was never definitely established.

Overt action came when mobs began preventing courts from sitting. Beginning in early September of 1786, a succession of courts were disrupted and prevented from conducting business by large groups of armed men: at Worcester, at Concord, at Taunton, at Great Barrington, and at Springfield. The legislature did not take the desired action, and a rebel force was organized. The climax of these events came in January of 1787. It is known as Shays' Rebellion, taking its name from one of its leaders, Daniel Shays. Massachusetts authorized an armed force to put down the rebellion, and the rebel force was dispersed on January 25. New Hampshire was threatened by a rebel force, but the movement was quickly put down by decisive action by Governor John Sullivan who had been a general during the late war.

The call for a convention to deal with constitutional matters had been issued prior to these events. It came from some delegates to what was supposed to have been a convention at Annapolis in 1786. The convention was supposed to have dealt with commercial matters, but it lacked a quorum of states, so a call was issued for a more general convention for next year. It did not take Shays' Rebellion to awaken some Americans to the need for constitutional revision.

Anyone who wanted a government for the United States could see that Congress was not supplying it. "Between October 1, 1785, and January 31, 1786, Congress had a quorum on only ten days, and never were more than seven states represented. Between October 1, 1785, and April 30, 1786, nine states—the minimum required to do any serious business—were represented on only three days."[18] As mobs began to intimidate courts in Massachusetts, one historian notes that "the Congress of the United States had likewise ceased to function."[19] As the riotous events moved to their culmination in early 1787, one state after another elected delegates to the Constitutional Convention. Finally, even Congress acted by recommending to the states that they send delegates. The fear of the rebellion spreading had apparently tipped the scales.

The site of the convention was Philadelphia, the time appointed to convene May 14, 1787, and the object was to contrive a government adequate to the common tasks of the United States.

16

Making the Constitution

> . . . I feel it a duty to express my profound and solemn
> conviction . . . that there never was an assembly of men
> charged with a great and arduous trust, who were more pure
> in their motives or more exclusively or anxiously devoted to
> the object committed to them to . . . best secure the perma-
> nent liberty and happiness of their country.
>
> —James Madison

> It is too probable that no plan we propose will be adopted.
> Perhaps another dreadful conflict is to be sustained. If to please
> the people, we offer what we ourselves disapprove, how can
> we afterwards defend our work? Let us raise a standard to
> which the wise and honest can repair. The event is in the hand
> of God.
>
> —George Washington

Even though this was an era studded with felicitously worded documents and momentous pronouncements, all of these pale beside the
Constitution of 1787—*the* United States Constitution. It stands alone
among them in the impact it has had, in its imitability, and in the role
it has had in the lives of generations that were then yet to come.

All this is quite remarkable. Certainly, Congress envisioned no such
document when it sent out a call for a convention. Nor could most of
those who assembled in convention see how, at the outset, they could
overcome the difficulties in the way of drawing a satisfactory constitution. Even were a masterpiece produced, it appeared most likely that
it would be rejected by the states. Few have ever remarked it, yet it
may well be that the most amazing thing of all is that the Constitution

was not the work of a single man, or even of two or three, but of a convention. It is a commonplace that committees produce little of value; but here, by a group larger than most committees, the exception was made to happen.

Some have described what happened as more than remarkable; it has even been called a miracle. George Washington wrote to Lafayette that it was "little short of a miracle that the delegates from so many different States (which States you know are different from each other), in their manners, circumstances and prejudices, should unite in forming a system of National Government, so little liable to well-founded objections."[1] Miss Catherine Drinker Bowen's recently published book on the convention is called *Miracle at Philadelphia*. Whatever it was, or should be called, all who are open to an examination of the evidence will admit that it was an extraordinary event.

Even so, the convention did not get underway any more auspiciously than did most other assemblages in that age; it was called for May 14, but there was not a quorum to do business until May 25. It was no easy matter to assemble men from over the length and breadth of the United States; delegates from Georgia, say, had a formidable distance to travel, and even an early start did not necessarily lead to a prompt arrival. In any case, promptness was better calculated in weeks than in hours.

The Virginia delegation was the first appointed by a legislature, and its members began to arrive in Philadelphia before other out-of-staters. It was an impressive delegation, including among its members some of that state's leading citizens: George Washington, Edmund Randolph, George Mason, and James Madison. (George Wythe, one of the best legal minds in America, put in an appearance but left shortly to attend his dying wife.) Most of the Pennsylvania delegates did not have to make a journey to get to Philadelphia, so that they were available from the beginning. It was an impressive delegation, for it included Benjamin Franklin, Robert Morris (who, if he was there, remained silent during the debates), Gouverneur Morris, and James Wilson.

The New England states were not only the slowest in appointing delegates but also theirs were among the last to arrive. Rhode Island rejected the invitation to appoint delegates. (The absence of Rhode Islanders was not considered a handicap during the convention, for that state's behavior was so universally deplored that men did not gladly seek the counsel of her citizens.) The New Hampshire delegates were exceedingly late; two of the four appointed finally arrived on July 23. (They could not come earlier because the state had not provided for their expenses.) New York appointed three delegates—Alexander Hamilton, Robert Yates, and John Lansing— rather reluctant ones, we

186

gather, for Yates and Lansing withdrew after a short period of attendance and Hamilton was absent for an extended period. Over all, 12 states had 55 delegates in attendance at one time or another. From most indications, the greatest concern for a stronger general government was among the delegates from the states located from New Jersey southward. The leadership in the convention came mainly from four states, and in this order: Virginia, Pennsylvania, Connecticut, and South Carolina. Two other states' delegations played some considerable role: New Jersey and Massachusetts. Delegates from other states were generally less conspicuous during the debates, though Luther Martin of Maryland and George Read of Delaware would have led if they could have attracted followers.

The delegates were as well qualified as could have been assembled in America, qualified both by experience and training. Among them were 39 who had served at one time or another in Congress, eight who had signed the Declaration of Independence, eight who had helped draw state constitutions, one, John Dickinson, who is credited with the first draft of the Articles of Confederation, seven who had been chief executives of their states, and 21 who had fought in the war. Thirty-three were lawyers, and ten of these had served as judges. About half of them were college graduates, more from Princeton than from any other institution.[2]

Both youth and advanced age were represented at the convention. The youngest delegate was Jonathan Dayton of New Jersey at 26; the oldest, Benjamin Franklin, who was, as he said, in his eighty-second year. The average age was in the low forties. Some of the leaders, however, were rather young: Charles Pinckney of South Carolina was only 29, Gouverneur Morris 35, and James Madison 36. They were counterbalanced by men of middling years and extensive experience, for example: John Dickinson 54, Roger Sherman 66, and John Langdon 67.

George Washington almost did not come, even though his presence at the convention was essential—for it was generally agreed that he was America's first personage. When he was informed of his election, he asked that someone else be appointed in his stead. He gave two reasons why he should be excused: one that now appears trivial, that he had already declined an invitation to attend the convention of the Society of the Cincinnati which would be meeting in Philadelphia at about the same time; the other, however, was good enough reason in any age, for he was suffering so from rheumatism that he could turn in bed only with the greatest difficulty, and men do not gladly leave the comforts of home when they are ill. Friends so earnestly urged him to attend, however, that he changed his mind.

Washington arrived in Philadelphia before the convention was scheduled to begin. It had long since become difficult for him to go anywhere quietly, and there was good reason to publicize this trip. He was met at Chester by a troop of horses which escorted him into Philadelphia where cannon were fired and bells rung.[3] The fact that Washington had arrived gave notice that the convention was important and that laggards should make haste to get there. When the convention was organized, Washington was elected, unanimously (as when was he not), to preside, an office which he took so seriously that he attended each session, though it was the most oppressively hot summer in the memory of Philadelphians. If Washington could endure it, others could and did. He was a man of stern visage, impressive physique, and high seriousness; with him in the chair, the convention could hardly be anything but what it was, a deliberative body which pursued its business in an absence of frivolity and without stooping to personalities. Though Washington did not participate in the debates until the closing days when he made a brief speech, there was no doubt where he stood on the Constitution. He signed it gladly, and took care to let men about the country know that he approved of it. The men in the convention were aware that when they looked toward the chair, they were gazing at the man who would almost certainly be the first President of the United States. This emboldened those who wanted a strong President to make the office powerful, for they were confident that Washington would not abuse such powers. Gouverneur Morris wrote to Washington a few weeks after the convention to describe the importance of his role:

> I have observed that your name to the new Constitution has been of infinite service. Indeed, I am convinced that if you had not attended the Convention, and the same paper had been handed out to the world, it would have met with a cooler reception, with fewer and weaker advocates, and with more and more strenuous opponents.[4]

Benjamin Franklin was the other most prominent American; his hold on the affections of his countrymen was not so great as that of Washington, but his international fame was such that any gathering which had the benefit of his counsels gained in reputation. Though he was getting old—in fact, was old—his mind was still clear, his vast fund of experience still at his command, and his accomplishments as a raconteur still led men to seek his company. He was not only aged but also infirm. He had to be carried in a sedan chair to the sessions, and he wrote out any but the briefest of remarks so that they could be read to the convention by his fellow Pennsylvanian, James Wilson. Franklin contributed most to the convention by avuncular admonitions to the delegates to compromise, to compose their differences, and to put aside so much of their personal desires as might be necessary to accomplish the object at hand. When the convention appeared to be nearly breaking up over the question of equal or proportional representation, Doctor Franklin said: "When a broad table is to be made, and edges of planks do not fit, the artist takes a little from both, and makes a good joint. In like manner here both sides must part with some of their demands, in order that they may join in some accommodating proposition."[5] At another point, he proposed that the sessions be opened with prayer, for he seemed to think that the influence of religion might link them together in their efforts to arrive at a new system. At the close of the convention, Franklin made an eloquent plea to get those who were holding out to sign what they had helped to make. In a speech, read by James Wilson, Franklin said, among other things:

> I confess that there are several parts of this constitution which I do not at present approve, but I am not sure I shall never approve them: For having lived long, I have experienced many instances of being obliged by better information, or fuller consideration, to change opinions even on important subjects, which I once thought right, but found to be otherwise. It is therefore that the older I grow, the more apt I am to doubt my own judgment, and to pay more respect to the judgment of others. . . .
>
> On the whole, Sir, I can not help expressing a wish that every member of the Convention who may still have objections to it, would with me, on this occasion doubt a little of his own infallibility, and to make manifest our unanimity, put his name to this instrument.[6]

His advanced age may have increased the influence of his spirit of accommodation, but he had been adept at the arts of politics and diplomacy long before the contentions of young men tired him.

Though the convention was not a large body, a few men did most of the speaking and a great deal of the other work of hammering out the Constitution. The leaders included: Madison, Mason and Randolph of Virginia, Gouverneur Morris and Wilson of Pennsylvania, Charles Pinckney and Rutledge of South Carolina, Ellsworth and Sherman of Connecticut, King and Gerry of Massachusetts, and, perhaps, Paterson of New Jersey. According to one tabulation, Gouverneur Morris spoke on 173 different occasions; Wilson, 168; Madison, 161; Sherman, 138; Mason, 136; and Gerry, 119.[7]

James Madison has frequently been described as the Father of the

Constitution. Certainly, he was one of its principal architects. He was not impressive to look at; judging by his appearance it would have been easy to mistake him for a clerk. He was quite short and thin, "Little Jemmy," they called him, "no bigger than a half cake of soap." Nor was he an orator; he spoke in such a low voice that those keeping journals often missed a part of what he said. He made up for these shortcomings, however, with intellectual acuity, sharp insight, and tenacity in the pursuit of his object. Moreover, he had prepared himself for the task of making a new constitution. Much of his time in the months before the convention had been spent in reading, and mastering, the literature on government. A plea to Jefferson in Paris had brought a plethora of books to augment his supply at home. The Virginia Plan, from which the Constitution emerged, was presented on the floor by Governor Randolph, but Madison had undoubtedly done much of the work on it. He might be said to have mothered the Constitution, too, because he devoted himself to it exclusively during the months of the convention. His recollection was that he not only attended every session but that he was never absent for more than a few minutes, and he was certain that he could not have missed a single speech of any duration. He kept copious notes of the speeches, and they are judged to be the most reliable record of what was said. This was a marathon undertaking itself, but he also spoke frequently, and at length, with a masterful show of erudition.

Gouverneur Morris was, however, the most dazzling speaker in the convention, an orator whose learning and close reasoning gave an irresistible thrust to his forensic skill. He had been maimed both in arm and leg, and stumped about on a wooden leg, but it is difficult to think of him as a cripple, for he was reputed to be quite a lady's man and known as a *bon vivant*. Madison and Morris were men who knew what they wanted, who pressed the convention step by step in their direction, who took care to see that what they had won by their reasoning was not lost in the maneuvers over detail, but who yielded gracefully when they were outvoted.

There must have been many moments of high drama during the convention, but I think the most eloquent speech fell from Gouverneur Morris. The occasion was the discussion of the counting of slaves for purposes of representation. "He never would concur in upholding domestic slavery." Morris said. "It was a nefarious institution. It was the curse of heaven on the States where it prevailed. . . . Proceed southwardly and every step you take through the great region of slaves presents a desert increasing, with the increasing proportion of these wretched beings. . . . The admission of slaves into the Representation when fairly examined comes to this: that the inhabitant of Georgia and South Carolina who goes to the Coast of Africa, and in defiance of the most sacred laws of humanity tears away his fellow creatures from their dearest connections and damns them to the most cruel bondages, shall have more votes in a Government instituted for the protection of the rights of mankind, than the Citizen of Pennsylvania or New Jersey who views with a laudable horror so nefarious a practice. . . . And what is the proposed compensation of the Northern States for a sacrifice of every principle of right, of every impulse of humanity. . . ? He would sooner submit himself to a tax for paying for all the negroes in the United States, than saddle posterity with such a Constitution."[8] It is generally believed, too, that Morris did much of the work of the committee on style which transformed the disparate elements which had survived the debates into the congruous whole we know as the Constitution—spare, brief, and potent with phrases that have since been etched into American consciousness by court decision and other action or inaction.

Impressions tumble over one another of the men during the sessions of the convention: of George Washington presiding from his high backed chair, leaning forward to try to discern the order of the proposals from amidst the welter of motions made from the floor, forbearing to speak on the issues because it would be improper; of James Madison, scribbling away at his notes, taking the floor to make a point, retiring to his quarters at the end of the day to flesh out his notes and review what had been done; of the proud and passionate Edmund Randolph, a young politician already in mid-career, presenting the Virginia Plan to the convention, vacillating on issues as the Constitution took shape, unwilling at last to sign the handiwork of the convention which had been shaped from his proposals; of James Wilson, tenaciously pressing for a national government, rising yet once again to support giving the people a more direct role in the government; of George Read, difficult to listen to but determined to be heard, single-mindedly arguing for a more powerful executive; of craggy Roger Sherman, whose face would stop a clock but whose arguments moved the convention toward the accomplishment of its task; of Charles Pinckney, young, brash, but sufficiently brilliant in debate to command the attention of the others; of George Mason, early and late a defender of the rights of man, working with obvious good will to shape the Constitution, but at last unwilling to sign it; of John Dickinson, theoretician of resistance in youth, coming to fame with his daring employment of reason, now grown older declaiming: "Experience must be our only guide. Reason may mislead us."[9]; and of Jonathan Dayton, the youngest man there, rising to second what had

191

not clearly been a motion by Gouverneur Morris on the evils of slavery and saying: "He did it . . . that his sentiments on the subject might appear whatever might be the fate of the amendment."[10]

Though the convention was composed of as impressive an assemblage of men as could have been gathered together at any time, there were some prominent Americans not there. John Adams was out of the country, doing his best to represent Congress before the royal court in London. Adams had lately published a book which surveyed the constitutional arrangements of various countries, a book whose influence might have been greater if its author had been present at the convention. Thomas Jefferson was in Paris as minister to France. Any gathering without him was lacking one of the American luminaries. Several of the firebrands of the Revolution were missing, if not missed, for they were better known for heat than light. Among them were: Samuel Adams who was not chosen, Richard Henry Lee and Patrick Henry who did not choose to attend, and Thomas Paine who was in Europe trying to promote a project for steel bridges in the interlude between revolutions. Probably if some of these men had been there they would have given such vociferous support to the idea of including a bill of rights that it would have been done, thus removing what turned out to be *the* major objection to the Constitution.

The convention was organized so as to proceed about its business without interference from outsiders or without inhibiting full discussion. The sessions were held behind closed doors; no record of what was said or being considered there was to be released without the approval of the convention. There were no galleries to be played to, no press to be placated. Strict rules governing the behavior of members were adopted. For example:

> Every member rising to speak, shall address the President; and whilst he shall be speaking, none shall pass between them, or hold discourse with another, or read a book, pamphlet or paper. . . .
>
> A member shall not speak oftener than twice, without special leave, upon the same question; and not the second time, before every other, who had been silent, shall have been heard, if he wish to speak.[11]

The convention operated on the rule that no decision on any particular of the constitution should be considered final. This enabled the convention to adjust the parts to one another as alterations were made.

The convention was remarkable both for its orderliness and for the absence of rancor among the members. On the one or two occasions when tempers flared, the strong feeling quickly subsided. Some did appear to be impatient in the last few days from going over ground already covered. Even so, an effort was made in the last days to make changes that might satisfy the few holdouts from signing. It is necessary to read but briefly into Madison's notes to get the feeling that these men were taking very seriously what they were doing, that though their task was urgent everything must be considered with great care. Above all, many were determined to stick with the undertaking until something had been completed to present to the public.

It was well that they were, for their object lay on the other side of a thicket of uncertainties, doubts, and differences. Even what they were supposed to do at the convention was in doubt. The resolution adopted by Congress calling the convention declared that it was to be for the "sole purpose of revising the Articles of Confederation." It was clear enough what Congress had said, but these men were gathered to represent their states and were supposed to act under their instructions, if any. The instructions differed enough one from the other that a good case could be made that the convention would do what its members thought best. Most of those gathered agreed with the idea that their task was to construct a plan for a new system of government, or accepted it without cavil. The few who did not could leave, and some did.

It was only with some difficulty that they agreed on how they would vote. Delegates from several states were bent on having representation in the new government based on population or wealth, as the Virginia Plan provided. They would have the best chance of getting this into a constitution if the states had votes in the convention proportionate to their populations. There was no likelihood, however, that the smaller states might agree to this, so the convention votes were by states, each state having one vote regardless of how many delegates there were, just as in the case of the Congress. If a state's delegation was tied in a vote, that state's vote would not be counted. A majority of the states present and voting was sufficient to any decision.

Sentiment had been building for some time that, if there was to be an effective union of the states, the general government must have the power to use force on individuals. This, as many saw it, was the only way to "render the constitution of the Federal Government adequate to the exigencies of the Union. . . ,"[12] as the declaration drawn at the Annapolis Convention the year before had described the need. A man named Stephen Higginson had written to General Knox earlier in 1787 describing precisely what needed to be done: "The Union must not only have the right to make laws and requisitions, but it must have the power of compelling obedience thereto. . . ."[13] Washington had written to Madison in March: "I confess . . . that my opinion of public virtue is so far changed, that I have my doubts whether any system, without the means of coercion in the sovereign will enforce due obedience to the ordinances of a General Government; without which every thing else fails. . . . But what kind of coercion, you may ask. This indeed will require thought. . . ."[14] Washington wrote to John Jay in the following vein: "I do not conceive we can exist long as a nation without having lodged somewhere a power which will pervade the whole Union in as energetic a manner, as the authority of the State Governments extends over the several States. . . ."[15]

There was no way, however, of contriving a general government which could compel obedience without encroaching on the powers of the states. Indeed, any attempt to work out such a plan had major obstacles in the way. Both theory and history militated against divided sovereignty. Theory said it could not be done; history afforded no clearcut examples of its having been successfully done. If sovereignty could not be divided, if a general government was to have coercive power, then the general government would have to be sovereign and the states become but districts in a nation. There were men at the convention who saw it this way and were ready to grasp the nettle.

But such a plan had little hope of ratification, if any. Madison described some of the difficulty in a letter to Edmund Pendleton before the convention:

> . . . The necessity of gaining the concurrence of the Convention in some system that will answer the purpose, the subsequent approbation of Congress, and the final sanction of the States, presents a series of chances which would inspire despair in any case where the alternative was less formidable.[16]

But if Madison had not known beforehand that the states would be jealous of their powers and prerogatives, he would have found out soon enough in the convention. George Mason, his fellow Virginian, expressed his determination to preserve the vitality of the states in calm but measured words: "He took this occasion to repeat, that notwithstanding his solicitude to establish a national Government, he never would agree to abolish the State Governments or render them absolutely insignificant. They were as necessary as the General Government and he would be equally careful to preserve them."[17] Luther Martin of Maryland said that he agreed with Mason "as to the importance of the State Governments. He would support them at the expense of the General Government which was instituted for the purpose of that support. . . . They are afraid of granting powers unnecessarily, lest they

194

should defeat the original end of the Union; lest the powers should prove dangerous to the sovereignties of the particular State which the Union was meant to support; and expose the lesser to being swallowed up by the larger."[18] Doctor Johnson in contrasting the Virginia and New Jersey Plans (the Virginia Plan calling for representation to be apportioned according to wealth and/or population while the New Jersey Plan called for representation by states), brought some of the difficulties out in the open. He noted that James Wilson and James Madison, advocates of the Virginia Plan, did not propose to destroy the states. "They wished," he said, "to leave the States in possession of a considerable, though a subordinate jurisdiction. They had not yet however shewn how this could consist with, or be secured against the general sovereignty and jurisdiction, which they proposed to give to the national Government."[19]

Some held that they were departing from experience even to try to contrive a government which depended upon divided sovereignty. Others argued that the American situation was unique, that history afforded no clear model for it, and that they must innovate. Charles Pinckney summed up the peculiar situation of America in this vigorous exposition:

> The people of this country are not only very different from the inhabitants of any State we are acquainted with in the modern world; but I assert that their situation is distinct from either the people of Greece or Rome, or of any State we are acquainted with among the ancients. . . .
>
> Our true situation appears to me to be this—a new extensive Country containing within itself the materials for forming a Government capable of extending to its citizens all the blessings of civil and religious liberty—capable of making them happy at home. . . .[20]

Reason is the sword of the young; experience the shield of age. Some of the young men at the convention were for casting a new system, but others wanted no such heady innovation. In any case, the states must be preserved.

Some of the proponents of an energetic general government declared that there was little danger to the states to be expected from it. They appealed to the history of confederacies to show that time and again it was the states who had intruded upon and broken up the general government. Others appealed to a broader experience to show that where power was confided in any government it tended to crush all opposing power.

The general government must have sufficient power and prestige to attract able and dedicated men into its service. The energy of government proceeds from the men in it, as John Francis Mercer of Maryland argued. "It is a great mistake to suppose that the paper we are to propose will govern the United States. It is the men whom it will bring into the Government and interest in maintaining it that is to govern them."[21] Americans of that time were familiar with something that their descendants know little about: government so lacking in power and prestige that able men would not deign to serve in it. A seat in the Congress was hardly coveted by the first citizens, and state governments found it difficult to attract men of ambition and integrity. Some men in the convention were loath to provide much reward for serving in the general government, on the ground that men would be attracted for reasons of personal gain rather than service. Alexander Hamilton answered the argument this way: "We must take man as we find him, and if we expect him to serve the public must interest his passions in doing so."[22] The idea was vigorously pushed in the convention of limiting the length of time a man might serve in the general government as well as making those who left office ineligible for appointive office for a time. James Wilson argued against this idea; he "animadverted on the impropriety of stigmatizing with the name of venality the laudable ambition of rising into the honorable offices of the Government. . . ."[23] James Madison said: "The objects to be aimed at were to fill all offices with the fittest characters, and to draw the wisest and most worthy citizens into the Legislative service."[24] He doubted that this could be done by hedging them around with ineligibilities and disqualifications.

Once it was granted that sufficient power be authorized to attract strong men who would impart energy to the general government and give it power to act directly upon individuals, then all were agreed that checks must be introduced on this power. Gouverneur Morris thought the following principles must be introduced:

> . . . Abilities and virtue, are equally necessary in both branches. Something more then is now wanted. 1. The checking branch must have a personal interest in checking the other branch, one interest must be opposed to another interest. 2. Vices as they exist must be turned against each other . . . 3. It should be independent.[25]

James Madison declared that if it "be essential to the preservation of liberty that the Legislative, Executive, and Judiciary powers be separate, it is essential to a maintenance of the separation, that they should be independent of each other."[26]

Yet, to accomplish this was a most difficult task. In the British system there were different classes to be represented, each class providing an independent base for its representatives. In America, there was no such actual division of the population. In Britain, the monarchy and the secular members of the House of Lords held hereditary positions, adding another dimension to their independence. But Americans neither had nor wanted hereditary officials. Hence, the problem: functions might be separated from one another readily, but how could those in the different branches have different sources of their power? Some were for having the executive chosen by Congress. But others pointed out that, if this were the case, he would be dependent on that body. Judges might be appointed by the Senate, but if that body might also remove them from office where was their independence? Probably, more time was spent on the question of how the executive should be chosen than any other, though it did not excite the emotions as did the question of whether representation in Congress should be based on population or by states.

Above all, there was the question of how those who were to govern could be made sufficiently independent of their electors to make wise decisions without posing fatal dangers to the liberties of the people. Undoubtedly, if the government was to be republican it must be based on voters from among the people. Nor, as some men never tired of saying, was it to be doubted that those whose rights were involved were the best protectors of them or that the ballot box was the place to do it. Some thought that frequent elections would be the best means of protecting the people. Roger Sherman observed that "Government is instituted for those who live under it. It ought therefore to be so constituted as not to be dangerous to their liberties. The more permanency it has the worse if it be a bad Government. Frequent elections are necessary to preserve the good behavior of rulers."[27] Others questioned this principle, for they noted that a too close dependence of the government on the people resulted not in wise and stable government but in the pandering of politicians to the temporary and changing opinions of the populace. Madison had said just prior to Sherman's remarks that the objective of the constitution was "first to protect the people against their rulers; secondly to protect the people against the transient impressions into which they themselves might be led. . . ." A "reflection . . . becoming a people . . . would be that they themselves . . . were liable to err . . . from fickleness and passion."[28] Alexander Hamilton pointed out that lately "the Government had entirely given way to the people, and had in fact suspended many of its ordinary functions in order to prevent those turbulent scenes which had appeared elsewhere."[29]

Perhaps, enough of the difficulties have been recounted to illustrate the fact that the Founders were wrestling with real practical and intellectual problems at the convention. Some twentieth century historians have attempted to interpret their differences in terms of class interests and other factors. It is not necessary to do this in order to account for the debates; it also drags in matters extraneous to the subjects at issue. Moreover, such an account does not explain the compromises that were eventually made; if men were moved only by narrow interests they would have been expected to cling to their views rather than compromise.

Compromise they did, however, in many matters that initially divided them. Indeed, some historians have gone so far as to describe the Constitution as a "bundle of compromises." The phrase has sometimes been used derogatorily to imply that on issue after issue men had yielded up their principles to the expediency of accommodating a welter of interests. Yet, a compromise need not be a yielding of a principle; it may well be the result of sacrificing narrow interest to the general well being. So it was, quite often, at the convention at Philadelphia; men advanced narrow and limited views in the debates but arrived at great principles through compromise. The stately, but simple, rhythms of the Constitution as it came from the committee on style captured principle after principle in its verbiage, meshed them together into a symphonic whole, and provided the plan for the government of an empire for liberty. That it could be done appeared most unlikely at the outset. That it had been done was not so clear at the time. That it was done seems now a miracle. It is, therefore, appropriate to examine these principles.

17

The Principles of
the Constitution

The questions at issue in the constitutional convention were rarely, if ever, philosophical in nature. The men gathered at Philadelphia in 1787 were practical men, by and large, going about the practical business of proposing how power would be disposed, arrayed, and distributed in the United States. Nor is the Constitution a treatise on philosophy; except for the preamble, the document deals exclusively with the practical and the mundane. Nonetheless, the debates were informed by principles, as remarks and occasional flights of oratory indicate, and the Constitution is based on high principles, which we may know both from analysis and an examination of the apologies for it.

These principles follow, if not inevitably then naturally enough, from the Founders' understanding of human nature. The same human nature which made government necessary, they thought, made certain principles appropriate to it and essential if it was to endure for any extended time. Government is made necessary because man is not perfect. James Madison put the matter succinctly:

> If men were angels, no government would be necessary.
> If angels were to govern men, neither external nor internal
> controls on government would be necessary.[1]

Obviously, Madison thought men are not angels; man is a flawed being needing restraints whether he belongs among the governed or the governors at any particular time.

There is no indication that any of the other Founders thought otherwise. Alexander Hamilton declared that "men are ambitious, vindictive, and rapacious."[2] Nor could he see that human nature was more dependable because the beings involved lived in republics rather than under monarchs:

> Has it not . . . invariably been found that momentary passions, and immediate interests, have a more active and imperious control over human conduct than general or remote considerations of policy, utility, or justice? Have republics in practice been less addicted to war than monarchies? Are there not aversions, predilections, rivalships, and desires of unjust acquisitions that affect nations as well as kings? Are not popular assemblies frequently subject to the impulses of rage, resentment, jealously, avarice, and of other irregular and violent propensities?[3]

Hamilton's low estimate of human nature is well known, but the gentle spoken Benjamin Franklin did not rate it much higher. He declared that when you "assemble a number of men to have the advantage of their joint wisdom, you inevitably assemble with those men, all their prejudices, their passions, their errors of opinion, their local interests, and their selfish views." He predicted that the government they were providing for in the convention "can only end in Despotism, as other forms have done before it, when the people shall become so corrupted as to need despotic Government, being incapable of any other."[4] A fair interpretation of this latter statement would be that man has an ingrained downward bent. The political implications were spelled out by Madison in this way: "In framing a government which is to be administered by men over men, the great difficulty lies in this: you must first enable the government to control the governed; and in the next place oblige it to control itself."[5]

It does not do justice to the Founders' conception of human nature simply to emphasize the flawed side. Man is a rational animal, they thought, i.e., capable of reason. He loves liberty, and needs it for the fulfillment of his possibilities. He is self-interested—a trait that can be turned to good use—but he is also capable of conceiving a general interest which embraces others as well as himself. He is an active, responsible being, capable of invention, construction, concern, and what goes by the name now of creativity. Put power in his hands over others, however, and he must be carefully watched. This was the cornerstone of their political faith.

With these views of human nature, the Founders combined an unusual mixture of hope and resignation about the government they were contemplating, hope that they could contrive a system that would be lasting but resigned to the likelihood that it would founder sooner or later on the shoals of the lust for power of those who governed and the bent to corruption of the governed. Many of the debates of the convention hovered around the question of whether too much or too little power was being conferred and whether those who would exercise it would have sufficient leeway to act energetically or be sufficiently restrained to prevent arbitrary and despotic action. The debates reflected these concerns; the Constitution embodied their conclusions. The convention was the forge; the Constitution was the finished and tempered metal. The following are its most salient principles:

I. FEDERAL SYSTEM OF GOVERNMENT

The federal system of government, as we know it, was invented at Philadelphia in 1787. Dictionaries, encyclopedias, and textbooks now define a "federal government" as one in which there is a division of powers between a general government, on the one hand, and local (or state) governments, on the other, both governments having jurisdictions over the citizenry within their bounds. A confederation is now held to differ from this arrangement in that under it the individual states retain the sole authority to use force on individuals. No such distinction appears to have existed in 1787. The only perceivable distinction was a grammatical one. "Confederation" was the noun form used to describe the organization of the states into a unit. "Federal" was the adjective form of the word "confederation." For example, Richard Henry Lee, who was opposing ratification of the Constitution, said that the "object has been all along to reform our federal system . . ."[6] He could only have been referring to the system under the Articles of Confederation as "federal." In adjoining sentences, Hamilton employed the words as if interchangeable in meaning.[7] Initially in the convention, those who favored a general government with sanctions referred to it as "national." They did not, however, get the system they had conceived, and in the course of the debates "national" took on an odious association. Those who favored adoption of the Constitution referred to themselves as "federalists," and to the government as a "federal" one,[8] in part, one suspects, to minimize the extent of the innovation. Clearly, what they had wrought was not a confederation, and it came to be called a "federal" government.

It made sense, once the American system had been devised, to use the words "federal" and "confederation" to call attention to structural differences in systems, but this development in language has tended to obscure the invention that took place. Occasionally, however, it has been pointed out. A present-day writer notes that the "United

States is regarded by many students as the archetype of a federal system. . . . Even general definitions of the term seem to derive from the American model."[9] James Madison wrote one passage, too, in which he called attention to the new character of what they had devised:

> The proposed Constitution . . . is, in strictness, neither a national nor a federal Constitution, but a composition of both. In its foundation it is federal, not national; in the sources from which the ordinary powers of the government are drawn, it is partly federal and partly national; in the operation of these powers, it is national not federal; in the extent of them, again, it is federal, not national; and finally in the authoritative mode of introducing amendments, it is neither wholly federal nor wholly national.[10]

It is a brilliant description of the complex arrangements in the Constitution, but, unfortunately, Madison is speaking in an unknown tongue so far as present-day Americans are concerned. Not only did the distinction between "federal" and "confederation" take place, but in contemporary usage "federal" is employed almost exclusively to refer to the general government and has, thus, become a synonym of "national." Whereas, Madison used "federal" to refer to those things in the Constitution in which the states retained their force and vigor.

At any rate, the main feature of the federal system of government is that the power of government was divided between the general government and the state governments. Such a division has the appearance of being a division of sovereignty, something which political theorists said could not be done. The Founders disposed of the theoretical problem by ignoring it in that they did not vest any such absolute authority as is described by sovereignty in any government. A political scientist has put the matter correctly in this discussion of the American government: "Sovereignty, in the classic sense, has no meaning; divided as power is, the element of absoluteness which is essential to the concept of sovereignty is not present."[11] The Constitution acknowledges the existence of the states and vests some of the powers of government in the United States. Power is dispersed rather than concentrated, and each of the coordinate (not levels of) governments has its own jurisdiction.

Both the general and the state governments are independent of each other to a degree but are also dependent on one another. These relationships are provided for by intricate arrangements. All elections take place within states and under their auspices. The Constitution was only to go into effect after the ratification by conventions held state by state. The selection of the personnel for the branches of the general government involved the states to greater or lesser degree depending upon the office involved. The House of Representatives was to be composed of members chosen from districts within states, and the number allotted to each state was to be based on population. Each state, on the other hand, has two Senators, providing for an equal representation of states in the upper house. This was worked out in what is sometimes called the Great Compromise of the convention, or the Connecticut Compromise. The President is selected by an electoral college, each state having as many electors as it has Representatives and Senators. The members of the courts were to be appointed by the President with the advice and consent of the Senate. The Senate was also given major powers in the approval of other appointments and in treaty making. The states retained a large role because of the preeminence of the Senate and because everything having to do with popular election is done by and within states.

The general government was clearly given control over the massive use of force and the states were left with the preponderant authority to use force ordinarily. The general government is authorized to raise and maintain armed forces and under its authority may call into action any state military force. Laws made pursuant to the Constitution are declared to be the supreme law of the land. The states retained most police powers, courts dealing with most civil and criminal matters, and much that has to do with the protection of life, liberty, and property. The general government is charged with protecting the states from foreign invasion and from one another. The line between the powers of the states and those of the general government was not marked by great detail; it was, no doubt, expected that they would contend with one another over various jurisdictions and thus limit one another. Such contentions were expected to counterbalance the extensive use of power by any government.

To say that federalism was an American invention is not to imply that it sprang from the head of Zeus fully clothed at Philadelphia in that summer. Actually, the Founders were encompassing a tradition when they devised the federal system. Elements of federalism were in the British colonial system. Each colony had its own government to deal with local matters. The British government exercised the type of powers over the colonies that were now to be vested in the general government. Moreover, the Congress under the Articles of Confederation had much of the authority which was not vested in the general government, even if it lacked the power for the full exercise of it. Most of the innovation was in the wresting of a pattern from an imperial system and installing it in a republican setting.

II REPUBLICAN FORM OF GOVERNMENT

There are two basic requirements which must be met if a government is to be styled a republic: (1) it must be popular in origin, i.e., draw its authority from an extensive electorate; and (2) power must be exercised by representatives. It is distinguished from an hereditary monarchy in that it is based on popular election and from a democracy in that power is wielded by representatives. Those who favored the new Constitution took pains to show that the government it provided for was republican in character.

James Madison showed that its powers were derived from the people by this explanation:

> The House of Representatives, like that of one branch at least of all the State legislatures, is elected immediately by the great body of the people. The Senate, like the Present Congress and the Senate of Maryland, derives its appointment indirectly from the people. [The Senate was chosen by state legislatures until the ratification of the 17th Amendment.] The President is indirectly derived from the choice of the people, according to the example in most of the States. Even the judges, with all other officers of the Union, will, as in the several States, be the choice, though a remote choice, of the people themselves.[12]

As they understood the difference between a republic and a democracy, it was a republic, not a democracy. Though it was based on the people, the people acted through representatives. Popular decision went through a series of filtrations, as Madison put it, before it became government action.

The United States was not a monarchy, and safeguards were introduced to prevent its becoming one, as Madison said:

> Could any further proof be required of the republican complexion of this system, the most decisive one might be found in its absolute prohibition of titles of nobility, both under the federal and State governments; and in its express guaranty of the republican to each of the latter.[13]

III SEPARATION AND BALANCE OF POWERS

If there was one principle upon which the Founders were agreed more than any other it was that of the separation of powers. Montesquieu had taught them that it was a requisite of good government. Both they and Montesquieu knew the separation of powers in principle from the British example. State governments already incorporated the principle, however imperfectly. Once it was decided that the power to coerce individuals would be lodged in the United States government there was little doubt that a system of checks and balances must be located in the system.

For this to be done, there must be several branches to limit one another. The branches, as constituted, made it a *mixed government*. This idea is not so well known anymore, for it comes from classical theory, which no longer is the basis of our studies as it was for the Founders. The idea is that there are three possible pure modes of rule: monarchy, aristocracy, and democracy. In this sense, both the United States and the states do not have a pure form of government; they are, instead, mixed. In the United States government, the President is based on the monarchical principle, the Senate the aristocratic, and the House the democratic (both because it has more members and is directly elected). It was not monarchy, aristocracy, or democracy, but rather drawn from principles of each of them as a form, i.e., from rule by one, rule by a few, and rule by the many.

The Founders had considerable difficulty devising a mixed government from a constituency which contained no fixed classes. As they saw it, it was very important that each branch be distinct from the other in the manner of its selection. A mixed government was desirable because there were differing functions of government which could best be entrusted to one, to a few, or to many. But, if the functions were best performed in this way, the division should not be watered down by having all the branches chosen by the same electorate. Perhaps it would be most accurate to say that they partially solved the problem. The members of the House were directly elected, and the number of them apportioned according to population. The Senate was to be elected by the state legislatures. This was natural enough and did base the choice on two different realities. But they never hit upon any comparable reality from which the President could be chosen. Electing him by an electoral college was an artificial expedient which, while it did give him an independent basis of selection, did not provide him with one that was organic to the country.

There was much talk in the convention of making each of the

branches independent of the other, and much was done to achieve this principle. The branches were not only given different sources of election but also were protected from one another. The houses of Congress make their own rules, are judges of the elections of their members, and jointly set their pay. They have a constitutionally established regular time of meeting, and may by agreement adjourn one house with the other. The President can protect himself by the use of the veto and by his powers of patronage. Moreover, he is commander-in-chief of the armed forces as well as having at his disposal the Federal constabulary. The members of the courts are to be paid according to a regular schedule; their salaries are not to be reduced during their tenure, which is for life or during good behavior.

But there is no denying that the branches are also interdependent and entwined in their operation. All legislation must pass both houses of Congress on the way to becoming law. Even appropriations, which must originate in the House, must still pass the Senate before they can go into effect. The President can veto acts of the Congress; in which case, such an act can only become law by being passed by at least a two-thirds majority in each house. The President and the Senate are particularly entwined in the appointive and treaty making powers. Amendments to the Constitution not only regularly involve both houses of the Congress but the state legislatures as well. The effect of all this interpendence is to require government by a consensus of the branches and, in the case of constitutional amendments, of the states also. The more important the decision, the broader its base for approval must be before it can be put into effect.

IV LIMITED GOVERNMENT

The crowning principle of the Constitution is limited government, for all the other principles tend toward and are caught up in this one. The federal system of government, the republican form of government, the principle of separation all place procedural limits on the powers of the governments. The independence of the branches, one of another, and of the state and general governments provides them with a base from which to check and limit one another. Their interpendence makes the concurrence of branches and governments necessary for action to be taken.

The Constitution provided not only for procedural limits on governments but for substantive ones as well. One way in which the general government is substantively limited is by enumerating its powers. This is done most directly in setting forth the legislative powers of the government, which are all vested in the Congress. They are contained in Section 8 of Article 1, and read, in part, as follows:

> The Congress shall have Power to lay and collect Taxes . . .
> To borrow Money on the credit of the United states;
> To regulate Commerce with foreign Nations, and among the several States, and with the Indian Tribes;
> To establish an uniform Rule of Naturalization . . .
> To coin money . . .
> To establish Post Offices and post Roads;. . . .
> To declare War, grant Letters of Marque and Reprisal, and make Rules concerning Captures on land and Water. . . .

To have placed all legislative authority in the Congress was a limitation on the other branches. To have enumerated the powers implied that those not listed were not included. Discussions within the convention bear this out. For example, the question was raised as to whether or not the general government ought to be granted the authority to construct canals. The idea was rejected on the ground that this would involve the general government in projects which would be mainly beneficial to the people of particular states. The point, however, is that they were operating on the assumption there that if the power were not listed it was not granted.

But it is not necessary to conclude only from the enumerated powers that the general government is limited by the Constitution. There are specific limitations contained in it. The Constitution required that all direct taxes be apportioned on the basis of population. (This prohibition was later removed by the 16th Amendment.) Other taxes must be levied uniformly throughout the United States. All taxation must be for the common defense and general welfare of the United States, which should be conceived as a major limitation. Specific restrictions on the general government are listed in Section 9 of Article I, of which the following is a partial list:

> The Privilege of the Writ of Habeas Corpus shall not be suspended, unless when in Cases of Rebellion or Invasion the public Safety may require it.
> No Bill of Attainder or ex post facto Law shall be passed . . .
> No Tax or Duty shall be laid on Articles exported from any State. . . .

No Money shall be drawn from the Treasury, but in Consequence of Appropriations made by Law. . . .

No Title of Nobility shall be granted by the United States.

State governments were also limited in the Constitution in several ways (Section 10, Article I). The following is an example:

No State shall enter into any Treaty, Alliance, or Confederation, grant Letters of Marque and Reprisal; coin Money, emit Bills of Credit; make any thing but gold and silver Coin a Tender in Payment of Debts; pass any Bill of Attainder or ex post facto Law, or Law impairing the Obligation of Contracts, or grant any Title of Nobility.

Some delegates to the convention were heartily in favor of a specific prohibition being placed in the Constitution against the United States government emitting bills of credit (i.e., issuing paper money). Others said that occasions might arise, such as during the late war, when the issuance of paper money might be necessary. The upshot was a silent compromise. Congress is not authorized to emit bills of credit, but neither is it specifically prohibited to do so. (The going assumption, however, was that what was not granted was prohibited.)

The other main limitation in the Constitution was the tacit limitation on the powers of the people. Much concern was expressed both in the constitutional convention and in the state ratifying conventions about limits on the people. The Founders perceived that a majority may be tyrannical; it may work its way to intrude on the rights of individuals, whose rights were considered the premier ones. Alexander Hamilton said: "The voice of the people has been said to be the voice of God; and, however generally this maxim has been quoted and believed, it is not true to fact. The people are turbulent and changing; they seldom judge or determine right."[14] Moses Ames, speaking in the Massachusetts convention to consider the ratification of the Constitution, said: "It has been said that a pure democracy is the best government for a small people who assemble in person. . . . It may be of some use in this argument . . . to consider, that it would be very burdensome, subject to faction and violence; decisions would often be made by surprise, in the precipitancy of passion, by men who either understand nothing or care nothing about the subject; or by interested men, or those who vote for their own idemnity. It would be a government not by laws, but by men."[15] James Madison declared that "on a candid examination of history, we shall find that turbulence, violence, and abuse of power, by the majority trampling on the rights of the minority, have produced factions and commotions, which, in republics, have more frequently than any other cause, produced despotism."[16]

The people were limited by the original Constitution in that they could act only through representatives, that except for the House of Representatives the branches were indirectly chosen, and that the courts were most remote from popular control. Both the government and the people are limited by the vesting of effective negative powers on any legislation in each of the houses, of a veto in the President, and the establishment of a Supreme Court which, it was understood, would have a final negative. Positive action requires a concurrence of the branches; while several of them have the power of negation. The direct power of the people is also limited by the staggering of the terms of offices. The House of Representatives is chosen every two years. Senators' terms are for six years, and approximately one-third of them are chosen every two years. The President's term is for four years, and the members of the courts serve during good behavior. This provided for stability in the government and a safeguard against the people working its will over the government while under the sway of some temporary passion.

V THE TRANSFORMATION OF EMPIRE

One of the least appreciated principles of the Constitution is that contained in the provision which makes it possible to dissolve an empire periodically by adding new states to the union. The United States had an empire from the beginning; indeed, writers and speakers frequently referred to the United States *as* an empire. At the least, however, the United States had a vast territory west of the Applachians and to the north and west of existing states. It was of considerable interest at the convention what provision should be made for the future of this territory. Should it be carved into provinces which, when any one of them became populous enough, would be admitted on equal terms with the older states? Gouverneur Morris, among others, argued vigorously that this should not be the case. He feared that in time the western states would outnumber the eastern states; "he wished therefore to put it in the power of the latter to keep a majority of votes in their own hands." He summed up his case in this way: "The busy haunts of men not the remote wilderness are the proper school of political talents. If the Western people get the power into their hands, they will ruin the Atlantic interests. The back members are always averse to the best measures."[17]

On this occasion, however, Morris was outpointed by the leaders of the Virginia delegation. George Mason said: "If the Western States are to be admitted into the Union, they must be treated as equals and subjected to no degrading discriminations. They will have the same pride and other passions which we have, and will either not unite with or will speedily revolt from the Union, if they are not in all respects placed on an equal footing with their brethern." Edmund Randolph declared that it was entirely "inadmissible that a larger and more populous district of America should hereafter have less representation than a smaller and less populous district." Madison joined in the colloquy by saying that "with regard to the Western States he was clear that no unfavorable distinctions were admissible, either in point of justice or policy."[18]

The Constitution simply states that "New States may be admitted by the Congress into this Union . . .", followed by some protections of the territory within existing states. The manner of providing for representation, however, assured that new states would be on a par with the original 13 when they came into the union. The effect of this has been the dissolution of empire by the admission of new states. In short, the Constitution provided for the transformation of empire into states which joined the union as full-fledged members of an expanding United States.

The state delegations present and voting in the convention at its close gave unanimous approval to the Constitution. Only a very few individuals refused to sign the handiwork of the convention. The document was submitted to the Congress, after which it was to go to the states which were asked to hold ratifying conventions. As the signing was taking place, Benjamin Franklin made the last public remarks recorded for the convention. James Madison described them this way:

> Whilst the last members were signing it Doctor Franklin looking toward the President's Chair, at the back of which a . . . sun happened to be painted, observed to a few members near him, that Painters have found it difficult to distinguish in their art a rising from a setting sun. I have, said he, often and often in the course of the Session, and the vicissitudes of my hopes and fears as to its issue, looked at that behind the President without being able to tell whether it was rising or setting: But now at length I have the happiness to know that it is a rising and not a setting sun.[19]

All who would having signed, the convention adjourned *sine die.*

18

The Bill of Rights

The thrust for a list of rights to be added to the Constitution gained momentum during the debates over ratification which took place in the states. No distinct statement of rights had been made a part of the Constitution, nor did it contain any systematic protection of those rights traditionally thought to be in special need of defenses. To some few within the convention and to a much larger number of those who were not there the omission was a deficiency that must be corrected or the Constitution rejected. In retrospect, it appears strange that the men who sat in the convention should have neglected to supply something that was so universally considered essential by Americans and whose absence so many would judge to be a fatal defect of their work. Among the reasons they did not were these: the leaders were focusing their efforts on getting a stronger general government, not upon restraining it; declarations of rights had not proved to be substantial deterrents to governments within the states; and, as some would argue, it was unnecessary to have such restrictions for a government possessing only enumerated powers. However good their reasons might be, the omission ran counter to American tradition and the predilections of the bulk of the populace.

The belief in the necessity of a bill of rights went deeper than the *American* tradition, too. Britons traced their liberties to restraints on government. That was the lesson, Americans thought, of the Magna Charta, the Petition of Right, and the Bill of Rights. That government should be restrained by documentary prohibitions was deeply ingrained in Americans with a British background.

Statement of rights, too, drew much force from natural law theory which underlay so much of American constitutional theory. The doctrine of natural rights not only held that man had certain rights in the nature

211

of things but that government which is charged with protecting them tends, if not restrained, to invade and diminish them. The accepted means for introducing protections of such rights into practice was by way of distinct bills of rights. By natural law theory they do not become rights because attention is called to them in fundamental instruments of government—they are inherent in the nature of things—, but many believed that there was greater likelihood of their being observed if they were written into fundamental law.

The example of the states appeared conclusive to many. If state governments which were much more closely dependent upon popular support had to be restrained then how much more necessary would be restraints on a general government which was remote from the people both in physical distance and by the manner in which its branches were to be chosen.

Conventions proceeded state by state to the consideration of and debate over ratification following the submission of the Constitution to the states in September of 1787. The Constitution provided for ratification by conventions made up of delegates chosen by electorates within states. For it to go into effect, it was mandatory that two-thirds of the state conventions approve the Constitution. Approval required only a majority vote. Whether a state which did not ratify would not be a part of the union was not stated in the Constitution, but presumably the state would have to take some kind of affirmative action to come into it. Most of the states acted with dispatch to hold elections followed in short order by conventions, but Rhode Island refused to hold a convention until 1790, and the North Carolina convention adjourned without acting on ratification in July of 1788.

The debates over ratification within the states have retained considerable historical interest. Perhaps the most important reason for this is that during these debates a thorough examination and exposition of the principles of the Constitution took place. Its strengths, weaknesses, and nature were thoroughly explored. The greatest brief in support of the Constitution was *The Federalist*, a book which was first published as newspaper articles for the express purpose of getting New York to ratify the Constitution. The articles were published under pseudonyms, but the bulk of them have since been attributed to Alexander Hamilton, a goodly number of the others to James Madison, and a few to John Jay. They are generally considered to be the most authoritative exposition of the original Constitution, despite the fact that they must have been composed in considerable haste for a specific occasion. Their success is a tribute not only to the brilliance of Hamilton and Madison particularly but also to the superiority of the analytical tools and rhetoric of an age. Though papers in opposition to ratification were published in a losing cause, some highly perceptive ones were brought forth; of these the most important were by George Mason, Richard Henry Lee, and Elbridge Gerry. In several of the conventions, spirited and lengthy debates took place. The debates in the Virginia convention were the most thorough, as befitted the leading state in America, followed by those in Massachusetts and New York.

The other matter to come out of the debates to make them lastingly important was the demand for, promise of, and eventual adoption of a Bill of Rights. There were many objections raised to the Constitution in the debates. Some saw it as establishing a general government of such powers that as they were augmented over the years would tend to extinguish the independence of the states. The powers of the President were much too great, critics declared, and since there was no barrier to re-election, he might become, in effect, a ruler for life. The Senate, too, came in for much criticism, since it was remote from the people, the terms of its members were long, and its powers were intertwined with those of the President. There was hardly a phrase or idea or provision of the Constitution that did not somewhere by somebody come under biting criticism. Even the phrase, "We the people," in the preamble was found to be offensive; reference should have been to the states rather than the people, some individuals thought. Much of the criticism was frivolous, some of it was entirely off the mark, and part of it arrived at by simply misconstruing what was provided in the Constitution. The heart of the criticism, however, was that a government was being set up unrestrained by sufficient protections of traditional and natural rights. Until this deficiency should be made up there were a great many who simply could not accept the Constitution.

Alexander Hamilton attempted to make as full answer as could be made to the proponents of a bill of rights in *The Federalist* number 84. He noted, first of all, that certain rights were protected within the Constitution, such as the right to a writ of *habeas corpus*, to trial by jury, and so forth. So far as particular bills of rights are concerned, he pointed out that they were, in their inception, instruments to restrain monarchs, hence, of doubtful appropriateness in a republic. Perhaps the most ingenious part of his argument is contained in the following, however:

> I go further and affirm that bills of rights, in the sense and to the extent in which they are contended for, are not only unnecessary in the proposed Constitution but would even be dangerous. They would contain various exceptions to powers which are not granted; and, on this very account, would afford a colorable pretext to claim more than were granted.

213

For why declare that things shall not be done which there is no power to do? Why, for instance, should it be said that the liberty of the press shall not be restrained, when no power is given by which restrictions may be imposed? I will not contend that such a provision would confer a regulating power; but it is evident that it would furnish, to men disposed to usurp, a plausible pretense for claiming that power . . . This may serve as a specimen of the numerous handles which would be given to the doctrine of constructive powers, by the indulgence of an injudicious zeal for bills of rights.[1]

Patrick Henry probably made as good answer as could be made to the argument Hamilton was making when he spoke on the subject in the Virginia convention:

Mr. Chairman, [he said] the necessity of a bill of rights appears to me to be greater in this government than ever it was in any government before. I have observed already, that the sense of the European nations, and particularly of Great Britain, is against the construction of rights being retained which are not expressly relinquished. I repeat, that all nations have adopted this construction—that all rights not expressly and unequivocally reserved to the people are impliedly and incidentally relinquished to rulers, as necessarily inseparable from the delegated powers. It is so in Great Britain; for every possible right, which is not reserved to the people by some express provision or compact, is within the king's prerogative. . . . It is so in Spain, Germany, and other parts of the world.

Whatever the merits of the arguments on either side, feeling was strong for a bill of rights and opposition was great to a Constitution which did not contain one specifically. As one recent account says, many were "sincere in deploring the failure of the Constitution to defend basic freedoms in so many words. At worst these prohibitions would do no harm, and might be expected to work much safety. America had recently, in the Revolution, freed itself from certain concrete oppressions by any eventuality."[2] Richard Henry Lee penned a poignant plea for just this during the debates:

. . . Fortunate it is for the body of a people, if they can continue attentive to their liberties, long enough to erect for them a temple, and constitutional barriers for their permanent security: when they are well fixed between the powers of the

214

rulers and the rights of the people, they become visible boundaries, constantly seen by all, and any transgression of them is immediately discovered: they serve as sentinels for the people at all times, and especially in those unavoidable intervals of inattention.[3]

Indeed, so strong was the sentiment for some sort of bill of rights that the Constitution received ratification in several crucial states only after the promise that one would be added.

Though the debates over ratification of the Constitution do provide valuable insights into it—and opponents did make some telling points —it is easy to make too much of them. Some twentieth century historians have alleged that the Constitution was unpopular, that its ratification was accomplished by underhanded maneuvers, and that had a larger electorate been consulted it might well not have been adopted. This is not only speculative but also argumentative, for it assumes that uninformed opinions should be given equal weight with those who had studied the questions carefully. In fact, in most places the Constitution had the support of the bulk of men of learning and substance as well as most of the leading characters in the country. Most of the more thoughtful opponents of ratification of it as it stood were by no means wholehearted in their opposition.

Besides, the vote in favor of ratification in most states was not close. Delaware ratified the Constitution December 7, 1787 by a vote of 30-0; Pennsylvania followed on December 12, by a vote of 46-23; New Jersey was unanimous for ratification a few days later, 39-0; Georgia unanimous on January 2, 1788, 26-0; Connecticut overwhelmingly approved, 128-40, on January 9. The vote was close in Massachusetts, 187-168, but ratification was achieved on February 16. The Maryland vote in favor of ratification was not even close; it was 63-11, despite the fact that several Maryland delegates to the Constitutional Convention at Philadelphia opposed it. Those in favor of ratification in South Carolina won handily, 149-73, on May 23; New Hampshire followed on June 21, 57-47. Nine states had now ratified it, and the Constitution could be put into effect. But the chances of succeeding with it without Virginia and New York were slim. Attention now focused on their conventions. In the Virginia convention which met for most of June, both sides were most reluctant to take a vote for fear of losing. This was one of the reasons the debates were so prolonged and the examination of the Constitution so thorough. James Madison was the leading exponent of the Constitution, ably assisted by John Marshall among others. Patrick Henry was the most tenacious opponent of ratification. When the vote was finally taken, it was 89 to 79 for ratification. The New York vote was even closer; that state ratified the Constitution by a vote of 30-27 on July 26. Thereafter, Americans turned to the task of organizing and getting the new government underway. North Carolina finally ratified the Constitution in November 1789 by a vote of 194-77. With all the other states in, and under the threat of a boycott, Rhode Island finally held a convention in 1790 which proceeded to the ratification of the Constitution by the narrowest possible margin, 34-32.[4] There were some close votes, then, but the composite picture is one of widespread willingness to try the new Constitution and almost universal acceptance of it when it had been amended. The fact that opposition dwindled into insignificance once it was ratified shows that the opponents only limitedly opposed it and could accept its adoption as a condition of political life which they found tolerable. The main questions about the Constitution now became how it should be amended and interpreted.

Of course, the opposition did not melt away until the Bill of Rights was made a part of the Constitution. Moreover, North Carolina's (and probably Rhode Island's) ratification of the Constitution was given impetus by the fact that such amendments were in the process of being adopted. Thus, while other things of great moment for the founding of the American Republic were taking place between 1788 and 1791, it is appropriate to complete at this point the discussion of the Bill of Rights.

Whether James Madison was the Father of the Constitution may forever remain debatable, but that he was the Father of the Bill of Rights is as near to being beyond dispute as such things can be. He examined the proposals as they had come from the state conventions, pondered the question of what rights were generally in greatest need of protection, and as a member of the first House of Representatives kept bringing the matter up until the House consented to act upon them. Moreover, Madison served on the committee which brought forth the proposals as well as on the joint House-Senate committee which worked out the final form of the amendments. There were suggestions at the time that he was less than enthusiastic about a bill of rights—as well as suggestions since that he deliberately made them vague and imprecise—but the record shows him working diligently to get something done when many of those who had been called Federalists were dragging their feet and some of the anti-Federalists were more inclined to niggling criticism than to working toward what could be achieved. Madison did oppose going into intricacies in the amendments; let us, he said, "confine ourselves to an enumeration of simple, acknowledged principles," for by doing so, "ratification will meet with but little difficulty."[5] Surely this was wise counsel.

Two pitfalls were avoided by the manner in which the Bill of Rights was made a part of the Constitution. It was passed by two-thirds majorities in the House and Senate and ratified by legislatures of the states, with concurrence by three-fourths of the states being necessary for adoption. The method used was one of amendment rather than of inserting these protections of rights within the body of the original Constitution. The first pitfall would have been the calling of another constitutional convention to produce a bill of rights. Those who wanted to get on with establishing a general government were most desirous of avoiding any such gathering, for it would most likely get out of hand and proceed to the undoing of the work of the first convention. To have the amendments advanced by Congress not only avoided that danger but also utilized the legislative branch of the new government in one of its more important functions, thus enhancing the prestige of the new government. Madison had at first thought that protections of rights should be placed within the original Constitution, but the House decided that they should be added as amendments. This, too, was a happy decision, for it avoided the spectacle of Congress tampering with the Constitution and setting the precedent for its being rewritten from time to time by the legislature.

The Bill of Rights was submitted to the states in September of 1789 and acquired a sufficient number of state votes of approval to go into effect in December of 1791. Twelve amendments were submitted, but two were not approved. The first of these dealt with apportioning representatives in the House and would have fitted poorly in a bill of rights. The second laid down rules about determining the pay of members of Congress and would have been equally ill placed at the head of an enumeration of rights and privileges. Madison had hoped to get an amendment passed which would have restricted the states as well as the general government from violating basic rights, but this proposal was turned down in the Senate.

The first ten amendments to the Constitution contain a list of restrictions, some specific, others more general, on the United States government. It would not be incorrect to call them a Bill of Prohibitions instead of a Bill of Rights, for they are of the nature of prohibitions. They are less a list of rights than they are a series of protections of rights. The phraseology is generally negative: "Congress shall make no law," "the right of the people to keep and bear arms, shall not be infringed," "no warrants shall issue," "no person shall be held," "no fact tried by a jury shall be otherwise re-examined," "excessive bail shall not be required," "shall not be construed," and "powers not delegated."

The meaning of this negative formulation and restrictive character can be succinctly stated. Some constitutions have contained declarations of rights which were more or less extensive lists of the rights supposed to belong to the people. Such lists tend to be ineffective and to amount to little more than pious wishes of those who state them. If one has a right, who is it against, and how is it to be enforced? For example, suppose it be declared that the people have the right to free speech. This is a noble sentiment, but unless there is a prohibition against someone who would violate it, it is of no use. Moreover, even if such a general right were enforced, it might well be done so as to limit someone else's speech.

The Founders were generally of the opinion that once law and order had been established the greatest danger to rights came from government itself. The movement for a bill of rights to be added to the United States Constitution came specifically from those who feared that the government it established would violate them. For example, Richard Henry Lee was involved in the debates in the Senate over the question of whether a bill of rights was necessary. Some said that they needed more experience to determine which and if amendments were necessary. Lee indicated in a letter that he thought there had been experience enough "to prove the propriety of those great principles of Civil liberty which the wisdom of the Ages has found to be necessary barriers against the encroachments of power in the hands of frail Man."[16] Wherever government power was lodged, there must be a variety of restrictions and limitations on its exercise if men's rights were to be protected, so thought most Americans of that day.

The first two amendments deal with certain specified rights. The first reads: "Congress shall make no law respecting an establishment of religion, or prohibiting the free exercise thereof; or abridging the freedom of speech, or of the press, or the right of the people peaceably to assemble, and to petition the Government for a redress of grievances." An established religion is one which is supported by government, i.e., by tax money, by requiring attendance, or other such aids and privileges. To say that Congress should make no law prohibiting the free exercise of religion would appear to mean that Congress should not concern itself with either prescribing or proscribing religious practices. (This prohibition did not extend to state governments, since they were left free to prescribe or proscribe religions, limited only by their own constitutions.) The right to believe and practice any or no religion was usually described at the time as the "right of conscience." Free speech, free press, peaceful assembly, and the right to petition did not mean so much as they might appear to. The historical problem had been that those who governed had restricted these to prevent criticism of themselves or influences upon their actions. What the Founders were primarily, probably exclusively, interested in protecting was the right of the people to speak, write, assemble, or petition so that they might characterize, criticize, or influence those who governed them with impunity. It is most doubtful, for example, that they conceived of the right to a free press as a right to publish pornography any more than they thought of the right to assemble as the right to intimidate. It is true, of course, that governments may restrict speech, the press, and assembly on other grounds than protecting those who govern from criticism and influence, but it is not clear what the incentive would be except for some public, as opposed to personal, reason. Be that as it may, the first amendment provides protections for several traditional rights generally most prized and often standing in need of protection.

The second amendment is the most peculiarly phrased of all of them, and for that reason its import is somewhat obscure. It says, "A well regulated Militia, being necessary to the security of a free State, the right of the people to keep and bear Arms, shall not be infringed." The first two phrases are surely rhetorical flourishes rather than prohibitions on government. The only rights involved are those of keeping and bearing arms. There is no mystery about the right to keep arms; it means simply the right to store them on one's property. The right to bear arms is subject to two interpretations. It might mean simply the right to carry them about from place to place. But in the context of the opening phrases, it might mean also the right to serve in the militia. The larger purpose of the amendment appears to have been to tip the scales in favor of citizen armies. Few things were more feared at the time than armies composed of foreign mercenaries. Indeed, standing armies from whatever source were considered a grave danger. A government with these at its disposal could go far to impose its will on the people, as had occurred at many times in the past. The suggestion of the amendment, perhaps it should be called a hint, is that the military force should be assembled from part-time soldiers who composed the militia. The effectiveness of the militia would be greatly enhanced, they thought, if its members were practiced in the use of firearms. This would be greatly facilitated if they were permitted to keep as well as to bear arms. Arms in the hands of the citizenry would also be a safeguard against either foreign mercenaries or standing armies.

Amendments three and four deal with both rights and procedures. The primary right involved is the right to the use of one's home in privacy and security. "A man's home is his castle," so goes an ancient saying, and these amendments were aimed to make this so as against the United States government. The third amendment prohibits the quartering of soldiers in private houses in time of peace without the consent of the owner and in time of war only according to rules laid down by law. The fourth deals with searches and seizures and prescribes the procedures by which they may be done.

Amendments five through eight are concerned almost entirely with processes by which government may take life, liberty, and property. They constitute restrictions which government is supposed to observe when it is going about the business of taking one or more of these from a person. It may appear ironic that a government which is supposed to protect life, liberty, and property may also take them on occasion. Yet it has been the considered judgment of most men through the ages that governments from time to time must take one or more of these from some individuals in order to protect the life, liberty, and property of the generality of people. It was also the view of the Founders that these are dread actions which must be hedged about with procedures and prohibitions to assure that men are not casually deprived of life, liberty, or property. Article V declares, in part, that no person shall be "deprived of life, liberty, or property without due process of law." Most of these processes are set forth in amendments five through eight, such as, trial by jury, indictment by a grand jury, compulsory processes for obtaining witnesses by the accused, and the right to counsel.

The courts exist, however, to settle disputes and to discover and punish malefactors. The primary purpose of the criminal courts is to protect the life, liberty, and property of peaceful persons by dealing sternly with those who violate them. They do not exist to protect criminals; if this were their purpose, it is doubtful that society would be sufficiently concerned to establish courts. Those who attend only to the Bill of Rights might suppose that our constitution-makers were concerned only with the rights of the accused. They were not, of course; the basic business of government and of the courts was assumed—so apparent as hardly to be worth stating—whereas, the supplementary matter of protecting the accused and the criminal was considered worthy of concentrated attention.

The ninth and tenth amendments provide the general protections of rights; they were drawn as an umbrella over the whole to protect the individual and the states from encroachment by the general government. The ninth specifies that "The enumeration in the Constitution of certain rights, shall not be construed to deny or disparage others retained by the people." Opponents of a bill of rights had pointed out that it would be impossible to spell out all the rights which men might justly claim. The listing of a few of them might set up the presumption that those not listed did not belong to men as rights. This article was intended to cover the matter, to make it as clear as could be that all manner of rights still belonged to the people, though no mention was made of them in the listing.

The tenth amendment puts the roof on the edifice, so to speak. It proclaims that "The powers not delegated to the United States by the Constitution, nor prohibited by it to the States, are reserved to the States respectively, or to the people." The language derives its impact from the natural law philosophy. In this view, rights belong to individuals in the nature of things. The powers of government are justly derived from the people, and since these governmental powers place some limit on individual rights they must be acquired by delegation (or by usurpation, which would be unjust, of course). The powers not delegated, then, whether it be to the general government or to the states, are reserved.

There were those who would have attached the modifier "specifically" to "delegated," but they were defeated in their efforts to do so. This raised the specter of endless wrangling over whether the power to perform acts in order to exercise the powers delegated had been granted or not. More deeply, the inclusion of the modifier would have posed the problem whether this government could exercise powers that are said to be inherent in government or not. Now, perhaps there was no need to retain the notion of powers inherent in government, but men who have just been engaged in the business of drawing up a constitution may be forgiven for being uncertain as to whether they had covered the whole ground or not. They might for all they knew, have failed to grant powers specifically which would shortly be necessary to the performance of functions which they had readily conceived. At any rate, the tenth amendment can be accurately construed as restrictive—that is surely its purpose—but not as confining as it would be if "specifically" were added to it.

Any amendment to the Constitution occupies a unique position in the American system. It supersedes anything preceding it which is contrary to it; that is, it becomes the governing article in the matters with which it deals. The first ten amendments, however, occupy an even more prominent place in the Constitution than their position as amendments would perforce give them. They were conceived as and quickly became known as the Bill of Rights. They were thought of, in part, as taking their place alongside Magna Carta, the Petition of Rights, and the British Bill of Rights. But the American Bill of Rights is significantly different from and more encompassing than these great British guarantors of the rights of Englishmen. For the British thought only to guarantee themselves against encroachment by the monarch. Whereas, the American Bill of Rights draws a line between the whole government and the citizenry which the government is not to transgress. In doing this, it differs somewhat from the original Constitution. That instrument generally grants and restricts powers in terms of branches. This mode was continued in the first amendment, then abandoned in the rest, so they may be interpreted as restraining the whole federal government.

The American Bill of Rights is inspired by the idea that it is not just the executive, not only the courts, but also the legislature that must be restrained. Government itself—in all its branches and so far as it may reach—is a potential threat to the people under it. If they are to be secure in their rights, if they are to enjoy their lives and possessions, that government over them must be kept to its appointed tasks and observe the procedures prescribed for it.

The adoption of the Bill of Rights reconciled most of the opponents of the Constitution to the new government. With it as a bulwark of defense against consolidated government, all the states could come into the union. The Bill of Rights did not yet reach through to all the inhabitants of the United States, but the provisions were such that all could desire to be covered by them.

19

Establishing the Government

"Great oaks from tiny acorns grow," run the words of an old saying. They seem particularly appropriate to the United States government, as we look back on its small, uncertain, and precarious beginnings from the twentieth century when the lineal descendant of that government has grown to immense proportions. It is difficult for us who are used to this Leviathan with its symmetry, stability, and massiveness even to imagine the frail beginnings and the contingency of its existence. The government which has long since proceeded on the momentum of an established institution once had to be made to go by conscious and concentrated effort, and a little of that story needs to be told.

The First Congress was so slow in assembling that there was some reason to doubt whether the government might even get underway. It was scheduled to begin with its sessions on March 4, 1789, in the city of New York. But only a few members of either house had arrived by that date. Historian Claude Bowers describes the further difficulties of Congress this way: "A week after the date set for the opening of Congress but six Senators had appeared, and a circular letter was sent to the others urging their immediate attendance. Two weeks more and neither House nor Senate could muster a quorum. . . . 'The people will forget the new government before it is born,' wrote [Fisher] Ames. 'The resurrection of the infant will come before its birth.' " This was unduly pessimistic, however, for the houses had the necessary quorums for organizing to do business on April 6.

A few days later, April 16, George Washington set out by carriage from Mount Vernon to make a journey to New York City to be inaugurated as the first President of the United States. The electors were unanimous in selecting him to the post, though their unanimity dissolved when it came to selecting John Adams as Vice President. Along

223

the way on his journey north Washington was greeted with pomp and ceremony and by throngs of people. The Governor of Pennsylvania, Thomas Mifflin, greeted Washington at the border of his state with a troop of calvary and escorted the President-elect into Philadelphia where his arrival was celebrated by thousands of inhabitants. Trenton, New Jersey, however, provided him the most effusive welcome. "There a triumphal arch composed of thirteen flower-bedecked pillars straddled the road. In front of it stood thirteen maidens in white, each with a flower basket on her arm. As the great man, now astride a white horse, rode into view the maidens burst into song."

> Virgins fair and matrons grave,
> Those thy conquering arm did save,
> Build for thee triumphal bowers;
> Strew, ye fair, his way with flowers
> Strew your hero's way with flowers.[1]

Republican simplicity had not yet replaced monarchical pomposity in America, but it is doubtful that any monarch was ever so genuinely admired, loved, and respected as the hero chosen to be chief of state of this Republic.

Quite a spectacle was prepared in New York City for Washington's arrival. Inauguration day was set for April 30. A splendid procession formed at Washington's residence to escort him to Federal Hall, the place of inauguration. He took the oath of office in public view, and then went into the Senate chamber to deliver his inaugural address to both houses of Congress there assembled. Washington had taken great care in preparing this address and had practiced the delivery of it before he had left Mount Vernon. Even so, he appears to have had great difficulty giving it utterance. Fisher Ames noted that the President was "grave, almost to sadness; his modesty, actually shaking; his voice deep, a little tremulous, and so low as to call for close attention."[2] Senator William Maclay of Pennsylvania declared that "this great man was agitated and embarrassed more than ever he was by the leveled cannon or pointed musket. He trembled, and several times could scarce make out to read."[3]

It is certain that Washington was no orator, nor was he comfortable in attempting to fulfill that office. But there was good reason aside from that for him to approach the highest office in the land tremulously. There is evidence that he entertained doubts as to his capabilities for the task ahead. One historian says that "Washington in some respects was a humble man, despite that massive outer shield of dignity which served to freeze the overfamiliar and even to awe his closest friends.

224

He knew his own limitations. He had a sufficient faith in his powers as a military strategist and commander in the field; he had no such confidence in his abilities as a statesman in time of peace."[4] But even a man lacking his modesty might well have blanched before the prospect of the difficulties he would face. Indeed, all those who undertook leading roles in the new government had their work cut out for them.

L. D. White, who made extensive studies of the early administrations, says that when Washington became "the first President under the new Constitution, he took over almost nothing from the dying Confederation. There was, indeed, a foreign office with John Jay and a couple of clerks to deal with correspondence. . . ; there was a Treasury Board with an empty treasury; there was a 'Secretary at War' with an authorized army of 840 men; there were a dozen clerks whose pay was in arrears, and an unknown but fearful burden of debt, almost no revenue, and a prostrate credit. But one could hardly perceive in the winter of 1789 a government of the Union."

Indeed, the problems of getting an effective government underway in early 1789 were greater than even the above would suggest. The population of the country was not so great, of course. The census of 1790 showed it to be just under 4,000,000. But it was spread over a vast area. Though the bulk of the population was on or near the Atlantic seaboard, that fact hardly indicated that the population was concentrated. The seaboard itself stretched for perhaps 1500 miles from Maine through Georgia. Along this great stretch of coast population was located mostly in clumps, and these were frequently separated from one another by considerable distances. Back of the seaboard was a vast area, split by the Appalachians, much of it inhabited by Indians, by and large still in its primeval condition, and most of it as yet unsurveyed. Travel from one place to another was often an unpleasant adventure, and from some parts of the country to others a virtual impossibility overland.

Although the preponderance of the population, save for the blacks, was British in background and tradition, there were many differences among the people in any given area in addition to regional differences. Americans as a whole had not yet been governed by a real government located on this continent, and even British rule had not bound them together; that had held them only to the mother country as best it could. There were differences of religion: they were Baptists, Methodists, Presbyterians, Congregationalists, Episcopalians, Quakers, and members of a multitude of small sects, though, again, Americans were usually Protestant. The middle states differed decidedly from the New England ones, and the Southern ones from all the rest. These diversities made any union by government appear unlikely, if not impossible.

The financial situation of the United States government was so precarious that it might well be said that the new government was receiver for the bankrupt Confederation. Even after the repudiation of the Continental currency the debts left over from the War were large and growing. In many instances not even the interest was being paid. In 1790, Alexander Hamilton estimated that the United States owed to foreign creditors $11,710,378, of which $1,640,071 was interest. The principal of the domestic debt he declared to be $27,383,917, to which would be added interest arrears to the amount of $13,030,168.[5] States had debts, too, which had been contracted during the war and which might be charged to the United States government.

To these difficulties were added those of dealing effectively with foreign powers. The United States had not yet earned the respect or fear of foreign countries. British troops still held sway in the Old Northwest from forts on the Great Lakes. The Spanish dominated much of the Mississippi River as well as egress from it. As if this were not enough, on July 14, 1789, only two-and-a-half months after Washington's inauguration, a mob in Paris stormed the Bastille, signaling the onset of the French Revolution. Undoubtedly many in America thought that the early events of the revolution were a good augury for the United States. Much of the rhetoric of the revolutionaries bore a family resemblance to that just used by Americans. (This was neither entirely coincidence nor attributable to the Zeitgeist alone; Thomas Paine devoted himself to the French cause as he had lately done to the American one.) This was to be a revolution in defense of the rights of man, so Americans heard, and were gladdened. Moreover, the French proclaimed a republic in 1792, and Americans were surely glad for company in that goal.

But out of the French Revolution grew such activities, contests, and, eventually, wars that all of Europe was caught up in them and repercussions were felt in much of the world. If George Washington had foreseen the trial that the wars and disturbances surrounding the French Revolution would be to the United States when he was preparing his inaugural address he might have given up in despair, although it was not in his character to do so. War broke out in Europe in 1793, receded and expanded, but continued until 1815 with only one intermission of peace for about a year. It involved not only all the European powers at one time or another, and most of them several times, but also their empires in the rest of the world and any neutral nations trading with Europe. The American Republic needed peace very much for the development of unity; instead it was pressed toward war and torn between warring parties.

To contend with these difficulties in 1789, the United States gov-

226

ernment had a Constitution—a piece of paper—consisting of a few articles setting forth a plan of government. The United States was a vision in 1789, its government a dream, its dominion over the vast continental territory based on a hope. Americans had proved themselves masters of rhetoric: they could pen declarations, draw up constitutions, add to them bills of rights; they had even fought a war successfully, but it was still doubtful whether they could effect a permanent union, submit to the necessary taxation to retire their debts, govern the domain, and take their place as a nation among nations.

Words are wonderful things; ideas move men; and plans contain the necessary patterns for human endeavor. But there is a missing link between words on paper—though they may compose a constitution or some noble document—and the realities of unity, government, stability, and liberty. That missing link, if it is supplied, is supplied by men. Man *is* a frail reed, but his proposals are evanescent without his energies. It was men who breathed the breath of life into the government, who provided the flesh to the bones of the Constitution, who in their contests with one another held the government in check, and who gave impetus and direction to it. But it was neither the majority of men who did this nor even all of those who held office in the government. Madison's comment after looking over the roll of those elected to the first Congress may have been somewhat harsh, but it was much to the point: he said that there were few members who would take an active hand "in the drudgery of the business."[6] That part would be played, as it usually is, by a few men with the tenacity, the ambition, the drive, and the determination to make the government work. Critics abound; leaders who get things done are few.

The number of the men who played the leading roles in making the new government work were few and can be named on the fingers of a single hand—almost. Of course, others played important parts, and no government could succeed without widespread support from the populace (and the social base which their activities provide), but given all these things, it still required and had the leadership of a remarkable set of men. The ones that stand out above all the others in the early years of the Republic are: George Washington, James Madison, Alexander Hamilton, Thomas Jefferson, John Adams, and John Marshall.

Americans were jealous of their rights and loath to grant that power over their lives and fortunes which is necessary even for limited government. Nor was it easy to reconcile them to the potential concentration of power that was vested in the office of President. If such power had to be vested in men, even many of those at the Constitutional Convention agreed, it would be better imparted to three men than one. What

227

made it finally acceptable to Americans to have a single man as President was that that single man would be George Washington at first. Washington's reaction is summed up in this way by a biographer:

> Even before the Constitution was adopted, public opinion had fixed on Washington as the first president. He repelled the suggestion when it was made to him and opposed it wherever he decently could. Fame he had never coveted and the purely military ambition of his youth had long since been burned out, as he had gained close acquaintance with the scourge of war. At the age of fifty-six he had no "wish beyond that of living and dying an honest man on my own farm."[7]

It was this modesty, this lack of personal ambition, this humility, and his sense of stewardship and honor that made him so right for the post. Washington could be trusted, that was the key: trusted to stick to his post until he had accomplished the goal, trusted to do the honorable thing, trusted with the affairs of the people, and trusted to think in terms of the Union. He would not be expected to achieve daring coups, to make risky innovations, or to use his office for purely personal ambitions. He would and did bring dignity to the office and make of it a symbol of unity for a people.

Wispy James Madison is a strange choice for one of the essential leaders in establishing the government. Historians and biographers did not make the choice, though it should be said that they have affirmed it. Nor could it be said that for most of his career he was the choice of the people. With his quiet voice, his unassuming manner, and his small stature, he was not one to be picked for leadership. The Virginia legislature passed over him for one of their Senators, and he had to make do with being a member of the House of Representatives. In a sense, Madison must have chosen himself for the role. He achieved it, at any rate, because of his cultivated intellect, his determination to have a national government, and because he spoke with such cogency and authority on the Constitution. Where others doubted or vacillated, he was certain and determined. He was the man who had so much to do with drawing the Constitution, getting it adopted, making a Bill of Rights, and guiding through the House the early legislation by which the government was established.

Alexander Hamilton was, and has remained, a controversial figure in the history of the early years of the Republic. Given his brilliance, his audacity, his drive, and his ambition it probably could not have been otherwise. He was the man with a plan, a plan he intended to see adopted, and a plan over whose merits men were sharply divided.

228

Perhaps what he achieved could have been accomplished without the acrimony he stirred up, but it is doubtful. He wanted an energetic government which men would look upon as *the* government, and any program to achieve it was bound to stir up deep animosities. Hamilton was a nationalist; much less than any other leading figure of these times was he associated by allegiance with any state. He was born and partially educated in the West Indies. He came to Boston in 1772 or 1773, somewhere between the ages of 15 and 18, depending on which birthdate is accepted and which year he arrived. Soon after he moved to New York. He had hardly arrived when he entered the lists of pamphleteers against British measures. He served in the army during the war, was appointed an aide to General George Washington and in that post learned much about the country. He was instrumental both in getting the Constitutional Convention called and less so in helping with its work. He was, however, a leading figure in securing its ratification in New York.

Washington appointed Hamilton to what many considered the most important post in the new government, that of Secretary of the Treasury. If it was not the most important, he acted as if it were, and from it he proceeded to establish a financial system for the United States. His overall achievement has been aptly described this way:

> He created as from a void a firm public credit; he strengthened the government by not merely placing it on a sure financial foundation, but also uniting great propertied interests behind it. . . . He saw the importance of what he called "energy in the administration". . . , and if only because he went further than any other member of the government in exercising the powers of the Constitution, he must rank as one of the boldest and most farsighted of the founders of the nation.[8]

Thomas Jefferson has had the loftiest of reputations among the Founders. There was something Olympian about him; he had more skills and abilities than any man ought to have: he was architect, inventor, lawyer, statesman, writer, and linguist, among other accomplishments. But his Olympian position may owe more to his absence from the center of most continental and national efforts during the crucial years of the late 1770's and the 1780's. When other prominent men were engaged in the War for Independence he was serving ineptly as Governor of Virginia. While the New Constitution was being drawn and ratified he was serving as Minister to France. While others were engaged in the heat of the contest for ratification or alteration, he could and did write calm and judicious letters about the document. Even after he was brought to the center of affairs in Washington's administration as Secretary of State he remained in the shade of the more energetic and imaginative Hamilton, and it would have been a sensible judgment that he was unsuited to the rough and tumble of politics. It is ironic, then, that he is included among the list of men who established the government for his role in partisan politics. Jefferson did grasp the nettle of involvement in the exercise of power, forge a political party which attracted a large national following, establish what became a succession of Presidents, and bring republican simplicity to government as well as make political parties another instrument in the balance and containment of power in America. He hardly wished to be remembered as a partisan politician, or even a politician for that matter, yet he adorns history books mainly in that role, and in an overall view this is as it should be. It is in the rough and tumble of politics that ideas are tested along with the mettle of those who advanced them. To be founder of a political party appears to be a lesser thing than to be "Father of the Constitution," but Jefferson's reputation has been more secure than that of James Madison. (Lest someone remind me that Jefferson wrote the Declaration of Independence, I note again that indeed he did, and maintain also that this authorship would have given him a secure place in American history but it would probably have no more made him a Founder than did Thomas Paine's authorship of *Common Sense* and *The Crisis*.)

Why include John Adams in the list of eminent establishers of the government? There is no doubt, of course, that he should have a secure niche among the Founders for his service over the years in working for independence and for his dogged diplomacy in Europe, Moreover, he was the first Vice President of the United States and the second President. These latter activities are the ones that give trouble, however, for he has frequently been judged a weak and ineffective President, one who inherited and kept a cabinet from Washington which he could not dominate and one who lacked the authority to keep the Federalists in line. The consensus of the opinion of historians has sometimes been more generous with him, however. About twenty years ago historian Arthur M. Schlesinger queried more than fifty prominent historians and political scientists and asked them to evaluate the Presidents on a scale ranging from Great to Failures. John Adams finished in the top ten, and was rated as near Great.[9] Perhaps, if the reason for rating him so high may be simplified, it is that as President he steered the United States on a course of neutrality and independence in the world, averted both serious internal troubles and a major foreign conflict, and achieved out of it an accord with France.

John Marshall came late to the role of establishing the government.

He did take part in the war and in politics during the 1770's and 1780's but in positions that did not bring him to the forefront of the attention of Americans. He was prominent in the Virginia convention which took up the question of ratification of the Constitution and debated in favor of adoption. But he only emerged as a major national figure in 1800 when John Adams appointed him Secretary of State. And, in 1801 he was made Chief Justice of the Supreme Court, a position which he occupied until his death in 1835. It was, of course, as Chief Justice that he distinguished himself and played a prominent part in giving stability to the United States government.

Marshall does not exactly fit our image of an eminent jurist. He was not particularly well stocked with formal education; his academic training in the law was restricted to a few lectures by George Wythe which he attended. A contemporary said he was " 'tall, meagre, emaciated,' loose-jointed, inelegant in 'dress, attitudes, gesture,' of swarthy complexion, and looking beyond his years, with a countenance 'small in proportion to his height' but pervaded with 'great good humour and hilarity. . . .' "[10] Even so, he came to dominate the court in fairly short order, a fact which is the more remarkable because he was a Federalist, and the men appointed to be his brothers on the court over the years were Republicans. He had a mind which could go to the nub of the matter; he was unencumbered by any great knowledge of the law; and he could carry the field with the force of an argument. His great strength lay in his devotion to the Constitution and his determination to have it hold sway regardless of what there might be in ordinary law to the contrary. The impact of his opinions on the Constitution raised that document far above the realm of ordinary law and did much to make the Constitution into a Higher Law. As Justice Story said in the dedication of his *Commentaries* to Marshall:

> Your expositions of constitutional law enjoy a rare and extraordinary authority. They constitute a monument of fame far beyond the ordinary memorials of political and military glory. They are destined to enlighten, instruct, and convince future generations; and can scarcely perish but with the memory of the constitution itself.[11]

The great task which confronted the men who would establish the government of the United States at the outset, aside from gaining respect for it, was to flesh out the very general outline for a government contained in the Constitution. Their work can be likened to that of a master carpenter whose task is to construct a house from a blueprint. The blueprint indicates what the house should be like, but it rarely tells in any detail how the effects are to be achieved. That is the work of the builder. So it was with the men who took the reins of the government. Moreover, they had the momentous job of deciding how things should be done with the knowledge that once one way was chosen it would serve as a precedent for the future. As the writers of a constitutional history text say:

> The decisions made by the statesmen who launched the new government were of especial importance, for the institutions they erected and the policies they inaugurated established precedents that were certain to affect profoundly the entire subsequent development of the constitutional system.[12]

There were many such precedential decisions in the early years, some trivial, or apparently so, others momentous. For example, the Senate spent some time under the spur of the presiding officer, John Adams, discussing a proper form of address for the President. A Senate committee actually recommended that Washington be addressed as "His Highness, the President of the United States of America, and Protector of their Liberties." Many in the Senate were outraged, and under Madison's leadership in the House, that body insisted that he be addressed as the Constitution implies, namely as "the President of the United States," and so he has been ever since.[13] There was considerable discussion over whether or not cabinet members should be permitted to appear before the houses of Congress to present and discuss legislation. The decision was against it. President Washington appears to have been uncertain himself as to how he was to get the "advice and consent" of the Senate to treaties. He came in person to the Senate to present his first treaty. He was so disgruntled at the proceedings there, however, that he vowed after a second visit over this same treaty that he would never return on a similar errand, and he did not. Since that time, Presidents have caused treaties to be drawn, have sent them along to the Senate for approval, amendment, or rejection, and have considered themselves to be thus complying with the Constitution.

Perhaps the best example of a precedent being set which men adhered to for a very long time was in the matter of the number of terms a President would serve. There had been considerable concern when the office was set up that election to the office would amount to election for life, for a President might be expected to be reelected time after time. No doubt, some even hoped this would be the case. George Washington, however, decided to retire after his second term. His example carried such weight that every other man who had the opportunity stepped down voluntarily after two terms for the next 144 years. Franklin D. Roosevelt was the first President to attempt to succeed himself for a third term. The precedent was still so highly valued, however, that the two term limit has since been made a part of the fundamental law.

The Congress had the most immediate task of getting the government underway. It had to pass legislation that would call into being powers and functions that had been authorized by the Constitution. The first order of business was to provide revenue for the government. The first act, then, was the Tariff Act passed July 4, 1789. Though there were some protectionist features to it, the average duties laid were only eight percent, making it an act for revenue primarily. On July 20, a Tonnage Act was passed, levying a tax on goods unloaded in American ports. The rate was to be 50 cents a ton on foreign shipping and six cents a ton on domestic. These duties, while not prohibitive, did obviously discriminate in favor of American ships. These things done, the Congress busied itself in the next couple of months creating government departments. The first departments called into being were State, War and Treasury, in that order, and these were followed shortly by authorization for a Postmaster General and an Attorney General, although these dignitaries did not yet oversee departments. A Federal Judiciary Act was passed on September 24, which provided for a Supreme Court with a Chief Justice and five associates. Three circuit courts were authorized, each of which was to have the attention of two Supreme Court justices. And 13 district courts were authorized. The establishment of lower United States courts was a decisive measure by the Congress, for though Congress had been empowered by the Constitution to establish such courts, it was a discretionary power, and by doing so Congress set the United States in the direction of having two distinct court systems, those of the United States and those of the states.

The leadership in originating and pressing through much of this legislation was assumed by James Madison. Of his role in getting through part of the legislation, one historian says: "In the formulation of the fiscal policies of the new government, James Madison asserted over Congress the same high order of leadership that he had exercised over the Constitutional Convention."[14]

It was now President Washington's turn to take the necessary actions to get the government functioning. Men had to be appointed to high offices with the consent of the Senate. Other men had to be appointed to do the more mundane jobs. Washington was finally able to persuade Thomas Jefferson to serve as the first Secretary of State. He persuaded his old comrade at arms, Henry Knox, to become Secretary of War which for him mainly involved continuing the post he occupied under the Confederation. Hamilton was the first Secretary of the Treasury, Edmund Randolph the first Attorney General, and John Jay the first Chief Justice of the Supreme Court. Department heads at first were not thought of as composing the President's Cabinet. They began to be convened as a Cabinet, however, when Washington found it more convenient to have their opinions in concert rather than as individuals on certain matters. However, the Cabinet, as such, has only such power and influence as the President accords it. With Washington this was considerable. "He surveyed his Cabinet with justifiable complacency. All were men of ability, and two were men of genius. With such as these, he wrote, 'I feel myself supported by able Co-adjutors, who harmonize well together.' "[15] This estimate, however, turned out to be much too optimistic.

The government slowly began to function. Some of the most basic laws had been passed, men appointed to posts, and the tasks of performing functions assigned. The three branches of government were ready to act, their separate functions becoming more clearly delineated, and the relationships among them being sorted out. What had been a dream and a hope only a few months before was by 1790 becoming a reality.

20

Steering the Course
of a Nation

Republics had been notoriously unstable, fiscally irresponsible, subject
to being pulled hither and yon by foreign influences, divided so as to
be laid open to civil commotions by partisan conflicts, and rent by contests over succession to leadership. No fact troubled the more thoughtful
of the Founders of the United States more than this one. The United
States had already witnessed before 1789 many of the results of the fatal
tendencies of republics. Monarchy had ever and again been revived to
solve the more tenacious problems of republics. Could the United States
be steered around the shoals on which other republics had foundered?
There were those who doubted it. After all, what would be the rock
to anchor a government against the storms without a monarch? The
answer seemed to be that there must be no storms, yet this would not
be. How could a country be made to yield to precedent, tradition, and
those founts of stability to government—awe and obedience—without
the bulwarks of established church, hereditary aristocracy, and
monarchy? Perhaps it could not be done, but if it could it would be
because the best and most able men should be engaged in political
leadership and they should set examples which lesser men would follow
in the course of time. The outstanding men had come to the fore and
taken their places, as we have seen; it now remained to be seen if they
could set a safe course.

I ERECTING A FINANCIAL STRUCTURE

It is all too easy to find fault with Hamilton and his programs. Much
of what his political foes said against him and them was true. He did
entertain great doubts about the political wisdom of the general

populace. He was a nationalist who cared little enough about the integrity of the states, if he thought they had any. He was mercantilist, or at least he was under the sway of the fag ends of mercantilist ideas. He was ambitious, aggressive, a broad constructionist, and he did intrude in foreign affaris. Those of us who differ with him in the main thrust of his economic policies may criticize him for his protectionist and pro-manufacturing posture.

Yet when all has been said against him and his programs, it should be granted that what he accomplished offsets much of it, and he emerges from an examination of his policies as one who if he did not always do right generally, did do well. There are few enough men with large vision, probably less who can conceive the programs necessary to realize it, and only a small number will labor tenaciously to get them in operation. It is easy enough, as I say, to criticize his financial program; but which one of his critics could establish the financial foundations of a nation?

Hamilton conceived a financial program which he hoped would provide the sinews of a nation. His task would have been hopeless enough if he had aimed only to get revenue to run the government, for Americans were loath to pay taxes of any kind, and politicians had shown themselves all too willing to adopt expedients which would enable them to operate for a time without the onerous necessity of taxes. But Hamilton wanted much more than a revenue. He wanted to establish the credit of the United States, when bankruptcy was the obvious outlet. And, he wanted to do so in such a way that he would tie men of wealth and position to the government, influence the people to view the United States government as *the* government, and make it clear that the general government would take care of national concerns.

Hamilton's program was presented in a series of reports to Congress in 1790-91, and most of it was enacted during the same years. The main acts dealt with the acceptance and funding of the national debt, the assumption of state debts, the creation of a Bank of the United States, and the establishment of an excise tax on whiskey.

Hamilton's first report which was on the public credit was presented January 14, 1790. In it, he argued vigorously that the domestic debt as well as the foreign debt should be assumed at the full value originally contracted. There were many of the opinion that the domestic debt should be discounted. Most of the obligations were held by speculators now, it was argued, men who had bought them at a fraction of their face value and who stood to be greatly enriched if they were paid off at full value. Hamilton approached the subject from the angle of establishing the credit of the government. "By what means is it to be effected?" he asked. "The ready answer to which question is, by good faith; by a punctual performance of contracts. States, like individuals, who observe their engagements are respected and trusted, while the reverse is the fate of those who pursue an opposite conduct."

> While the observance of that good faith, which is the basis of public credit, is recommended by the strongest inducements of political expediency, it is enforced by considerations of still greater authority. There are arguments for it which rest on the immutable principles of moral obligation. And in proportion as the mind is disposed to contemplate, in the order of Providence, an intimate connection between public virtue and public happiness, will be its repugnancy to a violation of those principles.
>
> This reflection derives additional strength from the nature of the debt of the United States. It was the price of liberty. The faith of America has been repeatedly pledged for it, and with solemnities that give peculiar force to the obligation . . .[1]

Hamilton's proposal to establish a fund for paying the national debt at face value was linked in the same bill with a plan for the assumption of state debts contracted during the War for Independence. Assumption was much more controversial than the other proposals. In fact, the idea bordered on the preposterous, in view of past history. At least some of the states had made headway in paying their debts; whereas, as yet, no United States government had demonstrated either the willingness or ability to service any debt. Moreover, there were differences in size of debt from state to state. However, adjustments were made for this, Hamilton did some horse trading with the Virginia delegation, and both funding and assumption passed. The United States issued new securities to replace the old, paid interest on them, and set aside funds to take care of them. No immediate progress was made, however, in actually paying off the debt. Even so, the credit of the United States began to improve.

Hamilton's next major proposal was for a United States bank. He proposed that it should be chartered as a corporation by the federal government, that the government should subscribe to 20 percent of the stock, and that the remainder should come from private investors. Federal funds were to be deposited in it, and the bank was to issue paper money which would become the main currency of the United States. Jefferson argued that there was no authority in the Constitution for chartering such a corporation, but Hamilton carried the field, and

Washington signed the bank bill into law February 25, 1791. Stock in the bank sold within hours after it went on the market.

Congress passed an excise tax on whiskey in March of 1791. This was the first tax levied by the United States government to be borne directly by American producers. It was much resented, particularly by western Pennsylvania farmers, who were accustomed to shipping their corn east in a liquid state. A rebellion broke out there in 1794, and it was put down by troops. Some Americans, at least, had felt the power of the new government directly.

Hamilton's most ambitious and extensive program was contained in his Report on Manufactures which he presented in December of 1791. In it, he clothed the argument for government intervention in its most attractive apparel. He held forth a vision of America drawn together in fraternal bonds through the interdependence of manufacturers, shippers, and farmers. North and South, East and West, would be drawn together in a great economic cornucopia. Few could disagree with him that there were advantages to the division of labor, to an American independence of foreign countries, or even that there was good reason to draw immigrants to American shores along with foreign capital. All of this was attractive background to an argument for government aid to manufacturing. "Such aid must consist of protective duties against competitive foreign manufactures, bounties for the establishment of new industries, premiums for excellence and quality of manufactured articles, exemptions of essential raw materials from abroad from import duties. . . , the encouragement of inventions, improvement in machinery and processes by substantial grants. . . , and, finally, the construction of roads and canals for a . . . flow of physical goods and materials."[2]

With such a program, however, Hamilton had bit off more than Congress could swallow. Even supposing the program to be desirable, which many doubted, where was the authority in the Constitution to spend the tax moneys taken from the generality of the people for such purposes? Hamilton argued that the power was there in the general welfare clause. If this were so, Madison declared, then "everything from the highest object of state legislation, down to the most minute object of policy would be thrown under the power of Congress."[3] Thus, the main elements of Hamilton's grandest scheme were turned back.

Even so, the broad lines of Hamilton's achievements have been enthusiastically summarized in this way by a present-day historian:

> By 1792, largely as a result of the leadership assumed by Alexander Hamilton, the heavy war debt dating from the struggle for independence had been put in the course of extinguishment, the price of government securities had been

stabilized close to their face value. . . , a Federal revenue system had been brought into being, a system of debt management had been created, the power of the Federal government had been decisively asserted. . . , and the credit of the Federal government had been solidly established.[4]

II INDEPENDENCE IN A HOSTILE WORLD

The United States was dependent upon European countries in the gaining of separation from England. The French alliance supplied both the naval power and a considerable army for the winning of the most impressive victory against the British on the American continent. That other nations were at war with or hostile to Britain made the American victory more certain. The favorable treaty gained by the United States at Paris in 1783 was made possible by the cross currents of animosities and jealousies among European powers. The United States staved off bankruptcy time and again in the 1780's with loans acquired in European countries.

One of the greatests tasks of the United States under the Constitution was to shake off the dependence upon Europe. Undoubtedly, European powers still viewed the United States as a potential pawn in their contests with one another. The French were inclined to think that they had a special claim on the good will of the United States. The British, on the other hand, could not view with equanimity anything less than restoring in some measure the old relationship of dependence. The Spanish were not resigned to the dominance by the United States of the eastern portion of the continent. Nor would the United States be independent of Europe until the British hold on the Great Lakes and the Spanish control of the Mississippi were broken.

The most attractive solution to this problem was for the United States to attach itself to some European power which would become its protector and champion its causes against all others. That is what, to a limited extent, had been done with France. But the French had been of very little help against Britain and Spain after the war. Moreover, the changes in France after 1792, and the new European war which broke out, made the French connection an almost certain liability and would have linked the United States to governments which not only changed frequently but also were tyrannical and oppressive. The course which Presidents Washington, Adams, and Jefferson chose successively was independence from all these powers. But it was easier to choose such a course than to steer it.

The first crisis of the Washington Administration came when the

French declared war on England, Spain, and Holland. The Franco-American Alliance committed the United States to the defense of the French West Indies and not to render aid to France's enemies. Washington issued a Neutrality Proclamation shortly after the war broke out, stating that the United States was at peace with both Great Britain and France, and warning Americans not to commit hostile acts against either side. Jefferson had raised some doubt as to Washington's authority to do this, but he did not push the point. A few days before Washington made his proclamation, a new Minister from France had arrived in the United States, a man known as Citizen Genêt. Genêt had no sooner arrived than he began to commission privateers from American ports to prey on British shipping. Washington warned him against this, but he persisted in similar activities, and the President eventually demanded his recall.

In 1794 Congress passed a Neutrality Act, which confirmed Washington's earlier proclamation, in effect, and put teeth into it. Already, relations with France had deteriorated considerably. When the United States came to terms with Britain in a treaty, relations grew worse. The accord with Britain is known as Jay's Treaty; it was signed by the diplomats in November of 1794 and ratified by the Senate June 24, 1795. By this treaty, Britain agreed to and did shortly withdraw her troops from the posts on the Great Lakes. It also opened up the East and West Indies to trade with the United States. A joint commission was appointed to deal with the debt claims, particularly of British merchants, which went back to colonial days, and a final settlement was made in 1802. British trade with the United States was placed on a most favored nation basis, which meant that any trade concession granted to any other nation would also be granted to British traders. This treaty settled most of the outstanding difficulties between the two countries, but in view of increasing difficulties with France, it was interpreted by that country as a slap in the face.

On the heels of Jay's Treaty came Pinckney's Treaty with Spain in 1795. By its terms, Spain acknowledged the boundaries of the United States as being those established by the Treaty of Paris (1783), agreed to the free navigation of the Mississippi, and accorded the right of deposit at New Orleans to Americans for a period of three years. By these two treaties the United States made great headway toward the practical attainment of an independence of Europe which had been sought in the Treaty of Paris.

However, the French government now posed increasing problems for the United States. It refused to receive Charles C. Pinckney as U.S. Minister to France when he arrived there in late 1796. Nor was the commission made up of Pinckney, John Marshall, and Elbridge Gerry, appointed by President Adams to negotiate a settlement, treated any better. The French government did not formally receive them, and agents of the foreign minister, Talleyrand, agents designated in dispatches as X, Y, and Z, suggested that the government would be happy to meet with them if they would pay a bribe and give France a loan. This XYZ affair stirred up much resentment in America when it was made public in 1798. Many expected that France would go to war with the United States at any time. Adams initiated such measures in preparation for the conflict as he thought prudent. And, an undeclared naval war between the two countries did take place, 1798-1800. Meanwhile, Adams continued efforts to reach an accord with France. This was achieved in what is known in diplomatic history as the Convention of 1800. France agreed to release the United States from the treaties made in 1778, and diplomatic relations between the two countries were resumed.

It would take us too far afield to go into any detail about the foreign relations of the next 25 years under Jeffersonian Republicans. They were, however, aimed at following an independent course in the world. This was made extremely difficult by the Napoleonic wars which embroiled Europe for the first 15 years of the new century. Both France and England continued pressure on the United States. The pressure of France was, however, greatly reduced by the Louisiana Purchase. But the pressure of Britain led eventually to the War of 1812, which some historians have called the Second War for Independence. Perhaps the culminating symbolic move in the establishment of American independence was the Monroe Doctrine set forth in 1823. By it, President Monroe announced that Americans were not subject to further colonization and by so saying attempted to place the Americas off limits to the European quest for empire and to free this continent from the struggles of Europe.

During these early years of trial a set of principles for American conduct with other nations had emerged from pronouncements and practice. The following is a summary of them, stated as imperatives:

The United States *should*

1. Establish and maintain a position of independence with regard to other countries.

2. Avoid *political* connection, involvement, or intervention in the affairs of other countries.

3. Make no permanent or entangling alliances.

4. Treat all nations impartially, neither granting nor accepting special privileges from any.

5. Promote commerce with all peoples and countries.

241

6. Cooperate with other countries to develop civilized rules of intercourse.

7. Act always in accordance with the "laws of nations."

8. Remedy all just claims of injury to other nations, and require just treatment from other nations, standing ready, if necessary, to punish offenders.

9. Maintain a defensive force of sufficient magnitude to deter aggressors.[5]

III THE RISE OF POLITICAL PARTIES

One of the unforeseen and, by some undesired developments in the early years of the Republic was the rise of political parties. No reference to any role for them was made in the Constitution. There had not been, as yet, any political parties in America; divisions were occasional or tied to factional leadership of some men, as a rule. To formalize such differences by organizing them into political parties would have appeared the height of folly to many of the Founders. In fact, there was good reason to suppose that if the Republic did not founder on the shoals of foreign entanglements it would split under the stress of partisan or factional contests, as republics had tended to do in times past.

George Washington, in his farewell address, warned the country "in the most solemn manner against the baneful effects of the spirit of party " generally. He declared that

It serves always to detract the public councils and enfeeble the public administration. It agitates the community with ill-founded jealousies and false alarms; kindles the animosity of one part against another; foments occasionally riot and insurrection. It opens the door to foreign influence and corruption, which find a facilitated access to the government itself through the channels of party passion. Thus the policy and the will of one country are subjected to the policy and will of another.

Washington admitted that the spirit of party arose out of human nature itself and was unlikely to be entirely extinguished, but he exhorted his countrymen that the "effort ought to be by force of public opinion to mitigate and assuage it."[6]

Washington had reason enough for his fears about the spirit of party. Even before he left office the lines of party were forming; his

Cabinet had already experienced the strain; and the country at large was about to witness some of the most acrimonious disputes ever to take place. It should be noted, however, that as yet disputants did not ordinarily mount the stump to address the people directly about their differences. Attacks usually appeared in newspapers, and more likely than not if major figures were involved they wrote or had their cases presented under pseudonyms. Such practices did not, however, promote restraint or prevent breaks between individuals which were difficult to heal. They may well have had the opposite result.

It is not difficult to see why parties and factions arise when men are free to hold and practice different views. Men simply do not see all questions from the same angle, and they do have, as individuals and groups, different interests from one another. And, men again and again are drawn to the conceit that what is to their advantage is also to the advantage of the majority of people. Those in power usually take a more generous view of the extent of their power than those without such power. There is, undoubtedly, a general welfare, but men hardly discern it and focus upon it exclusively in the course of their careers.

There were choices of course in plenty to divide Americans and provide the opportunity for politicians to capitalize on them in the early years of the republic. After all, the course of the nation was being set. Strong willed and determined men were placing their imprint upon it. Small wonder that those favoring and those opposing certain courses of action should form opposing factions which eventually assumed more permanent status. How should the Constitution be interpreted? Should it be broadly or strictly construed? Should the powers of the general government be greater, or those of the states preserved and enhanced? In foreign affairs, should the French Revolution be supported? Or should the United States link its fortunes to those of Britain? Or, if the United States was to be neutral, would this not benefit one side at war to the disadvantage of the other? More fundamentally, were there not choices to be made between order and liberty, between reason and experience, and between the individual and the community? If this latter formulation poses the distinctions too bluntly, it nevertheless indicates configurations of belief toward which men tended.

The two parties which emerged in the 1790's were called Federalist and Republican. Alexander Hamilton and John Adams are usually associated as leaders of the Federalist Party, which indicates also the early divisions in that party, a division which in the course of time sundered it. New England was the center of the strength of the Federalist Party, but it had devotees throughout the country. Thomas Jefferson and James Madison were the leaders of the Republican Party, and the bulk of its strength was from Pennsylvania southward. The Republican

Party was born in opposition, which probably made it considerably more united than the Federalist, which was born in power and suffered in the beginning from the stresses of power. It is much easier to be united in opposition and adversity than in possession of power and prosperity.

Though it must be understood that leaders of parties are not in perfect agreement, that men do not readily acknowledge either-or positions, that the following should not be taken as absolutes, Federalists and Republicans did tend to divide along the following lines. Federalists were more inclined to emphasize the depravity of man, particularly that of the generality of men, than were Republicans, although Madison readily declared man to be a frail vessel, and Jefferson would not deny it. Federalists emphasized the importance of experience, tradition, awe, and veneration, while Republicans were more hopeful about the benefits of reason. Federalists inclined to be nationalists (when they were in power), and the Republicans to favor state's rights. Federalists tended toward mercantilism in economic policy, while Republicans were more favorably disposed toward *laissez-faire*. Federalists favored industrializing, while Republicans wanted an agricultural economy with an emphasis on foreign trade. Republicans were much more favorably disposed toward France than were the British-leaning Federalists.

It is not to the purpose of this work to devote much attention to these conflicts. What is important is that they were there and that political parties took shape around them as issues. Nor is it so important that when the Republicans were in power for awhile they began to abandon the policies they had championed and to advance some of those they had opposed. Being in power is a severe test of anyone's beliefs, and there are usually excuses enough in changing circumstances for altering them. What is important is that although political parties are extra-constitutional they came to play an important role in buttressing and maintaining the Constitution.

One of the checks and balances on government not conceived and contrived in the Constitutional Convention was that provided by political parties. Perhaps the greatest check of all on those in power is provided by the opposition party and by its members who hold office, but not the power of determining policies. If the party in power takes a generous view of the powers available to its members, the one out of power uses the limited powers doctrine as one of its reasons for opposing the extension of power. The Jeffersonians out of power opposed the Sedition Act as unconstitutional. Federalists out of power opposed the Jeffersonian Embargo and defended state's rights. So it has frequently been throughout American history. The strict construction doctrine would sometimes have few advocates without a minority party.

The Jeffersonians brought particularly important counterbalances to

244

the Federalist emphasis. It probably was most useful that the early officials of the United States should have emphasized dignity, respect for law, pomp, and even ceremony. But Jefferson was much more in keeping with the genius of America in his emphasis upon republican simplicity and informality. Though the mercantile ideas of Hamilton may have served some temporary purpose, the Jeffersonians brought to the fore newer, fresher, and freer economic ideas, and there was no doubt that Jefferson believed in paying off the debt. Albert Gallatin, as Jefferson's Secretary of the Treasury, was a remarkable counterpart to Hamilton. He was equally brilliant, and his thought tended toward the freeing of enterprise. It may be of some use to quote him in a critique of the tariff system, a critique penned long after he had left the Treasury:

> Let it be recollected, that the system is in itself an infraction of an essential part of the liberty of the citizen. The necessity must be urgent and palpable, which authorizes any government to interfere in the private pursuits of individuals; to forbid them to do that which in itself is not criminal, and which every one would most certainly do, if not forbidden. Every individual, in every community, without exception, will purchase whatever he may want on the cheapest terms within his reach. The most enthusiastic restrictionist, the manufacturer, most clamorous for special protection, will, each individually, pursue the same course, and prefer any foreign commodity, or material, to that of domestic origin, if the first is cheaper, and the law does not forbid him. All men ever have acted, and continue, under any system, to act on the same principle. . . . The advocates of the tariff system affirm, that what is true of all men, individually, is untrue, when applied to them collectively. We cannot consider the adherence of enlightened nations to regulations of that description, but as the last relic of that system of general restrictions and monopolies, which had its origin in barbarous times. . . .[7]

Perhaps the greatest precedent set in the early years of the Republic grew out of party divisions. That precedent was the peaceful change from one set of rulers to another. The congressional elections are so staggered that at no time would there be an entirely new Congress. Even more is it unlikely that the personnel of the federal courts would all change at any time. The one crucial branch, then, for the above and other reasons, for a change from one group of rulers to another is the executive branch. There was no overall change in that branch until 1801. Though Washington stepped down in 1797, there was a clear continuity between his administration and that of Adams, for the members of the Cabinet were continued. Not so, when Jefferson came into office as President. Party divisions and loyalties had become so strong and determining, the feelings between Adams and Jefferson were so heated, that there could be no question of Jefferson's continuing with his Cabinet. Yet for all the strong feelings, the change from Adams to Jefferson was made peacefully. And so it has been ever since: Americans have become so accustomed to the peaceful change of rulers (or governors, if one's sensibilities are stirred by the other term) as not to remark it. Yet it is always a remarkable thing in history when a man with such powers yields them up to someone else without war. In a sense, our political contests are a means of shifting the conflict from the field of battle to the arena of ideas and words. The contest is usually sharp, but the loser retires gracefully from the field.

Were Washington's fears of parties groundless, then? Surely, they were not groundless; he could have called up much history in support of them. Nor did he expect that America would be without such divisions; he hoped only for a mitigation of the harshness of them. And, it can be reported that this occurred. Two major developments have made party contests less than seriously divisive, as a rule.

One is that the United States has usually had only two major parties. A multiplicity of parties does tend to divide the country into irreconcilable factions. Whereas, when there are only two major parties, they tend both to contain many people of similar views in each of them and to try to attract any considerable faction not yet within the party. But why, it is asked, has the United States had only two major parties? Some have supposed that the predilection to do this is peculiar to Anglo-Saxon peoples. But such an explanation is of doubtful validity. The more likely explanation is the winner-take-all practices, some in the Constitution, some added by the states. In elections to Congress, there is, as a rule, only one winner in a district and in a state. (On rare occasions, there occurs an election of two Senators from the same state in the same election. But in such a case, candidates run separately for the positions, since the term of one of the men elected would not be for the full six years.) The office of President is clearly a winner-take-all affair, and states have made this true for electors along party lines as well by giving the whole vote for electors to the party which attains a plurality. The effect of this practice (as contrasted with proportional representation) is that only major parties can sustain any considerable following over the years by patronage. And only two parties can reasonably expect to elect many to office. They do so, as a rule, only by appealing to a very broad electorate.

The other offset in the American system to the baneful effects of party is a little more complicated. Washington noted that in "governments of a monarchical cast" it is plausible to "look with indulgence, if not with favor, upon the spirit of party. But in those of the popular character, in government purely elective, it is a spirit not to be encouraged."[8] We can read between the lines of this a little and almost certainly infer his meaning. A land which has an hereditary monarch has continuity and stability. Governments change, cabinet officers come and go, a new election brings new members of the legislature, but the monarch remains. A republic, however, does not have this visible symbol of continuity and stability. When it is divided by parties, there is no man beyond these contesting groups to provide it. Yet the United States has had a sign and symbol—a veritable rock—to give it continuity and stability. It is, of course, the Constitution. Washington may be pardoned for not foreseeing that it would serve in that office.

IV THE CONSTITUTION AS HIGHER LAW

The most likely prognosis for the Constitution in 1789 was that in very short order it would become a dead letter. After all, it was only a "piece of paper," and power resided in the hands of men once the government was organized. The ways by which it might have become a dead letter are so numerous that only a few of them need be suggested. Once men had power in their hands, they might have gone their own way, using the Constitution only as a launching pad, as it were, to come to power, then ignoring its restrictions. The states, on the other hand, might have made of it a nullity by so circumscribing the actual exercise of powers that the general government would be of no account. The President might have become a dictator. The Constitution might have remained; all might have given it their vocal allegiance without allowing it to affect their actions.

We know, of course, that these things did not occur. Instead, the Constitution became, in fact, a Higher Law in the United States, a Constitution above constitutions, and a document to which men truly repaired for the resolution of vexed issues. That this occurred can be attributed to tradition, circumstances, and the efforts of leading men.

Americans had a tradition of higher law, and it needs to be only briefly recalled here. They were a people of the Book, to whom the Bible was a higher law. They accepted, also, the belief that natural law was higher law. In the British and colonial traditions, they had received the belief that certain basic documents constitute a higher law, i.e.,

247

charters, covenants, declarations, and acts of conventions. This is to say that Americans were predisposed to the acceptance of a higher law, and they were especially sensitized to written laws.

The circumstances under which the Constitution was drawn and ratified lent weight to giving it a unique place. It had been drawn in convention by some of the most prominent men in America. This had been done behind closed doors and by way of debates to which the public at large was not privy. It had been ratified by special conventions within the states by men chosen for the particular task. And, most of the prominent men in America came forth to serve in the government which it authorized.

George Washington gave the full weight of his prestige to the Constitution. He wanted only men in his government who were devoted to it, and in his appointments attempted to make this the first requirement. His public pronouncements were such as to add weight and authority to the document. In his First Inaugural Address, he referred "to the great constitutional charter under which you are assembled, and which, in defining your powers, designates the objects to which your attention is to be given."[9] He said in his Farewell Address that those entrusted with governmental powers should

> confine themselves within their respective constitutional spheres, avoiding in the exercise of the powers of one department to encroach upon another. The spirit of encroachment tends to consolidate the powers of all the departments in one, and thus to create, whatever the form of government, a real despotism. . . . If in the opinion of the people the distribution or modification of the constitutional powers be in any particular wrong, let it be corrected by an amendment in the way which the Constitution designates. But let there be no change by usurpation; for though this in one instance may be the instrument of good, it is the customary weapon by which free governments are destroyed.[10]

Other men who were or would be Presidents uttered similar messages. James Madison said in 1792:

> Liberty and order will never be *perfectly* safe, until a trespass on the constitutional provisions for either, shall be felt with the same keenness that resents an invasion of the dearest rights, until every citizen shall be an Argus to espy, and Aegeon to avenge, the unhallowed deed.

Thomas Jefferson declared in 1793:

> Our peculiar security is in the possession of a written Constitution. Let us not make a blank paper by construction. I say the same as to the opinion of those who consider the grant of the treaty-making power as boundless. If it is, then we have no Constitution. If it has bounds, they can be no other than the definitions of the powers which that instrument gives.

But it was John Marshall, as Chief Justice of the Supreme Court for 35 years, who raised the Constitution to the pinnacle as the Higher Law in the United States. Among the large number of decisions of the court written by Marshall, a goodly number were referred to the Constitution for resolution. Indeed, Marshall appears to have relished those instances when he could make of the question before the court a constitutional question. This judgment is based on the fact that some of them could have been decided readily on other than constitutional grounds. Marshall made the Constitution very much a live letter, by making it available as law on which decisions could rest, by bringing Congress to heel, by bringing the states to heel, and by using it both as authority and restraint. Marshall tried to make it clear always that those brought to heel were not brought to that posture by the court but by the Constitution. In Osborn v. U.S.Bank delivered in 1824, he said: "Judicial power, as contra-distinguished from the power of the law, has no existence. Courts are the mere instruments of the law, and can will nothing."[11] He viewed the Constitution as "intended to endure for ages to come," and made decisions designed to ensure that it would.

In Marbury v. Madison, delivered in 1803, Marchall declared that the Constitution limits the Congress. "The powers of the legislature are defined and limited; and that those limits may not be mistaken or forgotten, the constitution is written." When the legislature acts contrary to its constitutional authority, its acts are not to be put in force. For, he said, "the particular phraseology of the constitution of the United States confirms and strengthens the principle, supposed to be essential to all written constitutions, that a law repugnant to the constitution is void, and that courts, as well as other departments, are bound by that instrument."[12]

In Fletcher v. Peck (1810), Marshall spoke for a unanimous court when he held that the states were restrained by the Constitution. He said that Georgia "is a part of a large empire; she is a member of the American union; and that union has a constitution, the supremacy of which all acknowledge, and which imposes limits to the legislatures of the several states, which none claim a right to pass."[13]

Marshall could buttress his decisions with the broadest principles, but he could also construe the Constitution with great attention to distinctions. For example, the case of Craig, et. al., v. The State of Missouri involved the attempt to issue paper money by the state. The state contended that since this money was not made legal tender, it was permitted. Not so, said Marshall:

> The Constitution itself furnishes no countenance to this distinction. The prohibition is general. It extends to all bills of credit, not to bills of a particular description. . . . The Constitution . . . considers the emission of bills of credit and the enactment of tender laws as distinct operations, independent of each other, which may be separately performed. Both are forbidden. To sustain the one because it is not also the other; to say that bills of credit may be emitted if they be not made a tender in payment of debts, is in effect, to expunge that distinct independent prohibition, and to read the clause as if it had been entirely omitted. We are not at liberty to do this. . . .[14]

It has been commonly said of Marshall that in his decisions he construed the Constitution in a way to increase the power of the government, that he was a nationalist, and that he built the power of the United States government at the expense of the states. This view contains some truth, obviously, but it is not the most important thing to say about him. It can also be truly said that Marshall by the tone and character of his decisions gave the central role in expounding the Constitution to the Supreme Court, but that is not the most important thing to say about him, for that position can be and has been abused. What looms above all the other things he did as an enduring contribution is that he looked to and raised the Constitution to the position of Higher Law—a law to which courts, congresses, presidents, and states must yield. Above all, he professed to be bound by the Constitution. "This department," he said, "can listen only to the mandates of law, and can tread only that path which is marked out by duty."[15] The Supreme Court rose to high regard not because people believed that the Constitution was what the court said it was but because they believed that the court spoke not the will of its members but submitted their wills to the Constitution. John Marshall made such a view credible.

The course of the nation was set in the early years of the Republic.

The credit was established, and men came to believe that the obligations of the United States would be met. The United States adopted and followed an independent course in the world. The government was further checked and balanced by political parties. And the Constitution achieved a special place as a Higher Law binding all Americans.

21

Epilogue:
The Beacon of Liberty

Why should anyone bother to write the history of the founding of the American Republic? Or why, if it be written, should anyone bother to read or study it? Because, it has been asserted, it constitutes an epoch, and even an epic. That may be true enough, but if that epoch be wrenched out of its broader context, why should it be considered an epic? Here were some colonies on a remote continent which revolted from the empire of which they were a part and succeeded in effecting the separation. Having done so, they repudiated their paper money, could not meet many of their obligations, and lacked the respect of the great powers of the world. Their Confederation was without energy, and there was considerable doubt whether their state governments could maintain order. In these circumstances, they made a concerted effort to revamp and reorganize to produce a "more perfect Union." As we have left the story, they appear to have succeeded in doing this in considerable measure. Though this was an achievement to be admired, it would not suffice to make the story one of epic dimensions.

Nor should the account be read as a glorification of war. Even if war were worthy of glorification, the struggles in America would surely count as among its less notable episodes. There were few great battles; usually when one loomed ahead, a withdrawal occurred rather than a fight to the finish. The British used a great many foreign mercenaries. The Americans relied extensively on the militia, whose members would hardly qualify as soldiers. The Continental armies were ragtag bobtail aggregations with too little discipline and shortages of almost everything else that makes armies function. True, there were great acts of personal heroism, and there was the exemplary tenacity of a few leaders, but these were offset often enough by cowardice of militia, lack of resolution by governments, and a civilian population looking the other way when help was needed. In any case, it is unlikely that the miseries of the Continental armies would be recalled as a glorification of war.

This account is not to be understood as simply a veneration of government in general or of American governments in particular. Government is necessary; those of a pious bent may properly say that it is ordained. That is, man is such, and society is such, that government is required to maintain the peace. But if government were all that was wanted, it would be possible to construct a much simpler one than the federal system of government in these United States. The exercise of government power does not require checks and balances, the separation of power, two or more distinct jurisdictions, a duplication of court systems, nor a multiplicity of elected officials. Much of this is actually extraneous to the efficient exercise of governmental power.

What makes the story worth retelling, then, and gives it its epic dimensions, is neither war nor government. It is worth recalling because in the midst of war, diplomatic contests, internal divisions between Patriots and Loyalists, fiscal irresponsibilities, political squabbles, a sufficient number of Americans clung to a hope and an idea to bring it forth from the upheaval and make strides toward realizing it. That idea, if it must be put in a phrase, was the idea of ordered liberty, the idea that America should be a land where protections of liberty and property were firmly established, a refuge for the persecuted to come to, and a beacon shining forth as a guide for others to follow. George Washington could speak with the assurance that he knew his countrymen when he said, in his farewell address, "Interwoven as is the love of liberty with every ligament of your hearts, no recommendation of mine is necessary to fortify or confirm the attachment."

This epoch is raised to epic proportions, then, by the quality of the idea that nourished it and by the degree to which the men of that day were able to achieve it. The era is appreciated more for the epic that it was when it is seen in its proper context of past and future. It is what the United States became that justifies our attention to its beginnings, and it is that out of which it was wrought that gave it substance.

The epic of the founding of the American Republic is no less than the epic of the rebirth of liberty on the American continent. That is right; it was indeed a *re*birth.

It would have been quite strange if it had been other than a rebirth. All our births are but rebirths. They are not the less remarkable for that, for we celebrate and stand in awe of the succession of rebirths which give continuity to and perennially freshen and renew our world. What is spring but a rebirth of what was there the year before? Every child born of woman is a rebirth of the human form in new attire.

254

Rebirth stands at its peak when Christianity proclaims that you must be born again, that a rebirth in spirit is greater than the original birth. It is not for man to create; it is sufficient that he be able to take part in re-creation.

But there are facts enough to support the position that it was a rebirth of liberty that took place in America; it does not have to be made to follow from the universality of the phenomena. It was a rebirth of liberty because Americans took the elements from the past which they shaped into their own system for the protection of liberty. That is about all that history affords—elements—for they have all too seldom been drawn together in a working system. The story of mankind is full to overflowing with examples of oppressions, tyrannies, restrictions, and repressions. Arbitrary government has been the rule; government restrained is the exception. Yet here and there and from time to time there have been practices which ameliorated the oppressions and allowed for greater or lesser amounts of liberty. The Founders of these United States combed the pages of history, read the works of political thought, sought guidance from all sources known to them, and brought their own traditions to bear on the subject to learn what they could of how to establish governments that would provide ordered liberty.

The records of the Hebrew people contained in Scripture were of interest; the philosophers of Greece offered hints; the natural law philosophy in ancient Rome was a fount of inspiration; the separation of powers in the Middle Ages in abstracted form provided them a clue and example; the British tradition was ever at their back; and their own colonial experience provided them with numerous examples, bad and good. From these they drew and out of them they wove a frame of government with which to work. All that they had learned they viewed with a canny eye to discern where other systems had failed and what in their own would give way first before the bent of men toward power. Looking at the matter in the long run, they were reasonably certain that their labor was futile, for the work of men in the past had eventually fallen prey to man's interior bent to destruction; they saw little enough reason to suppose that theirs would meet with much better luck. Perhaps what was reborn would be a little stronger than what had gone before because its elements had been carefully selected, but that was the most to be hoped for.

The act of rebirth would not, however, have been worthy of extended attention if the infant had been stillborn or if it had been frail and sickly, destined shortly to pass away. What finally makes the founding of such significance is that the American story is, in most important ways, a success story. So it has been adjudged, and so it must be adjudged by the yardsticks that men apply to nations. Those English

Americans who had landed on some of the most forbidding territory, or that which was among the least promising in the new world, did, in the course of time, press on across the Appalachians, push their ways to the Mississippi, surge across the great plains, pick their way through the Rockies, and establish themselves on the Pacific. Everywhere they went, they carried with them their religion, institutions, language, and constitutions; all others yielded to them, by and large. Conquests there were, but that is not the main story. The main story is one of construction: of houses, of bridges, of fences, of factories, of roads, of canals, of railroads, of barns, of communities, and of cities. In time, they were so productive that the Europe which had once succored them would turn to America for sustenance. It is not a story, of course, in which the pure in heart can always rejoice and take comfort. None of the stories that involve men over any span of time are of that kind. But it has been a success story which could have been viewed by the Founders—who were mostly men who did not expect too much of the frail reed that is man and could therefore rejoice in what he did accomplish—with a measure of pride. They had laid a strong foundation for the United States.

Any historian worth his salt must pause to ponder the sources of this success, and, it should be said, a goodly number have. But the success of America has not been of academic interest alone; peoples around the world have had and have a considerable interest in America. They have poured in large number to American shores in search of refuge and opportunity. They have sought to abstract from the American system those features they hold responsible for the success. Of course, the successful are frequently envied, often despised, and sometimes hated, but they are, nonetheless, imitated.

It is common to ascribe the American success to a variety of causes, ranging from chance or luck to a favorable environment. Some declare that the United States was particularly fortunate during the nineteenth century because of the remoteness from Europe, or because of bountiful resources, or because Presidents were of a higher caliber than might have been expected, or because the British navy formed a protective shield, or because of a temperate climate which was mild enough to permit work the year round yet demanding enough to stir effort, or any of a large number of causes in combination. But the underlying explanation to which most who have written or spoken on the subject subscribe as judged by the attention given to it is American democracy. They have seen the greatness of America in the quest for democracy and the achievements of America as the fruit of democracy. It is this, above all else, that Americans have talked most about exporting in more

256

recent times and that other countries have most often made the most noise about imitating, however sincerely or with whatever results.

Now there is no denying that there are and have been democratic elements in the American political system. The Founders believed in popular government, up to a point, and many quotations could be brought forth to illustrate their argument that the Constitution provided for a government resting on the consent of the people. They held that popular consent was the source of governmental authority and the fount of its strength. It should be said, however, that what they meant was that government to be legitimate must have the consent of the property owners and taxpayers. But it is to seriously misinterpret what they thought and what they did to call it simply democratic; and it is an even graver error to ascribe to democracy the foundation of American liberty and success.

The matter can be put strongly, perhaps too strongly, by saying in philosophical terminology that the democratic features of the American political system are *accidents*. In common parlance, this is roughly equivalent to saying that the democratic features are incidental. Note well, however, that to call them philosophical accidents is not to declare them unimportant. It is an accident, in this sense of the word, that one man is born black, another white, one red, and another yellow. None will deny that much importance has been and some importance may attach to these distinctions. But they do not go to the heart of the matter of what a man is. Color is not *essential*—again, speaking philosophically, it is accidental or incidental to the nature of man. So democracy is accidental, that is, not of the essence of the American political system.

To put the matter another way, and to get closer to the point, the democratic (or republican, if one prefers) featur s of the political system are largely means to an end, and not to be confused with the end. They are means to legitimating government, selecting officials, and justifying the claims of government on the goods and services of the people. The end of government, so the Founders thought, is to provide order and to protect life, liberty, and property. Nor did they suppose these to be disparate ends. The surest means of promoting happiness (to which order is the one absolute requirement), they thought, is to protect individuals in their possession of life, liberty, and property. After all, the sources of disorder among men in community are the quest for power and the contentions over property. Indeed, so universal have been the contentions over property that some have supposed that if property be done away with so would the sources of conflict among men. There is no reason to suppose that this would follow, however, nor do such efforts as have been made to do so give evidence to support it. On the contrary, when property rights are abolished, the contest shifts to the arena of the quest for power and special privilege, which immeasurably worsens rather than improves the situation. At any rate, the Founders thought that order and liberty are correlative ends of government.

The *essence* of the American political system is *limited government*. This conclusion is supported in almost every paragraph of the Constitution. Limited government is the raison d'être of checks and balances, the separation of powers, the two branches of Congress, the presidential veto, the power of the courts to receive appeals, the enumeration of powers, the prohibitions against the exercise of certain powers, the staggered terms of elected officers, the indirect modes of election, the dispersion of powers among the states and the general government, and a Bill of Rights. One qualification should be made to classifying the democratic features as accidents; insofar as the necessity for popular consent limits government, it is essential to the American system.

Had the men who made the Constitution in Philadelphia in 1787 been concerned only with establishing a popular (or democratic) government their task would surely have been much simpler than it was, and they might have finished with it in short order. If they had considered a direct democracy impractical, which they did, of course, then all they would have needed to do would have been to compose a list of officials necessary to the exercise of governmental powers and provide for their election from time to time, by an explicit electorate. It is quite true, of course, that such a system might never have witnessed a second election. Anything added to it, however, would have been by way of limiting government, not of making it democratic.

This is by way of saying, of course, that the Founders conceived their task otherwise; what was uppermost in their minds was to confide governmental powers to a general government—to make these adequate to the exigencies of the Union—and then to see that both the general government and the state governments were restrained and confined. It was for these purposes that they scanned the records of history, consulted the best minds, and called upon their experience. It was for these ends that they made the system as complex as it is.

The *essence* of the *American* system—which is something much more than the political system—is *limited government* and *free men*. This is the clue to the productive and constructive successes of Americans. When the energies of peaceful men are released they are capable of and have achieved wonders of building, invention, production, transportation, and so forth. These activities proceed from people as individu-

258

als. They do not proceed from government, whether the government be democratic, aristocratic, or monarchical. Government is not capable, by nature, of being productive or constructive. In its capacity as government, it acts to restrain and restrict. When it uses these powers against those who would disturb the peace in one way or another it enables peaceful men to produce and construct. When it uses them to restrain peaceful men, it inhibits the constructive. Thus it is that limited government is the requirement for releasing the energies of men.

It would not be appropriate for Americans to be overly proud of their successes. Not only does pride go before a fall, but it is much less warranted than may be supposed. One need only to look casually at American history to see that Americans have quite often ignored and forgotten the principles of their political system, that they have confused means with ends and accidents with essences. The ink was hardly dry on the Constitution before some were conceiving of means to expand the powers of the general government. And it would be less than candid not to say here that in more recent times there have been increasing numbers who act as if their government were some sort of energizer and fount of construction and production. The powers exercised by all governments have been greatly expanded and the energies of individuals have been more and more channeled and confined. The means—the democratic features—have been made into an end—democracy—and many suppose that America comes closer and closer to its goal the more democratic that it is. American politicians have proven themselves to be as imaginative and inventive as those in government in any other land in devising justifications for the expansion of their powers. Bemused by the supposed attractions of democracy, many voters must suppose that their own powers are thus being increased, but they only increase the powers of those who hold the reins of government at their own expense.

It is not in pride, then, but with humility, that we return to an account of the foundations and of the Founders. It is to visit the scene of the beginnings of a great nation, but more than that to capture the sources of the greatness of it in the principles upon which it was founded. Out of the web of conflicts and contests of those years emerge the principles of liberty. They are, we may believe, enduring principles, not something invented by a generation of outstanding men. Indeed, the principles of liberty could probably be rediscovered by any man who would put his mind to the matter for long enough. But that is not necessary; they have long since been clearly discerned and written out. What distinguishes the Founders is that they were able to incorporate them into the fundamental laws of the land.

This epoch of history is an epic, finally, because of the quality of the work that was done, the caliber of the men who performed it, the nobility of the ideas that impelled the action, and the durability of the structure they devised. It was not uncommon for men during the days of the founding to declare that Americans had been especially blessed by the remarkable confluence of men, events, and happenings in the midst of which these United States were born. George Washington put the matter about as elegantly and reverently as could be in his First Inaugural Address:

> . . . No people can be bound to acknowledge and adore the Invisible Hand which conducts the affairs of men more than those of the United States. Every step by which they have advanced to the character of an independent nation seems to have been distinguished by some token of providential agency; and in the important revolution just accomplished in the system of their united government the tranquil deliberations and voluntary consent of so many distinct communities from which the event has resulted can not be compared with the means by which most governments have been established without some return of pious gratitude, along with an humble anticipation of the future blessings which the past seems to presage. . . .

One by one, the men who had so much to do with the founding passed on to their final reward. To close this historical account with a record of their departures may serve to remind us not only that all men are mortal but also that those who strive to know and realize great ideas leave a portion of their immortality here on earth.

James Otis died in 1783, the first of the notables of the epoch to go. He had been among the first to raise his voice against British repression, reached the peak of his forensic skill in the mid-1760's, thereafter succumbed to occasional bouts with madness, but recovered sufficiently to fight at the Battle of Bunker Hill.

Benjamin Franklin died in 1790. He was probably the first American of international fame. He had risen from obscurity to be a printer, postmaster, inventor, philosopher, diplomat, leader in his state, and elder statesman at the Constitutional Convention. His country had done well by him; he did even better by it.

George Mason died in 1792. His moment of national prominence came during the Convention, in whose deliberations he participated so well but whose product he rejected.

Roger Sherman died in 1793. This dour Connecticut Yankee performed yeoman service for his state and country over the years, never so outstandingly as at the Constitutional Convention. His last years were well spent in the Congress of the United States, where he supported the programs of Hamilton.

John Hancock died in 1793. His national fame probably rests almost solely on his efforts as presiding officer of the Second Continental Congress which enabled him to plant an oversized signature on the Declaration of Independence, but he was involved in the Patriot cause from the early years and was perennial governor of Massachusetts during most of the early years of that state.

Richard Henry Lee died in 1794. He joined early in the resistance to the oppressive acts of Britain, introduced the resolution for independence into the Second Continental Congress, was an opponent of the Constitution as it was drawn, but nevertheless served in the first Senate under it.

James Wilson died in 1798. He is remembered best for his work at the Constitutional Convention, but he was also the most able apologist for it at the state convention to consider ratification.

Patrick Henry died in June of 1799. His was for many years one of the most eloquent voices in America in defense of liberty. The making of strong and effective governments, however, was not his forte. During most of his years he could not forget that government remote from the people was a danger to their liberties.

George Washington died in December of 1799, probably as a result of the ministrations of his physicians, not an uncommon way to die in those days. Much of his adult life had been a sacrifice to the public service, for he ever longed to devote himself to his own affairs. Although he had frequently perforce to neglect his business affairs he did not, according to his accounts, neglect his private charities.

Samuel Adams died in 1803. His had been a leading role in arousing opposition to British acts in the 1760's and 1770's: to the Sugar Act, Stamp Act, Townshend Acts, and Tea Act. Once the revolt had succeeded, however, his public service was restricted to the state of Massachusetts.

Alexander Hamilton died in 1804. His death was caused by wounds suffered in a duel with Aaron Burr, making him the only one of the Founders to die of violence from the anger of another. It is not so surprising that this should have happened to someone, for quarrels were particularly acrimonious in those days. There are many impressions to be had of Hamilton, but it is perhaps most fitting that we take our leave of him by quoting a letter he wrote to his wife just before his death. It brings us more dramatically into another age than anything I know.

> This letter, my dear Eliza, will not be delivered to you, unless I shall first have terminated my earth career, to begin, as I humbly hope, from redeeming grace and divine mercy, a happy immortality. If it had been possible for me to have avoided the interview, my love for you and my precious children would have been alone a decisive motive. But it was not possible, without sacrifices which would have rendered me unworthy of your esteem. I need not tell you of the pangs I feel from the idea of quitting you, and exposing you to the anguish I know you would feel. Nor could I dwell on the topic, lest it should unman me. The consolations of religion, my beloved, can alone support you; and these you have a right to enjoy. Fly to the bosom of your God, and be comforted. With my last idea I shall cherish the sweet hope of meeting you in a better world. Adieu, best of wives—best of women. Embrace all my darling children for me.[1]

Henry Knox died in 1806, Robert Morris in the same year, Oliver Ellsworth in 1807, John Dickinson in 1808, Thomas Paine in 1809, Edmund Randolph in 1813, Elbridge Gerry in 1814, Gouverneur Morris in 1816, and Charles C. Pinckney in 1825.

Thomas Jefferson and John Adams died on the same day, of the same month, of the same year—July 4, 1826. There was more that was symbolic about this than their death on July 4, but that would have been enough, for both of them had been on the subcommittee for drawing the Declaration of Independence. There was more, however, for in some ways they came to represent the poles of political belief: Adams the proponent of awe, respect, and dignity of government, Jefferson the exemplar of republican simplicity; Adams the sturdy voice of conservative New England, Jefferson the eloquent spokesman for liberal Virginia; Adams, the Federalist, Jefferson, the Republican. They had been early believers in independence and had participated in many of the tasks by which it had been won. Partisan contests had made them the bitterest of political enemies by 1800. Time has a way of healing such wounds, however, and they were fortunate to live long enough to put behind them such animosities. Eventually, they resumed correspondence with one another, and continued the friendship until death.

John Jay died in 1829, Charles Carroll of Carrollton in 1832, and John Marshall in 1835.

Shortly before his death, James Madison concluded that he was the last of the men still living who had participated in making the Constitution. Indeed, he observed, wryly, that he might well be thought to have outlived himself. Frail "Jimmy" finally died in 1836 at the ripe age of 85. The last of that remarkable group of men called Founders had passed on.

They had relighted the beacon of liberty; it remains for those who come after to keep it burning.

Appendix A

The Declaration of
Stamp Act Congress

The members of this congress, sincerely devoted, with the warmest sentiments of affection and duty to his majesty's person and government; inviolably attached to the present happy establishment of the protestant succession, and with minds deeply impressed by a sense of the present and impending misfortunes of the British colonies on this continent; having considered as maturely as time would permit, the circumstances of the said colonies, esteem it our indispensable duty to make the following declarations, of our humble opinion, respecting the most essential rights and liberties of the colonists, and of the grievances under which they labor, by reason of several late acts of parliament.

1st. That his majesty's subjects in these colonies, owe the same allegience to the crown of Great Britain, that is owing from his subjects born within the realm, and all due subordination to that august body, the parliament of Great Britain.

2d. That his majesty's liege subjects in these colonies are entitled to all the inherent rights and privileges of his natural born subjects within the kingdom of Great Britain.

3d. That it is inseparably essential to the freedom of a people, and the undoubted rights of Englishmen, that no taxes should be imposed on them, but with their own consent, given personally, or by their representatives.

4th. That the people of these colonies are not, and from their local circumstances, cannot be represented in the house of commons in Great Britain.

5th. That the only representatives of the people of these colonies, are persons chosen therein, by themselves; and that no taxes ever have been, or can be constitutionally imposed on them, but by their respective legislatures.

6th. That all supplies to the crown, being free gifts of the people, it is unreasonable and inconsistent with the principles and spirit of the British constitution, for the people of Great Britain to grant to his majesty the property of the colonists.

7th. That trial by jury is the inherent and invaluable right of every British subject in these colonies.

8th. That the late act of parliament, entitled, an act for granting and applying certain stamp duties, and other duties in the British colonies and plantations in America, etc., by imposing taxes on the inhabitants of these colonies, and the said act, and several other acts, by extending the jurisdiction of the courts of admiralty beyond its ancient limits, have a manifest tendency to subvert the rights and liberties of the colonists.

9th. That the duties imposed by several late acts of parliament, from their peculiar circumstances of these colonies, will be extremely burthensome and grievous, and from the scarcity of specie, the payment of them absolutely impracticable.

10th. That as the profits of the trade of these colonies ultimately centre in Great Britain, to pay for the manufactures which they are obliged to take from thence, they eventually contribute very largely to all supplies granted there to the crown.

11th. That the restrictions imposed by several late acts of parliament, on the trade of these colonies, will render them unable to purchase the manufactures of Great Britain.

12th. That the increase, prosperity and happiness of these colonies, depend on the full and free enjoyment of their rights and liberties, and an intercourse, with Great Britain, mutually affectionate and advantageous.

13th. That it is the right of the British subjects in these colonies, to petition the king or either house of parliament.

Lastly, That it is the indispensable duty of these colonies to the best of sovereigns, to the mother country, and to themselves, to endeavor by a loyal and dutiful address to his majesty, and humble application to both houses of parliament, to procure the repeal of the act for granting and applying certain stamp duties, of all clauses of any other acts of parliament, whereby the jurisdiction of the admiralty is extended as aforesaid, and of the other late acts for the restriction of the American commerce.

Appendix B

Declaration of Independence

IN CONGRESS, JULY 4, 1776

THE UNAMINOUS DECLARATION OF THE THIRTEEN UNITED STATES OF AMERICA

When in the Course of human events, it becomes necessary for one people to dissolve the political bands which have connected them with another, and to assume among the Powers of the earth, the separate and equal station to which the Laws of Nature and of Nature's God entitle them, a decent respect to the opinions of mankind requires that they should declare the causes which impel them to the separation.

We hold these truths to be self-evident, that all men are created equal, that they are endowed by their Creator with certain unalienable Rights, that among these are Life, Liberty and the pursuit of Happiness. That to secure these rights, Governments are instituted among Men, deriving their just powers from the consent of the governed, That whenever any Form of Government becomes destructive of these ends, it is the Right of the People to alter or to abolish it, and to institute new Government, laying its foundation on such principles and organizing its powers in such form, as to them shall seem most likely to effect their Safety and Happiness. Prudence, indeed, will dictate that Governments long established should not be changed for light and transient causes; and accordingly all experience hath shown, that mankind are more disposed to suffer, while evils are sufferable, than to right themselves by abolishing the forms to which they are accustomed. But when a long train of abuses and usurpations, pursuing invariably the same Object evinces a design to reduce them under absolute Despotism, it is their right, it is their duty, to throw off such Government, and to provide new Guards for their future security. Such has been the patient sufferance of these Colonies; and such is now the necessity which constrains them to alter their former Systems of Government. The history of the present King of Great Britain is a history of repeated injuries and usurpations, all having in direct object the establishment of an absolute Tyranny over these States. To prove this, lets Facts be submitted to a candid world.

He has refused his Assent to Laws, the most wholesome and necessary for the public good.

He has forbidden his Governors to pass laws of immediate and pressing importance, unless suspended in their operation till his Assent should be obtained; and when so suspended, he has utterly neglected to attend to them.

He has refused to pass other Laws for the accommodation of large districts of people, unless those people would relinquish the right of Representation in the Legislature, a right inestimable to them and formidable to tyrants only.

He has called together legislative bodies at places unusual, uncomfortable, and distant from the depository of their Public Records, for the sole purpose of fatiguing them into compliance with his measures.

He has dissolved Representative Houses repeatedly, for opposing with manly firmness his invasions on the rights of the people.

He has refused for a long time, after such dissolutions, to cause others to be elected; whereby the Legislative Powers, incapable of Annihilation, have returned to the People at large for their exercise; the State remaining in the mean time exposed to all the dangers of invasion from without, and convulsions within.

He has endeavoured to prevent the population of these States; for that purpose obstructing the Laws for Naturalization of Foreigners; refusing to pass others to encourage their migration hither, and raising the conditions of new Appropriations of Lands.

He has obstructed the Administration of Justice, by refusing his Assent to Laws for establishing Judiciary Powers.

He has made Judges dependent on his Will alone, for the tenure of their offices, and the amount and payment of their salaries.

He has erected a multitude of New Offices, and sent hither swarms of Officers to harrass our People, and eat out their substance.

He has kept among us, in times of peace, Standing Armies without the Consent of our legislature.

He has affected to render the Military independent of and superior to the Civil Power.

He has combined with others to subject us to a jurisdiction foreign to our constitution, and unacknowledged by our laws; giving his Assent to their Acts of pretended Legislation:

For quartering large bodies of armed troops among us:

For protecting them, by a mock Trial, from Punishment for any Murders which they should commit on the Inhabitants of these States:

For cutting off our Trade with all parts of the world:

For imposing Taxes on us without our Consent:

For depriving us in many cases, of the benefits of Trial by Jury:

For transporting us beyond Seas to be tried for pretended offences:

For abolishing the free System of English Laws in a neighbouring Province, establishing therein an Arbitrary government, and enlarging its Boundaries so as to render it at once an example and fit instrument for introducing the same absolute rule into these Colonies:

For taking away our Charters, abolishing our most valuable Laws, and altering fundamentally the Forms of our Governments:

For suspending our own Legislatures, and declaring themselves invested with Power to legislate for us in all cases whatsoever.

He has abdicated Government here, by declaring us out of his Protection and waging War against us.

He has plundered our seas, ravaged our Coasts, burnt our towns, and destroyed the Lives of our people.

He is at this time transporting large Armies of foreign Mercenaries to compleat the works of death, desolation and tyranny, already begun with circumstances of Cruelty & perfidy scarcely paralleled in the most barbarous ages, and totally unworthy the Head of a civilized nation.

He has constrained our fellow Citizens taken Captive on the high Seas to bear Arms against their Country, to become the executioners of their friends and Brethren, or to fall themselves by their Hands.

He has excited domestic insurrections amongst us, and has endeavoured to bring on the inhabitants of our frontiers, the merciless Indian Savages, whose known rule of warfare, is an undistinguished destruction of all ages, sexes and conditions.

In every stage of these Oppresions We have Petitioned for Redress in the most humble terms: Our repeated Petitions have been answered only by repeated injury. A Prince, whose character is thus marked by every act which may define a Tyrant, is unfit to be the ruler of a free People.

Nor have We been wanting in attention to our British brethren. We have warned them from time to time of attempts by their legislature to extend an unwarrantable jurisdiction over us. We have reminded them of the circumstances of our emigration and settlement here. We have appealed to their native justice and magnanimity, and we have conjured them by the ties of our common kindred to disavow these usurpations, which would inevitably interrupt our connections and correspondence. They too have been deaf to the voice of justice and consanguinity. We must, therefore, acquiesce in the necessity, which denounces our Separation, and hold them, as we hold the rest of mankind, Enemies in War, in Peace Friends.

We, therefore, the Representatives of the United States of America, in General Congress, Assembled, appealing to the Supreme Judge of the world for the rectitude of our intentions, do, in the Name, and by Authority of the good People of these Colonies, solemnly publish and declare, That these United Colonies are, and of Right ought to be Free and Independent States; that they are Absolved from all Allegiance to the British Crown, and that all political connection between them and the State of Great Britain, is and ought to be totally dissolved; and that as Free and Independent States, they have full Power to levy War, conclude Peace, contract Alliances, establish Commerce, and to do all other Acts and Things which Independent States may of right do. And for the support of this Declaration, with a firm reliance on the Protection of Divine Providence, we mutually pledge to each other our Lives, our Fortunes and our sacred Honor.

John Hancock

New Hampshire

Josiah Bartlett,   Matthew Thornton.
Wm. Whipple,

Massachusetts Bay

Saml. Adams,   Robt. Treat Paine,
John Adams,   Elbridge Gerry.

Rhode Island

Step. Hopkins,   William Ellery

Connecticut

Roger Sherman,   Wm. Williams,
Sam'el Huntington,   Oliver Wolcott.

New York

Wm. Floyd,   Francis Lewis,
Phil. Livingston,   Lewis Morris.

270

New Jersey

Richd. Stockton,
Jno. Witherspoon,
Fras. Hopkinson,

John Hart,
Abra. Clark.

Pennsylvania

Robt. Morris,
Benjamin Rush,
Benja. Franklin,
John Morton,
Geo. Clymer,

Jas. Smith,
Geo. Taylor,
James Wilson,
Geo. Ross.

Delaware

Caesar Rodney,
Geo. Read,

Tho. M'Kean.

Maryland

Samuel Chase,
Wm. Paca,
Thos. Stone,

Charles Carroll of
Carrollton.

Virginia

George Wythe,
Richard Henry Lee,
Th. Jefferson,
Benja. Harrison,

Thos. Nelson, Jr.,
Francis Lightfoot Lee,
Carter Braxton.

North Carolina

Wm. Hooper,
Joseph Hewes,

John Penn.

South Carolina

Edward Rutledge,
Thos. Heyward, Junr.,

Thomas Lynch, Junr.,
Arthur Middleton.

Georgia

Button Gwinnett,
Lyman Hall,

Geo. Walton.

Appendix C

Virginia Bill of Rights

ARTICLE I
BILL OF RIGHTS

A declaration of rights made by the representatives of the good people of Virginia, assembled in full and free convention; which rights do pertain to them and their posterity, as the basis and foundation of government.

1. That all men are by nature equally free and independent, and have certain inherent rights, of which, when they enter into a state of society, they cannot, by any compact, deprive or divest their posterity; namely the enjoyment of life and liberty, with the means of acquiring and possessing property, and pursuing and obtaining happiness and safety.

2. That all power is vested in, and consequently derived from, the people; that magistrates are their trustees and servants, and at all times amenable to them.

3. That government is, or ought to be, instituted for the common benefit, protection, and security of the people, nation, or community; of all the various modes and forms of government, that is best which is capable of producing the greatest degree of happiness and safety, and is most effectually secured against the danger of maladministration; and that when any government shall be found inadequate or contrary to these purposes, a majority of the community hath an indubitable, unalienable, and indefeasible right to reform, alter, or abolish it, in such manner as shall be judged most conducive to the public weal.

4. That no man, or set of men, are entitled to exclusive or separate emoluments or privileges from the community, but in consideration of public services; which, not being descendible, neither ought the offices of magistrate, legislator, or judge to be hereditary.

5. That the legislative and executive powers of the state should be separate and distinct from the judiciary; and that the members of the two first may be restrained from oppression, by feeling and participating the burthens of the people, they should, at fixed periods, be reduced to a private station, return into that body from which they were originally taken, and the vacancies be supplied by frequent, certain, and regular election, in which all or any part of the former members to be again eligible or ineligible, as the law shall direct.

6. That elections of members to serve as representatives of the people in assembly ought to be free; and that all men having sufficient evidence of permanent common interest with, and attachment to the community, have the right of suffrage, and cannot be taxed or deprived of their property for publick uses, without their own consent, or that of their representatives so elected, nor bound by any law to which they have not, in like manner, assented for the public good.

7. That all power of suspending laws or the execution of laws by any authority, without consent of the representatives of the people, is injurious to their rights, and ought not to be exercised.

8. That in all capital or criminal prosecutions a man hath a right to demand the cause and nature of his accusation, to be confronted with the accusers and witnesses, to call for evidence in his favor, and to a speedy trial by an impartial jury, of his vicinage, without whose unanimous consent he cannot be found guilty; nor can he be compelled to give evidence against himself; that no man be deprived of his liberty, except by the law of the land or the judgment of his peers.

9. That excessive bail ought not to be required, nor excessive fines imposed, nor cruel and unusual punishments inflicted.

10. That general warrants, whereby an officer or messenger may be commanded to search suspected places without evidence of a fact committed, or to seize any person or persons not named, or whose offence is not particularly described and supported by evidence, are grievous and oppressive, and ought not be granted.

11. That in controversies respecting property, and in suits between man and man, the ancient trial by jury is preferable to any other, and ought to be held sacred.

12. That the freedom of the press is one of the great bulwarks of liberty, and can never by restrained but by despotic governments.

13. That a well-regulated militia, composed of the body of the people trained to arms, is the proper, natural, and safe defence of a free State; that standing armies in time of peace should be avoided as dangerous to liberty; and that in all cases the military should be under strict subordination to and governed by the civil power.

14. That the people have a right to uniform government; and,

therefore, that no government separate from or independent of the government of Virginia ought to be erected or established within the limits thereof.

15. That no free government, or the blessings of liberty, can be preserved to any people but by a firm adherence to justice, moderation, temperance, frugality and virtue, and by a frequent recurrence to fundamental principles.

16. That religion, or the duty which we owe to our Creator, and the manner of discharging it, can be directed only by reason and conviction, not by force or violence; and, therefore, all men are equally entitled to the free exercise of religion, according to the dictates of conscience; and that it is the mutual duty of all to practise Christian forbearance, love, and charity towards each other.

Appendix D

Articles of Confederation

TO ALL TO WHOM THESE PRESENTS SHALL COME, WE THE
UNDERSIGNED
DELEGATES OF THE STATES AFFIXED TO OUR NAMES SEND
GREETING.

Whereas the Delegates of the United States of America in Congress
assembled did on the fifteenth day of November in the Year of our Lord
One Thousand Seven Hundred and Seventyseven, and in the Second
Year of the Independence of America agree to certain articles of Confederation and perpetual Union between the States of NewHampshire,
Massachusetts-bay, Rhodeisland and Providence Plantations, Connecticut, New York, New Jersey, Pennsylvania, Delaware, Maryland,
Virginia, North-Carolina, South-Carolina and Georgia in the Words following, viz.

"Articles of Confederation and perpetual Union between the
States of Newhampshire, Massachusetts-bay, Rhodeisland
and Providence Plantations, Connecticut, New-York,
New-Jersey, Pennsylvania, Delaware, Maryland, Virginia,
North-Carolina, South-Carolina and Georgia.

ARTICLE I. The stile of this confederacy shall be "The United
States of America."
ARTICLE II. Each State retains its sovereignty, freedom and
independence, and every power, jurisdiction and right, which is not
by this confederation expressly delegated to the United States, in Congress assembled.
ARTICLE III. The said States hereby severally enter into a firm

league of friendship with each other, for their common defence, the security of their liberties, and their mutual and general welfare, binding themselves to assist each other, against all force offered to, or attacks made upon them, or any of them, on account of religion, sovereignty, trade, or any other pretence whatever.

ARTICLE IV. The better to secure and perpetuate mutual friendship and intercourse among the people of the different States in this Union, the free inhabitants of each of these States, paupers, vagabonds and fugitives from justice excepted, shall be entitled to all privileges and immunities of free citizens in the several States; and the people of each State shall have free ingress and regress to and from any other State, and shall enjoy therein all the privileges of trade and commerce, subject to the same duties, impositions and restrictions as the inhabitants thereof respectively, provided that such restrictions shall not extend so far as to prevent the removal of property imported into any State, to any other State of which the owner is an inhabitant; provided also that no imposition, duties or restriction shall be laid by any State, on the property of the United States, or either of them.

If any person guilty of, or charged with treason, felony, or other high misdemeanor in any State, shall flee from justice, and be found in any of the United States, he shall upon demand of the Governor or Executive power, of the State from which he fled, be delivered up and removed to the State having jurisdiction of his offence.

Full faith and credit shall be given in each of these States to the records, acts and judicial proceedings of the courts and magistrates of every other State.

ARTICLE V. For the more convenient management of the general interests of the United States, delegates shall be annually appointed in such manner as the legislature of each State shall direct, to meet in Congress on the first Monday in November, in every year, with a power reserved to each State, to recall its delegates, or any of them, at any time within the year, and to send others in their stead, for the remainder of the year.

No State shall be represented in Congress by less than two, nor by more than seven members; and no person shall be capable of being a delegate for more than three years in any term of six years; nor shall any person, being a delegate, be capable of holding any office under the United States, for which he, or another for his benefit receives any salary, fees or emolument of any kind.

Each State shall maintain its own delegates in a meeting of the States, and while they act as members of the committee of the States.

In determining questions in the United States, in Congress assembled, each State shall have one vote.

278

Freedom of speech and debate in Congress shall not be impeached or questioned in any court, or place out of Congress, and the members of Congress shall be protected in their persons from arrests and imprisonments, during the time of their going to and from, and attendance on Congress, except for treason, felony, or breach of the peace.

ARTICLE VI. No State without the consent of the United States in Congress assembled, shall send any embassy to, or receive any embassy from, or enter into any conference, agreement, alliance or treaty with any king, prince or state; nor shall any person holding any office of profit or trust under the United States, or any of them, accept of any present, emolument, office or title of any kind whatever from any king, prince or foreign state; nor shall the United States in Congress assembled, or any of them, grant any title of nobility.

No two or more States shall enter into any treaty, confederation or alliance whatever between them, without the consent of the United States in Congress assembled, specifying accurately the purposes for which the same is to be entered into, and how long it shall continue.

No State shall lay any imposts or duties, which may interfere with any stipulations in treaties, entered into by the United States in Congress assembled, with any king, prince or state, in pursuance of any treaties already proposed by Congress, to the courts of France and Spain.

No vessels of war shall be kept up in time of peace by any State, except such number only, as shall be deemed necessary by the United States in Congress assembled, for the defence of such State, or its trade; nor shall any body of forces be kept up by any State, in time of peace, except such number only, as in the judgment of the United States, in Congress assembled, shall be deemed requisite to garrison the forts necessary for the defence of such State; but every State shall always keep up a well regulated and disciplined militia, sufficiently armed and accoutred, and shall provide and constantly have ready for use, in public stores, a due number of field pieces and tents, and a proper quantity of arms, ammunition and camp equipage.

No State shall engage in any war without the consent of the United States in Congress assembled, unless such State be actually invaded by enemies, or shall have received certain advice of a resolution being formed by some nation of Indians to invade such State, and the danger is so imminent as not to admit of a delay, till the United States in Congress assembled can be consulted; nor shall any State grant commissions to any ships or vessels of war, nor letters of marque or reprisal, except it be after a declaration of war by the United States in Congress assembled, and then only against the kingdom or state and the subjects thereof, against which war has been so declared, and under such regulations as shall be established by the United States in Congress assembled, unless such State be infested by pirates, in which case vessels of war may be fitted out for that occasion, and kept so long as the danger shall continue, or until the United States in Congress assembled shall determine otherwise.

ARTICLE VII. When land-forces are raised by any State for the common defence, all officers of or under the rank of colonel, shall be appointed by the Legislature of each State respectively by whom such forces shall be raised, or in such manner as such State shall direct, and all vacancies shall be filled up by the State which first made the appointment.

ARTICLE VIII. All charges of war, and all other expenses that shall be incurred for the common defence or general welfare, and allowed by the United States in Congress assembled, shall be defrayed out of a common treasury, which shall be supplied by the several States, in proportion to the value of all land within each State, granted to or surveyed for any person, as such land and the buildings and improvements thereon shall be estimated according to such mode as the United States in Congress assembled, shall from time to time direct and appoint.

The taxes for paying that proportion shall be laid and levied by the authority and direction of the Legislatures of the several States within the time agreed upon by the United States in Congress assembled.

ARTICLE IX. The United States in Congress assembled, shall have the sole and exclusive right and power of determining on peace and war, except in the cases mentioned in the sixth article - of sending and receiving ambassadors - entering into treaties and alliances, provided that no treaty of commerce shall be made whereby the legislative power of the respective States shall be restrained from imposing such imposts and duties on foreigners, as their own people are subjected to, or from prohibiting the exportation or importation of any species of goods or commodities whatsoever - of establishing rules for deciding in all cases, what captures on land or water shall be legal, and in what manner prizes taken by land or naval forces in the service of the United States shall be divided or appropriated - of granting letters of marque and reprisal in times of peace - appointing courts for the trial of piracies and felonies committed on the high seas and establishing courts for receiving and determining finally appeals in all cases of captures, provided that no member of Congress shall be appointed a judge of any of the said courts.

The United States in Congress assembled shall also be the last resort on appeal in all disputes and differences now subsisting or that hereafter may arise between two or more States concerning boundary, jurisdiction or any other cause whatever; which authority shall always be exercised in the manner following. Whenever the legislative or executive authority or lawful agent of any State in controversy with another shall present a petition to Congress, stating the matter in question and praying for a hearing, notice thereof shall be given by order of Congress to the legislative or executive authority of the other State in controversy, and a day assigned for the appearance of the parties by their lawful agents, who shall then be directed to appoint by joint consent, commissioners or judges to constitute a court for hearing and determining the matter in question: but if they cannot agree, Congress shall name three persons out of each of the United States, and from the list of such persons each party shall alternately strike out one, the petitioners beginning, until the number shall be reduced to thirteen; and from that number not less than seven, nor more than nine names as Congress shall direct, shall in the presence of Congress be drawn out by lot, and the persons whose names shall be so drawn or any five of them, shall be commissioners or judges, to hear and finally determine the controversy, so always as a major part of the judges who shall hear the cause shall agree in the determination: and if either party shall neglect to attend at the day appointed, without showing reasons, which Congress shall judge sufficient, or being present shall refuse to strike, the Congress shall proceed to nominate three persons out of each State, and the Secretary of Congress shall strike in behalf of such party absent or refusing; and the judgment and sentence of the court to be appointed, in the manner before prescribed, shall be final and conclusive; and if any of the parties shall refuse to submit to the authority of such court, or to appear or defend their claim or cause, the court shall nevertheless proceed to pronounce sentence, or judgment, which shall in like manner be final and decisive, the judgment or sentence and other proceedings being in either case transmitted to Congress, and lodged among the acts of Congress for the security of the parties concerned: provided that every commissioner, before he sits in judgment, shall take an oath to be administered by one of the judges of the supreme or superior court of the State where the cause shall be tried, "well and truly to hear and determine the matter in question, according to the best of his judgment, without favour, affection or hope of reward:" provided also that no State shall be deprived of territory for the benefit of the United States.

All controversies concerning the private right of soil claimed under different grants of two or more States, whose jurisdiction as they may respect such lands, and the States which passed such grants are adjusted, the said grants or either of them being at the same time claimed to have originated antecedent to such settlement of jurisdiction, shall on the petition of either party to the Congress of the United States, be finally determined as near as may be in the same manner as is before prescribed for deciding disputes respecting territorial jurisdiction between different States.

The United States in Congress assembled shall also have the sole and exclusive right and power of regulating the alloy and value of coin struck by their own authority, or by that of the respective States, - fixing the standard of weights and measures throughout the United States, - regulating the trade and managing all affairs with the Indians, not members of any of the States, provided that the legislative right of any State within its own limits be not infringed or violated - establishing and regulating post-offices from one State to another, throughout all the United States, and exacting such postage on the papers passing thro' the same as may be requisite to defray the expenses of the said office - appointing all officers of the land forces, in the service of the United States, excepting regimental officers - appointing all the officers of the naval forces, and commissioning all officers whatever in the service of the United States - making rules for the government and regulation of the said land and naval forces, and directing their operations.

The United States in Congress assembled shall have authority to appoint a committee, to sit in the recess of Congress, to be denominated "a Committee of the States," and to consist of one delegate from each State; and to appoint such other committees and civil officers as may be necessary for managing the general affairs of the United States under their direction - to appoint one of their number to preside, provided that no person be allowed to serve in the office of president more than one year in any term of three years; to ascertain the necessary sums of money to be raised for the service of the United States, and to appropriate and apply the same for defraying the public expenses - to borrow money, to emit bills on the credit of the United States, transmitting every half year to the respective States an account of the sums of money so borrowed or emitted, - to build and equip a navy - to agree upon the number of land forces, and to make requisitions from each State for its quota, in proportion to the number of white inhabitants in such State; which requisition shall be binding, and thereupon the Legislature of each State shall appoint the regimental officers, raise the men and cloath, arm and equip them in a soldier like manner, at the expense of the United States; and the officers and men so cloathed, armed and equipped shall march to the place appointed, and within the time agreed on by the United States in Congress assembled: but if the United States in Congress assembled shall, on consideration of circumstances judge proper that any State should not raise men, or should raise a smaller number of men than the quota thereof, such extra number shall be raised, officered, cloathed, armed and equipped in the same manner as the quota of such State, unless the legislature of such State shall judge that such extra number cannot be safely spared out of the same, in which case they shall raise, officer, cloath, arm and equip as many of such extra number as they judge can be safely spared. And the officers and men so cloathed, armed and equipped, shall march to the place appointed, and within the time agreed on by the United States in Congress assembled.

The United States in Congress assembled shall never engage in a war, nor grant letters of marque and reprisal in time of peace, nor enter into any treaties or alliances, nor coin money, nor regulate the value thereof, nor ascertain the sums and expenses necessary for the defence and welfare of the United States, or any of them, nor emit bills, nor borrow money on the credit of the United States, nor appropriate money, nor agree upon the number of vessels of war, to be built or purchased, or the number of land or sea forces to be raised, nor appoint a commander in chief of the army or navy, unless nine States assent to the same: nor shall a question on any other point, except for adjourning from day to day be determined, unless by the votes of a majority of the United States in Congress assembled.

The Congress of the United States shall have power to adjourn to any time within the year, and to any place within the United States, so that no period of adjournment be for a longer duration than the space of six months, and shall publish the journal of their proceedings monthly, except such parts thereof relating to treaties, alliances, or military operations, as in their judgment require secresy; . . . and the delegates of a State, or any of them, at his or their request shall be furnished with a transcript of the said journal, except such parts as are above excepted, to lay before the Legislatures of the several States.

ARTICLE X. The committee of the States, or any nine of them, shall be authorized to execute, in the recess of Congress, such of the powers of Congress as the United States in Congress assembled, by the consent of nine States, shall from time to time think expedient to vest them with; provided that no power be delegated to the said committee, for the exercise of which, by the articles of confederation, the voice of nine States in the Congress of the United States assembled is requisite.

ARTICLE XI. Canada acceding to this confederation, and joining in the measures of the United States, shall be admitted into, and entitled to all the advantages of this Union: but no other colony shall be admitted into the same, unless such admission be agreed to by nine States.

ARTICLE XII. All bills of credit emitted, monies borrowed and debts contracted by, or under the authority of Congress, before the assembling of the United States, in pursuance of the present confederation, shall be deemed and considered as a charge against the United States, for payment and satisfaction whereof the said United States, and the public faith are hereby solemnly pledged.

ARTICLE XIII. Every State shall abide by the determinations of the United States in Congress assembled, on all questions which by this confederation are submitted to them. And the articles of this confederation shall be inviolably observed by every State, and the Union shall be perpetual; nor shall any alteration at any time hereafter be made in any of them; unless such alteration be agreed to in a Congress of the United States, and be afterwards confirmed by the Legislatures of every State.

And whereas it has pleased the Great Governor of the world to incline the hearts of the Legislatures we respectively represent in Congress, to approve of, and to authorize us to ratify the said articles of confederation and perpetual union. Know ye that we the undersigned delegates, by virtue of the power and authority to us given for that purpose, do by these presents, in the name and in behalf of our respective constituents, fully and entirely ratify and confirm each and every of the said articles of confederation and perpetual union, and all and singular the matters and things therein contained: and we do further solemnly plight and engage the faith of our respective constituents, that they shall abide by the determinations of the United States in Congress assembled, on all questions, which by the said confederation are submitted to them. And that the articles thereof shall be inviolably observed by the States we re(s)pectively represent, and that the Union shall be perpetual.

In witness whereof we have hereunto set our hands in Congress. Done at Philadelphia in the State of Pennsylvania the ninth day of July in the year of our Lord one thousand seven hundred and seventy-eight, and in the third year of the independence of America.

Appendix E

The Federalist, No. X

TO THE PEOPLE OF THE STATE OF NEW YORK:

Among the numerous advantages promised by a well-constructed Union, none deserves to be more accurately developed than its tendency to break and control the violence of faction. The friend of popular governments never finds himself so much alarmed for their character and fate, as when he contemplates their propensity to this dangerous vice. He will not fail, therefore, to set a due value on any plan which, without violating the principles to which he is attached, provides a proper cure for it. The instability, injustice, and confusion introduced into the public councils, have, in truth, been the mortal diseases under which popular governments have everywhere perished; as they continue to be the favorite and fruitful topics from which the adversaries to liberty derive their most specious declamations. The valuable improvements made by the American constitutions on the popular models, both ancient and modern, cannot certainly be too much admired; but it would be an unwarrantable partiality, to contend that they have as effectually obviated the danger on this side, as was wished and expected. Complaints are everywhere heard from our most considerate and virtuous citizens, equally the friends of public and private faith, and of public and personal liberty, that our governments are too unstable, that the public good is disregarded in the conflicts of rival parties, and that measures are too often decided, not according to the rules of justice and the rights of the minor party, but by the superior force of an interested and overbearing majority. However anxiously we may wish that these complaints had no foundation, the evidence, of known facts will not permit us to deny that they are in some degree true. It will be found, indeed, on a candid review of our situation, that some of the distresses under which we labor have been erroneously charged on the operation of our governments; but it will be found, at the same time, that other causes will not alone account for many of our heaviest misfortunes; and, particularly, for that prevailing and increasing distrust of public engagements, and alarm for private rights, which are echoed from one end of the continent to the other. These must be chiefly, if not wholly, effects of the unsteadiness and injustice with which a factious spirit has tainted our public administrations.

By a faction, I understand a number of citizens, whether amounting to a majority or a minority of the whole, who are united and actuated by some common impulse of passion, or of interest, adverse to the rights of other citizens, or to the permanent and aggregate interests of the community.

There are two methods of curing the mischiefs of faction: the one, by removing its causes; the other, by controlling its effects.

There are again two methods of removing the causes of faction: the one, by destroying the liberty which is essential to its existence; the other, by giving to every citizen the same opinions, the same passions, and the same interests.

It could never be more truly said than of the first remedy, that it was worse than the disease. Liberty is to faction what air is to fire, an element without which it instantly expires. But it could not be less folly to abolish liberty, which is essential to political life, because it nourishes faction, than it would be to wish the annihilation of air, which is essential to animal life, because it imparts to fire its destructive agency.

The second expedient is as impracticable as the first would be unwise. As long as the reason of man continues fallible, and he is at liberty to exercise it, different opinions will be formed. As long as the connection subsists between his reason and his self-love, his opinions and his passions will have a reciprocal influence on each other; and the former will be objects to which the latter will attach themselves. The diversity in the faculties of men, from which the rights of property originate, is not less an insuperable obstacle to a uniformity of interests. The protection of these faculties is the first object of government. From the protection of different and unequal faculties of acquiring property, the possession of different degrees and kinds of property immediately results; and from the influence of these on the sentiments and views of the respective proprietors, ensues a division of the society into different interests and parties.

The latent causes of faction are thus sown in the nature of man; and we see them everywhere brought into different degrees of activity, according to the different circumstances of civil society. A zeal for different opinions concerning religion, concerning government, and many other points, as well of speculation as of practice; an attachment to different leaders ambitiously contending for pre-eminence and power; or to persons of other descriptions whose fortunes have been interesting to the human passions, have, in turn, divided mankind into parties, inflamed them with mutual animosity, and rendered them much more disposed to vex and oppress each other than to co-operate for their common good. So strong is this propensity of mankind to fall into mutual animosities, that where no substantial occasion presents itself, the most frivolous and fanciful distinctions have been sufficient to kindle their unfriendly passions and excite their most violent conflicts. But the most common and durable source of factions has been the various and unequal distribution of property. Those who hold and those who are without property have ever formed distinct interests in society. Those who are creditors, and those who are debtors, fall under a like discrimination. A landed interest, a manufacturing interest, a mercantile interest, a moneyed interest, with many lesser interests, grow up of necessity in civilized nations, and divide them into different classes, actuated by different sentiments and views. The regulation of these various and interfering interests forms the principal task of modern legislation, and involves the spirit of party and faction in the necessary and ordinary operations of the government.

No man is allowed to be a judge in his own cause, because his interest would certainly bias his judgment, and, not improbably, corrupt his integrity. With equal, nay with greater reason, a body of men are unfit to be both judges and parties at the same time; yet what are many of the most important acts of legislation, but so many judicial determinations, not indeed concerning the rights of single persons, but concerning the rights of large bodies of citizens? And what are the different classes of legislators but advocates and parties ot the causes which they determine? Is a law proposed concerning private debts? It is a question to which the creditors are parties on one side and the debtors on the other. Justice ought to hold the balance between them. Yet the parties are, and must be, themselves the judges; and the most numerous party, or, in other words, the most powerful faction must be expected to prevail. Shall domestic manufactures be encouraged, and in what degree, by restrictions on foreign manufactures? are questions which would be differently decided by the landed and the manufacturing classes, and probably by neither with a sole regard to justice and the public good. The apportionment of taxes on the various descriptions of property is an act which seems to require the most exact impartiality; yet there is, perhaps, no legislative act in which greater opportunity and temptation

287

are given to a predominant party to trample on the rules of justice. Every shilling with which they overburden the inferior number, is a shilling saved to their own pockets.

It is in vain to say that enlightened statesmen will be able to adjust these clashing interests, and render them all subservient to the public good. Enlightened statesmen will not always be at the helm. Nor, in many cases, can such an adjustment be made at all without taking into view indirect and remote considerations, which will rarely prevail over the immediate interest which one party may find in disregarding the rights of another or the good of the whole.

The inference to which we are brought is, that the causes of faction cannot be removed, and that relief is only to be sought in the means of controlling its effects.

If a faction consists of less than a majority, relief is supplied by the republican principle, which enables the majority to defeat its sinister views by regular vote. It may clog the administration, it may convulse the society; but it will be unable to execute and mask its violence under the forms of the Constitution. When a majority is included in a faction, the form of popular government, on the other hand, enables it to sacrifice to its ruling passion or interest both the public good and the rights of other citizens. To secure the public good and private rights against the danger of such a faction, and at the same time to preserve the spirit and the form of popular government, is then the great object to which our inquiries are directed. Let me add that it is the great desideratum by which this form of government can be rescued from the opprobrium under which it has so long labored, and be recommended to the esteem and adoption of mankind.

By what means is this object attainable? Evidently by one of two only. Either the existence of the same passion or interest in a majority at the same time must be prevented, or the majority, having such coexistent passion or interest, must be rendered, by their number and local situation, unable to concert and carry into effect schemes of oppression. If the impulse and the opportunity be suffered to coincide, we well know that neither moral nor religious motives can be relied on as an adequate control. They are not found to be such on the injustice and violence of individuals, and lose their efficacy in proportion to the number combined together, that is, in proportion as their efficacy becomes needful.

From this view of the subject it may be concluded that a pure democracy, by which I mean a society consisting of a small number of citizens, who assemble and administer the government in person, can admit of no cure for the mischiefs of faction. A common passion or interest will, in almost every case, be felt by a majority of the whole;

a communication and concert result from the form of government itself; and there is nothing to check the inducements to sacrifice the weaker party or an obnoxious individual. Hence it is that such democracies have ever been spectacles of turbulence and contention; have ever been found incompatible with personal security or the rights of property; and have in general been as short in their lives as they have been violent in their deaths. Theoretic politicians, who have patronized this species of government, have erroneously supposed that by reducing mankind to a perfect equality in their political rights, they would, at the same time, be perfectly equalized and assimilated in their possessions, their opinions, and their passions.

A republic, by which I mean a government in which the scheme of representation takes place, opens a different prospect, and promises the cure for which we are seeking. Let us examine the points in which it varies from pure democracy, and we shall comprehend both the nature of the cure and the efficacy which it must derive from the Union.

The two great points of difference between a democracy and a republic are: first, the delegation of the government, in the latter, to a small number of citizens elected by the rest; secondly, the greater number of citizens, and greater sphere of country, over which the latter may be extended.

The effect of the first difference is, on the one hand, to refine and enlarge the public views, by passing them through the medium of a chosen body of citizens, whose wisdom may best discern the true interest of their country, and whose patriotism and love of justice will be least likely to sacrifice it to temporary or partial considerations. Under such a regulation, it may well happen that the public voice, pronounced by the representatives of the people, will be more consonant to the public good than if pronounced by the people themselves, convened for the purpose. On the other hand, the effect may be inverted. Men of factious tempers, of local prejudices, or of sinister designs, may, by intrigue, by corruption, or by other means, first obtain the suffrages, and then betray the interests, of the people. The question resulting is, whether small or extensive republics are more favorable to the election of proper guardians of the public weal, and it is clearly decided in favor of the latter by two obvious considerations:

In the first place, it is to be remarked that, however small the republic may be, the representatives must be raised to a certain number, in order to guard against the cabals of a few; and that, however large it may be, they must be limited to a certain number, in order to guard against the confusion of a multitude. Hence, the number of representatives in the two cases not being in proportion to that of the two constituents, and being proportionally greater in the small republic, it follows that, if the proportion of fit characters be not less in the large than in the small republic, the former will present a greater option, and consequently a greater probability of a fit choice.

In the next place, as each representative will be chosen by a greater number of citizens in the large than in the small republic, it will be more difficult for unworthy candidates to practice with success the vicious arts by which elections are too often carried; and the suffrages of the people being more free, will be more likely to centre in men who possess the most attractive merit and the most diffusive and established characters.

It must be confessed that in this, as in most other cases, there is a mean, on both sides of which inconveniences will be found to lie. By enlarging too much the number of electors, you render the representatives too little acquainted with all their local circumstances and lesser interests; as by reducing it too much, you render him unduly attached to these, and too little fit to comprehend and pursue great and national objects. The federal Constitution forms a happy combination in this respect; the great and aggregate interests being referred to the national, the local and particular to the State legislatures.

The other point of difference is, the greater number of citizens and extent of territory which may be brought within the compass of republican than of democratic government; and it is this circumstance principally which renders factious combinations less to be dreaded in the former than in the latter. The smaller the society, the fewer probably will be the distinct parties and interests composing it; the fewer the distinct parties and interests, the more frequently will a majority be found of the same party; and the smaller the number of individuals composing a majority, and the smaller the compass within which they are placed, the more easily will they concert and execute their plans of oppression. Extend the sphere, and you take in a greater variety of parties and interests; you make it less probable that a majority of the whole will have a common motive to invade the rights of other citizens; or if such a common motive exists, it will be more difficult for all who feel it to discover their own strength, and to act in unison with each other. Besides other impediments, it may be remarked that, where there is consciousness of unjust or dishonorable purposes, communication is always checked by distrust in proportion to the number whose concurrence is necessary.

Hence, it clearly appears, that the same advantage which a republic has over a democracy, in controlling the effects of faction, is enjoyed by a large over a small republic,—is enjoyed by the Union over the States composing it. Does the advantage consist in the substitution of representatives whose enlightened views and virtuous sentiments render them superior to local prejudices and schemes of injustice? It will not be denied that the representation of the Union will be most likely to possess these requisite endowments. Does it consist in the greater security afforded by a greater variety of parties, against the event of any one party being able to outnumber and oppress the rest? In an equal degree does the increased variety of parties comprised within the Union, increase this security? Does it, in fine, consist in the greater obstacles opposed to the concert and accomplishment of the secret wishes of an unjust and interested majority? Here, again, the extent of the Union gives it the most palpable advantage.

The influence of factious leaders may kindle a flame within their particular States, but will be unable to spread a general conflagration through the other States. A religious sect may degenerate into a political faction in a part of the Confedracy; but the variety of sects dispersed over the entire face of it must secure the national councils against any danger from that source. A rage for paper money, for an abolition of debts, for an equal division of property, or for any other improper or wicked project, will be less apt to pervade the whole body of the Union than a particular member of it; in the same proportion as such a malady is more likely to taint a particular county or district, than an entire State.

In the extent and proper structure of the Union, therefore, we behold a republican remedy for the diseases most incident to republican government. And according to the degree of pleasure and pride we feel in being republicans, ought to be our zeal in cherishing the spirit and supporting the character of Federalists.

Appendix F

The Constitution of 1787

We the People of the United States, in order to form a more perfect Union, establish Justice, insure domestic Tranquility, provide for the common defence, promote the general Welfare, and secure the Blessings of Liberty to ourselves and our Posterity, do ordain and establish this *Constitution* for the United States of America.

ARTICLE I

SECTION 1. All legislative Powers herein granted shall be vested in a Congress of the United States, which shall consist of a Senate and House of Representatives.

SECTION 2. The House of Representatives shall be composed of Members chosen every second Year by the People of the several States, and the Electors in each State shall have the Qualifications requisite for Electors of the most numerous Branch of the State Legislature.

No person shall be a Representative who shall not have attained to the Age of twenty five Years and been seven Years a Citizen of the United States, and who shall not, when elected, be an Inhabitant of that State in which he shall be chosen.

Representatives and direct Taxes shall be apportioned among the several States which may be included within this Union, according to their respective Numbers, which shall be determined by adding to the whole Number of Free persons, including those bound to Service for a Term of Years, and excluding Indians not taxed, three fifths of all other Persons. The actual Enumeration shall be made within three Years after the first Meeting of the Congress of the United States, and within every subsequent Term of ten Years, in such Manner as they shall by Law direct. The Number of Representatives shall not exceed one for every thirty Thousand, but each State shall have at Least one Representative; and until such enumeration shall be made, the State of New Hampshire shall be entitled to chuse three, Massachusetts eight, Rhode Island and Providence Plantations one, Connecticut five, New York six, New Jersey four, Pennsylvania eight, Delaware one, Maryland six, Virginia ten, North Carolina five, South Carolina five, and Georgia three.

When vacancies happen in the Representation from any State, the Executive Authority thereof shall issue Writs of Election to fill such Vacancies.

The House of Representatives shall chuse their Speaker and other Officers; and shall have the sole Power of Impeachment.

SECTION 3. The Senate of the United States shall be composed of two Senators from each State, chosen by the Legislature thereof, for six Years; and each Senator shall have one Vote.

Immediately after they shall be assembled in Consequence of the first Election, they shall be divided as equally as may be into three Classes. The seats of the Senators of the first Class shall be vacated at the Expiration of the second year, of the second Class at the Expiration of the fourth Year, and of the third Class at the Expiration of the sixth Year, so that one-third may be chosen every second Year; and if Vacancies happen by Resignation, or otherwise, during the Recess of the Legislature of any State, the Executive thereof may make temporary Appointments until the next Meeting of the Legislature, which shall then fill such Vacancies.

No Person shall be a Senator who shall not have attained to the Age of thirty Years, and been nine Years a Citizen of the United States, and who shall not, when elected, be an Inhabitant of that State for which he shall be chosen.

The Vice President of the United States shall be President of the Senate, but shall have no Vote, unless they be equally divided.

The Senate shall chuse their other Officers, and also a President pro tempore, in the Absence of the Vice President, or when he shall exercise the Office of President of the United States.

The Senate shall have the sole Power to try all impeachments. When sitting for that Purpose, they shall be on Oath or Affirmation. When the President of the United States is tried, the Chief Justice shall preside: and no Person shall be convicted without the Concurence of two thirds of the Members present.

Judgment in Cases of Impeachment shall not extend further than to removal from Office, and disqualification to hold and enjoy any Office of honor, Trust or Profit under the United States: but the Party convicted shall nevertheless be liable and subject to Indictment, Trial, Judgment and Punishment, according to Law.

SECTION 4. The Times, Places and manner of holding Elections for Senators and Representatives, shall be prescribed in each State by the Legislature thereof; but the Congress may at any time by Law make or alter such Regulations, except as to the Places of chusing Senators.

The Congress shall assemble at least once in every Year, and such Meeting shall be on the first Monday in December, unless they shall by Law appoint a different Day.

SECTION 5. Each House shall be the Judge of the Elections, Returns and Qualifications of its own Members, and a Majority of each shall constitute a Quorum to do Business; but a smaller Number may adjourn from day to day, and may be authorized to compel the Attendance of absent Members, in such Manner, and under such Penalties as each House may provide.

Each House may determine the Rules of its Proceedings, punish its Members for disorderly Behaviour, and, with the Concurrence of two thirds, expel a Member.

Each House shall keep a Journal of its Proceedings, and from time to time publish the same, excepting such Parts as may in their judgment require Secrecy; and the Yeas and Nays of the Members of either House on any question shall, at the desire of one fifth of those Present, be entered on the Journal.

Neither House, during the Session of Congress, shall, without the Consent of the other, adjourn for more than three days, nor to any other Place than that in which the two Houses shall be sitting.

SECTION 6. The Senators and Representatives shall receive a Compensation for their Services, to be ascertained by Law, and paid out of the Treasury of the United States. They shall in all Cases, except Treason, Felony and Breach of the Peace, be privileged from Arrest during their Attendance at the Session of their respective Houses, and in going to and returning from the same; and for any Speech or Debate in either House, they shall not be questioned in any other place.

No Senator or Representative shall, during the Time for which he was elected, be appointed to any civil Office under the Authority of the United States, which shall have been created, or the Emoluments whereof shall have been encreased during such time; and no Person holding any Office under the United States, shall be a Member of either House during his Continuance in Office.

SECTION 7. All Bills for raising Revenue shall originate in the House of Representatives; but the Senate may propose or concur with Amendments as on other Bills.

Every Bill which shall have passed the House of Representatives and the Senate, shall, before it become a Law, be presented to the President of the United States; If he approve he shall sign it, but if not he shall return it, with his Objections to that House in which it shall have originated, who shall enter the Objections at large on their Journal, and proceed to reconsider it. If after such Reconsideration two thirds of that House shall agree to pass the Bill, it shall be sent, together with the Objections, to the other House, by which it shall likewise be reconsidered, and if approved by two thirds of that House, it shall become a Law. But in all such Cases the Votes of both Houses shall be determined by yeas and Nays, and the Names of the Persons voting for and against the Bill shall be entered on the Journal of each House respectively. If any Bill shall not be returned by the President within ten Days (Sundays excepted) after it shall have been presented to him, the Same shall be a Law, in like Manner as if he had signed it, unless the Congress by their Adjournment prevent its Return, in which Case it shall not be a Law.

Every Order, Resolution, or Vote to which the Concurrence of the Senate and House of Representatives may be necessary (except on a question of Adjournment) shall be presented to the President of the United States; and before the Same shall take Effect, shall be approved by him, or being disapproved by him, shall be repassed by two thirds of the Senate and House of Representatives, according to the Rules and Limitations prescribed in the Case of a Bill.

SECTION 8. The Congress shall have Power to lay and collect Taxes, Duties, Imposts and Excises, to pay the Debts and provide for the common Defence and general Welfare of the United States; but all Duties, Imposts and Excises shall be uniform throughout the United States;

To borrow Money on the credit of the United States;

To regulate Commerce with foreign Nations, and among the several States, and with the Indian Tribes;

To establish an uniform Rule of Naturalization, and uniform Laws on the subject of Bankruptcies throughout the United States;

To coin Money, regulate the Value thereof, and of foreign Coin, and fix the Standard of Weights and Measures;

To provide for the Punishment of counterfeiting the Securities and current Coin of the United States;

To establish Post Offices and post Roads;

To promote the Progress of Science and useful Arts, by securing for limited Times to Authors and Inventors the exclusive Right to their respective Writings and Discoveries;

To constitute Tribunals inferior to the supreme Court;

To define and punish Piracies and Felonies committed on the high Seas, and Offences against the Law of Nations;

To declare War, grant Letters of Marque and Reprisal, and make Rules concerning Captures on Land and Water;

To raise and support Armies, but no Appropriation of Money to that Use shall be for a longer Term than two Years;

To provide and maintain a Navy;

To make Rules for the Government and Regulation of the land and naval Forces;

To provide for calling forth the Militia to execute the Laws of the Union, suppress Insurrections and repel Invasions;

To provide for organizing, arming, and disciplining, the Militia, and for governing such Part of them as may be employed in the Service of the United States, reserving to the States respectively, the Appointment of the Officers, and the Authority of training the Militia according to the discipline prescribed by Congress;

To exercise exclusive Legislation in all Cases whatsoever, over such District (not exceeding ten Miles square) as may, by Cession of particular States, and the Acceptance of Congress, become the Seat of the Government of the United States, and to exercise like Authority over all Places purchased by the Consent of the Legislature of the State in which the Same shall be, for the Erection of Forts, Magazines, Arsenals, dock-Yards, and other needful Buildings; - And

To make all Laws which shall be necessary and proper for carrying into Execution the foregoing Powers, and all other Powers vested by this Constitution in the Government of the United States, or in any Department or Officer thereof.

SECTION 9. The Migration or Importation of such Persons as any of the States now existing shall think proper to admit, shall not be prohibited by the Congress prior to the Year one thousand eight hundred and eight, but a Tax or duty may be imposed on such Importation, not exceeding ten dollars for each Person.

The Privilege of the Writ of Habeas Corpus shall not be suspended, unless when in Cases of Rebellion or Invasion the public Safety may require it.

No Bill of Attainder or ex post facto Law shall be passed.

No Capitation, or other direct, tax shall be laid, unless in Proportion to the Census or Enumeration herein directed to be taken.

No Tax or Duty shall be laid on Articles exported from any State.

No Preference shall be given by any Regulation of Commerce or

Revenue to the Ports of one State over those of another: nor shall Vessels bound to, or from, one State, be obliged to enter, clear, or pay Duties in another.

No Money shall be drawn from the Treasury, but in Consequence of Appropriations made by Law; and a regular Statement and Account of the Receipts and Expenditures of all public Money shall be published from time to time.

No Title of Nobility shall be granted by the United States: And no Person holding any Office of Profit or Trust under them, shall, without the Consent of the Congress, accept of any present, Emolument, Office, or Title, of any kind whatever, from any King, Prince, or foreign State.

SECTION 10. No State shall enter into any Treaty, Alliance, or Confederation; grant Letters of Marque and Reprisal; coin Money; emit Bills of Credit; make any Thing but gold and silver Coin a Tender in Payment of Debts; pass any Bill of Attainder, ex post facto Law, or Law impairing the Obligation of Contracts, or grant any Title of Nobility.

No State shall, without the Consent of the Congress, lay any Imposts or Duties on Imports or Exports, except what may be absolutely necessary for executing it's inspection Laws: and the net Produce of all Duties and Imposts, laid by any State on Imports or Exports, shall be for the Use of the Treasury of the United States; and all such Laws shall be subject to the Revision and Controul of the Congress.

No State shall, without the Consent of Congress, lay any Duty of Tonnage, keep Troops, or Ships of War in time of Peace, enter into any Agreement or Compact with another State, or with a foreign Power, or engage in War, unless actually invaded, or in such imminent Danger as will not admit of delay.

ARTICLE II

SECTION 1. The executive Power shall be vested in a President of the United States of America. He shall hold his Office during the Term of four Years, and, together with the Vice President, chosen for the same Term, be elected, as follows:

Each State shall appoint, in such Manner as the Legislature thereof may direct, a Number of Electors, equal to the whole Number of Senators and Representatives to which the State may be entitled in the Congress: but no Senator or Representative, or Person holding an Office of Trust or Profit under the United States, shall be appointed an Elector.

The Electors shall meet in their respective States, and vote by Ballot for two persons, of whom one at least shall not be an Inhabitant of the same State with themselves. And they shall make a List of all the Persons voted for, and of the Number of Votes for each; which List they shall sign and certify, and transmit sealed to the Seat of the Government of the United States, directed to the President of the Senate. The President of the Senate shall, in the Presence of the Senate and House of Representatives, open all the Certificates, and the Votes shall then be counted. The Person having the greatest Number of Votes shall be the President, if such Number be a Majority of the whole Number of Electors appointed; and if there be more than one who have such Majority, and have an equal Number of Votes, then the House of Representatives shall immediately chuse, by Ballot one of them for President; and if no Person have a Majority, then from the five highest on the List, the said House shall in like manner chuse the President. But in chusing the President, the Votes shall be taken by States, the Representation from each State having one vote; A quorum for this Purpose shall consist of a Member or Members from two thirds of the States, and a Majority of all the States shall be necessary to a Choice. In every Case, after the Choice of the President, the Person having the greatest Number of Votes of the Electors shall be the Vice President. But if there should remain two or more who have equal Votes, the Senate shall chuse from them by Ballot the Vice-President.

The Congress may determine the Time of chusing the Electors, and the Day on which they shall give their Votes; which Day shall be the same throughout the United States.

No person except a natural born Citizen, or a Citizen of the United States, at the time of the Adoption of this Constitution, shall be eligible to the Office of President; neither shall any Person be eligible to that office who shall not have attained to the Age of thirty five Years, and been fourteen Years a Resident within the United States.

In Case of the Removal of the President from Office, or of his Death, Resignation or Inability to discharge the Powers and Duties of the said Office, the Same shall devolve on the Vice President, and the Congress may by Law provide for the Case of Removal, Death, Resignation or Inability, both of the President and Vice President, declaring what Officer shall then act as President, and such Officer shall act accordingly, until the Disability be removed, or a President shall be elected.

The President shall, at stated Times, receive for his Services, a Compensation, which shall neither be encreased nor diminished during the Period for which he shall have been elected, and he shall not receive within that Period any other Emolument from the United States, or any of them.

Before he enter on the Execution of his Office, he shall take the following Oath or Affirmation: -"I do solemnly swear (or affirm) that I will faithfully execute the Office of President of the United States, and will to the best of my Ability, preserve, protect and defend the Constitution of the United States."

SECTION 2. The President shall be Commander in Chief of the Army and Navy of the United States, and of the Militia of the several States, when called into the actual Service of the United States; he may require the Opinion, in writing, of the principal Officer in each of the executive Departments, upon any Subject relating to the Duties of their respective Offices, and he shall have Power to grant Reprieves and Pardons for Offences against the United States, except in Cases of Impeachment.

He shall have Power, by and with the Advice and Consent of the Senate, to make Treaties, provided two thirds of the Senators present concur; and he shall nominate, and by and with the Advice and Consent of the Senate, shall appoint Ambassadors, other public Ministers and Consuls, Judges of the supreme Court, and all other Officers of the United States, whose Appointments are not herein otherwise provided for, and which shall be established by Law: but the Congress may by Law vest the Appointment of such inferior Officers, as they think proper, in the President alone, in the Courts of Law, or in the Heads of Departments.

The President shall have Power to fill up all Vacancies that may happen during the Recess of the Senate, by granting Commissions which shall expire at the End of their next session.

SECTION 3. He shall from time to time give to the Congress Information of the State of the Union, and recommend to their Consideration such Measures as he shall judge necessary and expedient; he may, on extraordinary Occasions, convene both Houses, or either of them, and in Case of Disagreement between them, with Respect to the time of Adjournment, he may adjourn them to such Time as he shall think proper; he shall receive Ambassadors and other public Ministers; he shall take Care that the Laws be faithfully executed, and shall commission all the Officers of the United States.

SECTION 4. The President, Vice President, and all civil Officers of the United States, shall be removed from Office on Impeachment for, and Conviction of, Treason, Bribery, or other high Crimes and Misdemeanors.

ARTICLE III

SECTION 1. The Judical Power of the United States, shall be vested in one supreme Court, and in such inferior Courts as the Congress may from time to time ordain and establish. The Judges, both of the supreme and inferior Courts, shall hold their Offices during good Behaviour, and shall, at stated Times, receive for their Services, a Compensation, which shall not be diminished during their Continuance in Office.

SECTION 2. The judicial Power shall extend to all Cases, in Law and Equity, arising under this Constitution, the Laws of the United States, and Treaties made, or which shall be made, under their Authority;--to all Cases affecting Ambassadors, other public Ministers and Consuls;--to all Cases of admiralty and maritime Jurisdiction;--to Controversies to which the United States shall be a Party;--to Controversies between two or more States;--between a State and Citizens of another State;--between Citizens of different States,--between Citizens of the same State claiming Lands under Grants of different States, and between a State, or the Citizens thereof, and foreign States, Citizens or Subjects.

In all Cases affecting Ambassadors, other public Ministers and Consuls, and those in which a State shall be Party, the supreme Court shall have original Jurisdiction. In all the other Cases before mentioned, the supreme Court shall have appellate Jurisdiction, both as to Law and Fact, with such Exceptions, and under such Regulations as the Congress shall make.

The Trial of all Crimes except in Cases of Impeachment, shall be by Jury; and such Trial shall be held in the State where the said Crimes shall have been committed; but when not committed within any State, the Trial shall be at such Place or Places as the Congress may by Law have directed.

SECTION 3. Treason against the United States, shall consist only in levying War against them, or in adhering to their Enemies, giving them Aid and Comfort. No Person shall be convicted of Treason unless on the Testimony of two Witnesses to the same overt Act, or on Confession in open Court.

The Congress shall have Power to declare the Punishment of Treason, but no Attainder of Treason shall work Corruption of Blood, or Forfeiture except during the Life of the Person attained.

ARTICLE IV

SECTION 1. Full Faith and Credit shall be given in each State to the public Acts, Records, and judicial Proceedings of every other State. And the Congress may by general Laws prescribe the Manner in which such Acts, Records and Proceedings shall be proved, and the Effect thereof.

SECTION 2. The Citizens of each State shall be entitled to all Privileges and Immunities of Citizens in the several States.

A person charged in any State with Treason, Felony, or other Crime, who shall flee from Justice, and be found in another State shall on Demand of the executive Authority of the State from which he fled, be delivered up to be removed to the State having Jurisdiction of the Crime.

No person held to Service or Labour in one State, under the Laws thereof, escaping into another, shall, in Consequence of any Law or Regulation therein, be discharged from such Service or Labour, but shall be delivered up on Claim of the Party to whom such Service or Labour may be due.

SECTION 3. New States may be admitted by the Congress into this Union; but no new State shall be formed or erected within the Jurisdiction of any other State; nor any State be formed by the Junction of two or more States, or Parts of States, without the Consent of the Legislatures of the States concerned as well as of the Congress.

The Congress shall have Power to dispose of and make all needful Rules and Regulations respecting the Territory or other Property belonging to the United States; and nothing in this Constitution shall be so construed as to Prejudice any Claims of the United States, or of any particular State.

SECTION 4. The United States shall guarantee to every State in this Union a Republican Form of Government, and shall protect each of them against Invasion; and on Application of the Legislature, or of the Executive (when the Legislature cannot be convened) against domestic Violence.

ARTICLE V

The Congress, whenever two thirds of both Houses shall deem it necessary, shall propose amendments to this Constitution, or, on the Application of the Legislatures of two thirds of the several States, shall call a Convention for proposing Amendments, which, in either Case, shall be valid to all Intents and Purposes, as Part of this Constitution, when ratified by the Legislatures of three fourths of the several States, or by Conventions in three fourths thereof, as the one or the other Mode of Ratification may be proposed by the Congress; Provided that no Amendment which may be made prior to the Year One thousand eight hundred and eight shall in any Manner affect the first and fourth Clases in the Ninth Section of the first Article; and that no State, without its Consent, shall be deprived of its equal Suffrage in the Senate.

ARTICLE VI

All Debts contracted and Engagements entered into, before the Adoption of this Constitution, shall be as valid against the United States under this Constitution, as under the Confederation.

This Constitution, and the Laws of the United States which shall be made in Pursuance thereof; and all Treaties made, or which shall be made, under the Authority of the United States, shall be the supreme Law of the Land; and the Judges in every State shall be bound thereby, any Thing in the Constitution or Laws of any State to the Contrary notwithstanding.

The Senators and Representatives before mentioned, and the Members of the several State Legislatures, and all executive and judicial Officers, both of the United States and of the several States, shall be bound by Oath or Affirmation, to support this Constitution; but no religious Test shall ever be required as a Qualification to any Office or public Trust under the United States.

ARTICLE VII

The Ratification of the Conventions of nine States, shall be sufficient for the Establishment of this Constitution between the States so ratifying the Same.

Done in Convention by the Unanimous Consent of the States present the Seventeenth Day of September in the Year of our Lord one thousand seven hundred and Eighty seven and of the Independence of the United States of America the Twelfth IN WITNESS whereof We have hereunto subscribed our Names,
G⁰: Washington—Presidt.
and deputy from Virginia

Attest William Jackson Secretary

New Hampshire	John Langdon
	Nicholas Gilman
Massachusetts	Nathaniel Gorham
	Rufus King
Connecticut	Wm: Saml. Johnson
	Roger Sherman
New York . . .	Alexander Hamilton
New Jersey	Wil: Livingston
	David Brearley.
	Wm. Paterson.
	Jona: Dayton
Pennsylvania	B. Franklin
	Thomas Mifflin
	Robt. Morris
	Geo. Clymer
	Thos. Fitz Simons
	Jared Ingersoll
	James Wilson
	Gouv Morris
Delaware	Geo: Read
	Gunning Bedford jun
	John Dickinson
	Richard Bassett
	Jaco: Broom
Maryland	James McHenry
	Dan of St Thos. Jenifer
	Danl Carroll
Virginia	John Blair—
	James Madison Jr.
North Carolina	Wm: Blount
	Richd. Dobbs Spaight.
	Hu Williamson

304

South Carolina	J. Rutledge,
	Charles Pinckney,
	Charles Cotesworth Pinckney,
	Pierce Butler.
Georgia	William Few,
	Abr. Baldwin.
Attest:	William Jackson, Secretary.

Appendix G

First Ten Amendments

(ARTICLE I)

Congress shall make no law respecting an establishment of religion, or prohibiting the free exercise thereof; or abridging the freedom of speech, or of the press; or the right of the people peaceably to assemble, and to petition the Government for a redress of grievances.

(ARTICLE II)

A well regulated Militia, being necessary to the security of a free State, the right of the people to keep and bear Arms, shall not be infringed.

(ARTICLE III)

No Soldier shall, in time of peace, be quartered in any house, without the consent of the Owner, nor in time of war, but in a manner to be prescribed by law.

(ARTICLE IV)

The right of the people to be secure in their persons, houses, papers, and effects, against unreasonable searches and seizures, shall not be violated, and no Warrants shall issue, but upon probable cause,

supported by Oath or affirmation, and particularly describing the place
to be searched, and the persons or things to be seized.

(ARTICLE V)

No person shall be held to answer for a capital, or otherwise infamous crime, unless on a presentment or indictment of a Grand Jury,
except in cases arising in the land or naval forces, or in the Militia,
when in actual service in time of War or public danger; nor shall any
person be subject for the same offence to be twice put in jeopardy of
life or limb; nor shall be compelled in any Criminal Case to be a witness
against himself, nor be deprived of life, liberty, or property, without
due process of law; nor shall private property be taken for public use,
without just compensation.

(ARTICLE VI)

In all criminal prosecutions, the accused shall enjoy the right to
a speedy and public trial, by an impartial jury of the State and district
wherein the crime shall have been committed, which district shall have
been previously ascertained by law, and to be informed of the nature
and cause of the accusation; to be confronted with the witnesses against
him; to have compulsory process for obtaining witnesses in his favor,
and to have the Assistance of Counsel for his defence.

(ARTICLE VII)

In suits at common law, where the value in controversy shall exceed
twenty dollars, the right of trial by jury shall be preserved, and no fact
tried by a jury shall be otherwise re-examined in any Court of the
United States, than according to the rules of the common law.

(ARTICLE VIII)

Excessive bail shall not be required, nor excessive fines imposed,
nor cruel and unusual punishments inflicted.

(ARTICLE IX)

The enumeration in the Constitution, of certain rights, shall not be construed to deny or disparage others retained by the people.

(ARTICLE X)

The powers not delegated to the United States by the Constitution, nor prohibited by it to the States, are reserved to the States respectively, or to the people.

Appendix H

Washington's Farewell Address

Friends and Fellow-Citizens:

The period for a new election of a citizen to administer the Executive Government of the United States being not far distant, and the time actually arrived when your thoughts must be employed in designating the person who is to be clothed with that important trust, it appears to me proper, especially as it may conduce to a more distinct expression of the public voice, that I should now apprise you of the resolution I have formed to decline being considered among the number of those out of whom a choice is to be made.

I beg you at the same time to do me the justice to be assured that this resolution has not been taken without a strict regard to all the considerations appertaining to the relation which binds a dutiful citizen to his country; and that in withdrawing the tender of service, which silence in my situation might imply, I am influenced by no diminution of zeal for your future interest, no deficiency of grateful respect for your past kindness, but am supported by a full conviction that the step is compatible with both.

The acceptance of and continuance hitherto in the office to which your suffrages have twice called me have been a uniform sacrifice of inclination to the opinion of duty and to a deference for what appeared to be your desire. I constantly hoped that it would have been much earlier in my power, consistently with motives which I was not at liberty to disregard, to return to that retirement from which I had been reluctantly drawn. The strength of my inclination to do this previous to the last election had even led to the preparation of an address to declare it to you; but mature reflection on the then perplexed and critical posture of our affairs with foreign nations and the unanimous advice of persons entitled to my confidence impelled me to abandon the idea. I rejoice that the state of your concerns, external as well as internal, no longer renders the pursuit of inclination incompatible with the sentiment of duty or propriety, and am persuaded, whatever partiality may be retained for my services, that in the present circumstances of our country you will not disapprove my determination to retire.

The impressions with which I first undertook the arduous trust were explained on the proper occasion. In the discharge of this trust I will only say that I have, with good intentions, contributed toward the organization and administration of the Government the best exertions of which a very fallible judgment was capable. Not unconscious in the outset of the inferiority of my qualifications, experience in my own eyes, perhaps still more in the eyes of others, has strengthened the motives to diffidence of myself; and every day the increasing weight of years admonishes me more and more that the shade of retirement is as necessary to me as it will be welcome. Satisfied that if any circumstances have given peculiar value to my services they were temporary, I have the consolation to believe that, while choice and prudence invite me to quit the political scene, patriotism does not forbid it.

In looking forward to the moment which is intended to terminate the career of my political life my feelings do not permit me to suspend the deep acknowledgment of that debt of gratitude which I owe to my beloved country for the many honors it has conferred upon me; still more for the steadfast confidence with which it has supported me, and for the opportunities I have thence enjoyed of manifesting my inviolable attachment by services faithful and persevering, though in usefulness unequal to my zeal. If benefits have resulted to our country from these services, let it always be remembered to your praise and as an instructive example in our annals that under circumstances in which the passions, agitated in every direction, were liable to mislead; amidst appearances sometimes dubious; vicissitudes of fortune often discouraging; in situations in which not unfrequently want of success has countenanced the spirit of criticism, the constancy of your support was the essential prop of the efforts and a guaranty of the plans by which they were effected. Profoundly penetrated with this idea, I shall carry it with me to my grave as a strong incitement to unceasing vows that Heaven may continue to you the choicest tokens of its beneficence; that your union and brotherly affection may be perpetual; that the free Constitution which is the work of your hands may be sacredly maintained; that its administration in every department may be stamped with wisdom and virtue; that, in fine, the happiness of the people of these States, under the auspices of liberty, may be made complete by so careful a preservation and so prudent a use of this blessing as will acquire to them the glory of recommending it to the applause, the affection, and adoption of every nation which is yet a stranger to it.

Here, perhaps, I ought to stop. But a solicitude for your welfare which can not end but with my life, and the apprehension of danger natural to that solicitude, urge me on an occasion like the present to offer to your solemn contemplation and to recommend to your frequent review some sentiments which are the result of much reflection, of no inconsiderable observation, and which appear to me all important to the permanency of your felicity as a people. These will be offered to you with the more freedom as you can only see in them the disinterested warnings of a parting friend, who can possibly have no personal motive to bias his counsel. Nor can I forget as an encouragement to it your indulgent reception of my sentiments on a former and not dissimilar occasion.

Interwoven as is the love of liberty with every ligament of your hearts, no recommendation of mine is necessary to fortify or confirm the attachment.

The unity of government which constitutes you one people is also now dear to you. It is justly so, for it is a main pillar in the edifice of your real independence, the support of your tranquillity at home, your peace abroad, of your safety, of your prosperity, of that very liberty which you so highly prize. But as it is easy to foresee that from different causes and from different quarters much pains will be taken, many artifices employed, to weaken in your minds the conviction of this truth, as this is the point in your political fortress against which the batteries of internal and external enemies will be most constantly and actively (though often covertly and insidiously) directed, it is of infinite moment that you should properly estimate the immense value of your national union to your collective and individual happiness; that you should cherish a cordial, habitual, and immovable attachment to it; accustoming yourselves to think and speak of it as of the palladium of your political safety and prosperity; watching for its preservation with jealous anxiety; discountenancing whatever may suggest even a suspicion that it can in any event be abandoned, and indignantly frowning upon the first dawning of every attempt to alienate any portion of our country from the rest or to enfeeble the sacred ties which now link together the various parts.

For this you have every inducement of sympathy and interest. Citizens by birth or choice of a common country, that country has a right to concentrate your affections. The name of American, which belongs to you in your national capacity, must exalt the just pride of patriotism more than any appellation derived from local discriminations. With slight shades of difference, you have the same religion, manners, habits,

313

and political principles. You have in a common cause fought and triumphed together. The independence and liberty you possess are the work of joint councils and joint efforts, of common dangers, sufferings, and successes.

But these considerations, however powerfully they address themselves to your sensibility, are greatly outweighed by those which apply more immediately to your interest. Here every portion of our country finds the most commanding motives for carefully guarding and preserving the union of the whole.

The *North*, in an unrestrained intercourse with the *South*, protected by the equal laws of a common government, finds in the productions of the latter great additional resources of maritime and commercial enterprise and precious materials of manufacturing industry. The *South*, in the same intercourse, benefiting by the same agency of the *North*, sees its agriculture grow and its commerce expand. Turning partly into its own channels the seamen of the *North*, it finds its particular navigation invigorated; and while it contributes in different ways to nourish and increase the general mass of the national navigation, it looks forward to the protection of a maritime strength to which itself is unequally adapted. The *East*, in a like intercourse with the *West*, already finds, and in the progressive improvement of interior communications by land and water will more and more find, a valuable vent for the commodities which it brings from abroad or manufactures at home. The *West* derives from the *East* supplies requisite to its growth and comfort, and what is perhaps of still greater consequence, it must of necessity owe the secure enjoyment of indispensable *outlets* for its own productions to the weight, influence, and the future maritime strength of the Atlantic side of the Union, directed by an indissoluble community of interest as *one nation*. Any other tenure by which the *West* can hold this essential advantage, whether derived from its own separate strength or from an apostate and unnatural connection with any foreign power, must be intrinsically precarious.

While, then, every part of our country thus feels an immediate and particular interest in union, all the parts combined can not fail to find in the united mass of means and efforts greater strength, greater resource, proportionably greater security from external danger, a less frequent interruption of their peace by foreign nations, and what is of inestimable value, they must derive from union an exemption from those broils and wars between themselves which so frequently afflict neighboring countries not tied together by the same governments, which their own rivalships alone would be sufficient to produce, but which opposite foreign alliances, attachments, and intrigues would stimulate and imbitter. Hence, likewise, they will avoid the necessity

314

of those overgrown military establishments which, under any form of government, are inauspicious to liberty, and which are to be regarded as particularly hostile to republican liberty. In this sense it is that your union ought to be considered as a main prop of your liberty, and that the love of the one ought to endear to you the preservation of the other.

These considerations speak a persuasive language to every reflecting and vertuous mind, and exhibit the continuance of the union as a primary object of patriotic desire. Is there a doubt whether a common government can embrace so large a sphere? Let experience solve it. To listen to mere speculation in such a case were criminal. We are authorized to hope that a proper organization of the whole, with the auxiliary agency of governments for the respective subdivisions, will afford a happy issue to the experiment. It is well worth a fair and full experiment. With such powerful and obvious motives to union affecting all parts of our country, while experience shall not have demonstrated its impracticability, there will always be reason to distrust the patriotism of those who in any quarter may endeavor to weaken its bands.

In contemplating the causes which may disturb our union it occurs as matter of serious concern that any ground should have been furnished for characterizing parties by *geographical* discriminations--*Northern* and *Southern, Atlantic* and *Western*--whence designing men may endeavor to excite a belief that there is a real difference of local interests and views. One of the expedients of party to acquire influence within particular districts is to misrepresent the opinions and aims of other districts. You can not shield yourselves too much against the jealousies and heartburnings which spring from these misrepresentations; they tend to render alien to each other those who ought to be bound together by fraternal affection. The inhabitants of our Western country have lately had a useful lesson on this head. They have seen in the negotiation by the Executive and in the unanimous ratification by the Senate of the treaty with Spain, and in the universal satisfaction at that event throughout the United States, a decisive proof how unfounded were the suspicions propagated among them of a policy in the General Government and in the Atlantic States unfriendly to their interests in regard to the Mississippi. They have been witnesses to the formation of two treaties--that with Great Britain and that with Spain--which secure to them everything they could desire in respect to our foreign relations toward confirming their prosperity. Will it not be their wisdom to rely for the preservation of these advantages on the union by which they were procured? Will they not henceforth be deaf to those advisers, if such there are, who would sever them from their brethren and connect them with aliens?

To the efficacy and permanency of your union a government for the whole is indispensable. No alliances, however strict, between the parts can be an adequate substitute. They must inevitably experience the infractions and interruptions which all alliances in all times have experienced. Sensible of this momentous truth, you have improved upon your first essay by the adoption of a Constitution of Government better calculated than your former for an intimate union and for the efficacious management of your common concerns. This Government, the off-spring of our own choice, uninfluenced and unawed, adopted upon full investigation and mature deliberation, completely free in its principles, in the distribution of its powers, uniting security with energy, and containing within itself a provision for its own amendment, has a just claim to your confidence and your support. Respect for its authority, compliance with its laws, acquiescence in its measures, are duties enjoined by the fundamental maxims of true liberty. The basis of our political systems is the right of the people to make and to alter their constitutions of government. But the constitution which at any time exists till changed by an explicit and authentic act of the whole people is sacredly obligatory upon all. The very idea of the power and the right of the people to establish government presupposes the duty of every individual to obey the established government.

All obstructions to the execution of the laws, all combinations and associations, under whatever plausible character, with the real design to direct, control, counteract, or awe the regular deliberation and action of the constituted authorities, are destructive of this fundamental principle and of fatal tendency. They serve to organize faction; to give it an artificial and extraordinary force; to put in the place of the delegated will of the nation the will of a party, often a small but artful and enterprising minority of the community, and, according to the alternate triumphs of different parties, to make the public administration the mirror of the ill-concerted and incongruous projects of faction rather than the organ of consistent and wholesome plans, digested by common counsels and modified by mutual interests.

However combinations or associations of the above description may now and then answer popular ends, they are likely in the course of time and things to become potent engines by which cunning, ambitious, and unprincipled men will be enabled to subvert the power of the people, and to usurp for themselves the reins of government, destroying afterwards the very engines which have lifted them to unjust dominion.

Toward the preservation of your Government and the permanency of your present happy state, it is requisite not only that you steadily discountenance irregular opposition to its acknowledged authority, but also that you resist with care the spirit of innovation upon its principles, however specious the pretexts. One method of assault may be to effect

316

in the forms of the Constitution alterations which will impair the energy of the system, and thus to undermine what can not be directly overthrown. In all the changes to which you may be invited remember that time and habit are at least as necessary to fix the true character of governments as of other human institutions; that experience is the surest standard by which to test the real tendency of the existing constitution of a country; that facility in changes upon the credit of mere hypothesis and opinion exposes to perpetual change, from the endless variety of hypothesis and opinion; and remember especially that for the efficient management of your common interests in a country so extensive as ours a government of as much vigor as is consistent with the perfect security of liberty is indispensable. Liberty itself will find in such a government, with powers properly distributed and adjusted, its surest guardian. It is, indeed, little else than a name where the government is too feeble to withstand the enterprises of faction, to confine each member of the society within the limits prescribed by the laws, and to maintain all in the secure and tranquil enjoyment of the rights of person and property.

I have already intimated to you the danger of parties in the State, with particular reference to the founding of them on geographical discriminations. Let me now take a more comprehensive view, and warn you in the most solemn manner against the baneful effects of the spirit of party generally.

This spirit, unfortunately, is inseparable from our nature, having its root in the strongest passions of the human mind. It exists under different shapes in all governments, more or less stifled, controlled, or repressed; but in those of the popular form it is seen in its greatest rankness and is truly their worst enemy.

The alternate domination of one faction over another, sharpened by the spirit of revenge natural to party dissension, which in different ages and countries has perpetrated the most horrid enormities, is itself a frightful despotism. But this leads at length to a more formal and permanent despotism. The disorders and miseries which result gradually incline the minds of men to seek security and repose in the absolute power of an individual, and sooner or later the chief of some prevailing faction, more able or more fortunate than his competitors, turns this disposition to the purposes of his own elevation on the ruins of public liberty.

Without looking forward to an extremity of this kind (which nevertheless ought not to be entirely out of sight), the common and continual mischiefs of the spirit of party are sufficient to make it the interest and duty of a wise people to discourage and restrain it.

It serves always to distract the public councils and enfeeble the public administration. It agitates the community with ill-founded jealousies and false alarms; kindles the animosity of one part against another; foments occasionally riot and insurrection. It opens the door to foreign influence and corruption, which find a facilitated access to the government itself through the channels of party passion. Thus the policy and the will of one country are subjected to the policy and will of another.

There is an opinion that parties in free countries are useful checks upon the administration of the government, and serve to keep alive the spirit of liberty. This within certain limits is probably true; and in governments of a monarchical cast patriotism may look with indulgence, if not with favor, upon the spirit of party. But in those of the popular character, in governments purely elective, it is a spirit not to be encouraged. From their natural tendency it is certain there will always be enough of that spirit for every salutary purpose; and there being constant danger of excess, the effort ought to be by force of public opinion to mitigate and assuage it. A fire not to be quenched, it demands a uniform vigilance to prevent its bursting into a flame, lest, instead of warming, it should consume.

It is important, likewise, that the habits of thinking in a free country should inspire caution in those intrusted with its administration to confine themselves within their respective constitutional spheres, avoiding in the exercise of the powers of one department to encroach upon another. The spirit of encroachment tends to consolidate the powers of all the departments in one, and thus to create, whatever the form of government, a real despotism. A just estimate of that love of power and proneness to abuse it which predominates in the human heart is sufficient to satisfy us of the truth of this position. The necessity of reciprocal checks in the exercise of political power, by dividing and distributing it into different depositories, and constituting each the guardian of the public weal against invasions by the others, has been evinced by experiments ancient and modern, some of them in our country and under our own eyes. To preserve them must be as necessary as to institute them. If in the opinion of the people the distribution or modification of the constitutional powers be in any particular wrong, let it be corrected by an amendment in the way which the Constitution designates. But let there be no change by usurpation; for though this in one instance may be the instrument of good, it is the customary weapon by which free governments are destroyed. The precedent must always greatly overbalance in permanent evil any partial or transient benefit which the use can at any time yield.

Of all the dispositions and habits which lead to political prosperity, religion and morality are indispensable supports. In vain would that man claim the tribute of patriotism who should labor to subvert these great pillars of human happiness--these firmest props of the duties of men and citizens. The mere politician, equally with the pious man, ought to respect and to cherish them. A volume could not trace all their connections with private and public felicity. Let it simply be asked, Where is the security for property, for reputation, for life, if the sense of religious obligation *desert* the oaths which are the instruments of investigation in courts of justice? And let us with caution indulge the supposition that morality can be maintained without religion. Whatever may be conceded to the influence of refined education on minds of peculiar structure, reason and experience both forbid us to expect that national morality can prevail in exclusion of religious principle.

It is substantially true that virtue or morality is a necessary spring of popular government. The rule indeed extends with more or less force to every species of free government. Who that is a sincere friend to it can look with indifference upon attempts to shake the foundation of the fabric? Promote, then, as an object of primary importance, institutions for the general diffusion of knowledge. In proportion as the structure of a government gives force to public opinion, it is essential that public opinion should be enlightened.

As a very important source of strength and security, cherish public credit. One method of preserving it is to use it as sparingly as possible, avoiding occasions of expense by cultivating peace, but remembering also that timely disbursements to prepare for danger frequently prevent much greater disbursements to repel it; avoiding likewise the accumulation of debt, not only by shunning occasions of expense, but by vigorous exertions in time of peace to discharge the debts which unavoidable wars have occasioned, not ungenerously throwing upon posterity the burthen which we ourselves ought to bear. The execution of these maxims belongs to your representatives; but it is necessary that public opinion should cooperate. To facilitate to them the performance of their duty it is essential that you should practically bear in mind that toward the payment of debts there must be revenue; that to have revenue there must be taxes; that no taxes can be devised which are not more or less inconvenient and unpleasant; that the intrinsic embarrassment inseparable from the selection of the proper objects (which is always a choice of difficulties), ought to be a decisive motive for a candid construction of the conduct of the Government in making it, and for a spirit of acquiescence in the measures for obtaining revenue which the public exigencies may at any time dictate.

Observe good faith and justice toward all nations. Cultivate peace and harmony with all. Religion and morality enjoin this conduct. And can it be that good policy does not equally enjoin it? It will be worthy

319

of a free, enlightened, and at no distant period a great nation to give to mankind the magnanimous and too novel example of a people always guided by an exalted justice and benevolence. Who can doubt that in the course of time and things the fruits of such a plan would richly repay any temporary advantages which might be lost by a steady adherence to it? Can it be that Providence has not connected the permanent felicity of a nation with its virtue? The experiment, at least, is recommended by every sentiment which ennobles human nature. Alas! is it rendered impossible by its vices?

In the execution of such a plan nothing is more essential than that permanent, inveterate antipathies against particular nations and passionate attachments for others should be excluded, and that in place of them just and amicable feelings toward all should be cultivated. The nation which indulges toward another an habitual hatred or an habitual fondness is in some degree a slave. It is a slave to its animosity or to its affection, either of which is sufficient to lead it astray from its duty and its interest. Antipathy in one nation against another disposes each more readily to offer insult and injury, to lay hold of slight causes of umbrage, and to be haughty and intractable when accidental or trifling occasions of dispute occur.

Hence frequent collisions, obstinate, envenomed, and bloody contests. The nation prompted by ill will and resentment sometimes impels to war the government contrary to the best calculations of policy. The government sometimes participates in the national propensity, and adopts through passion what reason would reject. At other times it makes the animosity of the nation subservient to projects of hostility, instigated by pride, ambition, and other sinister and pernicious motives. The peace often, sometimes perhaps the liberty, of nations has been the victim.

So, likewise, a passionate attachment of one nation for another produces a variety of evils. Sympathy for the favorite nation, facilitating the illusion of an imaginary common interest in cases where no real common interest exists, and infusing into one the enmities of the other, betrays the former into a participation in the quarrels and wars of the latter without adequate inducement or justification. It leads also to concessions to the favorite nation of privileges denied to others, which is apt doubly to injure the nation making the concessions by unnecessarily parting with what ought to have been retained, and by exciting jealousy, ill will, and a disposition to retaliate in the parties from whom equal privileges are withheld; and it gives to ambitious, corrupted, or deluded citizens (who devote themselves to the favorite nation) facility to betray or sacrifice the interests of their own country without odium, sometimes even with popularity, gilding with the appearances of a virtuous sense of obligation, a commendable deference for public opinion, or a laudable zeal for public good the base or foolish compliances of ambition, corruption, or infatuation.

As avenues to foreign influence in innumerable ways, such attachments are particularly alarming to the truly enlightened and independent patriot. How many opportunities do they afford to tamper with domestic factions, to practice the arts of seduction, to mislead public opinion, to influence or awe the public councils! Such an attachment of a small or weak toward a great and powerful nation dooms the former to be the satellite of the latter. Against the insidious wiles of foreign influence (I conjure you to believe me, fellow-citizens) the jealousy of a free people ought to be *constantly* awake, since history and experience prove that foreign influence is one of the most baneful foes of republican government. But that jealousy, to be useful, must be impartial, else it becomes the instrument of the very influence to be avoided, instead of a defense against it. Excessive partiality for one foreign nation and excessive dislike of another cause those whom they actuate to see danger only on one side, and serve to veil and even second the arts of influence on the other. Real patriots who may resist the intrigues of the favorite are liable to become suspected and odious, while its tools and dupes usurp the applause and confidence of the people to surrender their interests.

The great rule of conduct for us in regard to foreign nations is, in extending our commercial relations to have with them as little *political* connection as possible. So far as we have already formed engagements let them be fulfilled with perfect good faith. Here let us stop.

Europe has a set of primary interests which to us have none or a very remote relation. Hence she must be engaged in frequent controversies, the causes of which are essentially foreign to our concerns. Hence, therefore, it must be unwise in us to implicate ourselves by artificial ties in the ordinary vicissitudes of her politics or the ordinary combinations and collisions of her friendships or enmities.

Our detached and distant situation invites and enables us to pursue a different course. If we remain one people, under an efficient government, the period is not far off when we may defy material injury from external annoyance; when we may take such an attitude as will cause the neutrality we may at any time resolve upon to be scrupulously respected; when belligerent nations, under the impossibility of making acquisitions upon us, will not lightly hazard the giving us provocation; when we may choose peace or war, as our interest, guided by justice, shall counsel.

Why forego the advantages of so peculiar a situation? Why quit our own to stand upon foreign ground? Why, by interweaving our destiny with that of any part of Europe, entangle our peace and prosperity in the toils of European ambition, rivalship, interest, humor, or caprice?

It is our true policy to steer clear of permanent alliances with any portion of the foreign world, so far, I mean, as we are now at liberty to do it; for let me not be understood as capable of patronizing infidelity to existing engagements. I hold the maxim no less applicable to public than to private affairs that honesty is always the best policy. I repeat, therefore, let those engagements be observed in their genuine sense. But in my opinion it is unnecessary and would be unwise to extend them.

Taking care always to keep ourselves by suitable establishments on a respectable defensive posture, we may safely trust to temporary alliances for extraordinary emergencies.

Harmony, liberal intercourse with all nations are recommended by policy, humanity, and interest. But even our commercial policy should hold an equal and impartial hand, neither seeking nor granting exclusive favors or preferences; consulting the natural course of things; diffusing and diversifying by gentle means the streams of commerce, but forcing nothing; establishing with powers so disposed, in order to give trade a stable course, to define the rights of our merchants, and to enable the Government to support them, conventional rules of intercourse, the best that present circumstances and mutual opinion will permit, but temporary and liable to be from time to time abandoned or varied as experience and circumstances shall dictate; constantly keeping in view that it is folly in one nation to look for disinterested favors from another; that it must pay with a portion of its independence for whatever it may accept under that character; that by such acceptance it may place itself in the condition of having given equivalents for nominal favors, and yet of being reproached with ingratitude for not giving more. There can be no greater error than to expect or calculate upon real favors from nation to nation. It is an illusion which experience must cure, which a just pride ought to discard.

In offering to you, my countrymen, these counsels of an old and affectionate friend I dare not hope they will make the strong and lasting impression I could wish-that they will control the usual current of the passions or prevent our nation from running the course which has hitherto marked the destiny of nations. But if I may even flatter myself that they may be productive of some partial benefit, some occasional good--that they may now and then recur to moderate the fury of party spirit, to warn against the mischiefs of foreign intrigue, to guard against the impostures of pretended patriotism-this hope will be a full recompense for the solicitude for your welfare by which they have been dictated.

How far in the discharge of my official duties I have been guided by the principles which have been delineated the public records and other evidences of my conduct must witness to you and to the world. To myself, the assurance of my own conscience is that I have at least believed myself to be guided by them.

In relation to the still subsisting war in Europe my proclamation of the 22nd of April, 1793, is the index to my plan. Sanctioned by your approving voice and by that of your representatives in both Houses of Congress, the spirit of that measure has continually governed me, uninfluenced by any attempts to deter or divert me from it.

After deliberate examination, with the aid of the best lights I could obtain, I was well satisfied that our country, under all the circumstances of the case, had a right to take, and was bound in duty and interest to take, a neutral position. Having taken it, I determined as far as should depend upon me to maintain it with moderation, perseverance, and firmness.

The considerations which respect the right to hold this conduct it is not necessary on this occasion to detail. I will only observe that, according to my understanding of the matter, that right, so far from being denied by any of the belligerent powers, has been virtually admitted by all.

The duty of holding a neutral conduct may be inferred, without anything more, from the obligation which justice and humanity impose on every nation, in cases in which it is free to act, to maintain inviolate the relations of peace and amity toward other nations.

The inducements of interest for observing that conduct will best be referred to your own reflections and experience. With me a predominant motive has been to endeavor to gain time to our country to settle and mature its yet recent institutions, and to progress without interruption to that degree of strength and consistency which is necessary to give it, humanly speaking, the command of its own fortunes.

Though in reviewing the incidents of my Administration I am unconscious of intentional error, I am nevertheless too sensible of my defects not to think it probable that I may have committed many errors. Whatever they may be, I fervently beseech the Almighty to avert or mitigate the evils to which they may tend. I shall also carry with me the hope that my country will never cease to view them with indulgence, and that, after forty-five years of my life dedicated to its service with an upright zeal, the faults of incompetent abilities will be consigned to oblivion, as myself must soon be to the mansions of rest.

Relying on its kindness in this as in other things, and actuated by that fervent love toward it which is so natural to a man who views in it the native soil of himself and his progenitors for several generations, I anticipate with pleasing expectation that retreat in which I promise myself to realize without alloy the sweet enjoyment of partaking in the midst of my fellow-citizens the benign influence of good laws under a free government--the ever-favorite object of my heart, and the happy reward, as I trust, of our mutual cares, labors, and dangers.

Appendix I

Jefferson's First Inaugural Address

Friends and Fellow-Citizens.

Called upon to undertake the duties of the first executive office of our country, I avail myself of the presence of that portion of my fellow-citizens which is here assembled to express my grateful thanks for the favor with which they have been pleased to look toward me, to declare a sincere consciousness that the task is above my talents, and that I approach it with those anxious and awful presentiments which the greatness of the charge and the weakness of my powers so justly inspire. A rising nation, spread over a wide and fruitful land, traversing all the seas with the rich productions of their industry, engaged in commerce with nations who feel power and forget right, advancing rapidly to destinies beyond the reach of mortal eye—when I contemplate these transcendent objects, and see the honor, the happiness, and the hopes of this beloved country committed to the issue and the auspices of this day, I shrink from the contemplation, and humble myself before the magnitude of the undertaking. Utterly, indeed, should I despair did not the presence of many whom I here see remind me that in the other high authorities provided by our Constitution I shall find resources of wisdom, of virtue, and of zeal on which to rely under all difficulties. To you, then, gentlemen, who are charged with the sovereign functions of legislation, and to those associated with you, I look with encouragement for that guidance and support which may enable us to steer with safety the vessel in which we are all embarked amidst the conflicting elements of a troubled world.

During the contest of opinion through which we have passed the animation of discussions and of exertions has sometimes worn an aspect which might impose on strangers unused to think freely and to speak and to write what they think; but this being now decided by the voice of the nation, announced according to the rules of the Constitution, all will, of course, arrange themselves under the will of the law, and unite in common efforts for the common good. All, too, will bear in mind this sacred principle, that though the will of the majority is in all cases to prevail, that will to be rightful must be reasonable; that the minority possess their equal rights, which equal law must protect, and to violate would be oppression. Let us, then, fellow-citizens, unite with one heart and one mind. Let us restore to social intercourse that harmony and affection without which liberty and even life itself are but dreary things. And let us reflect that, having banished from our land that religious intolerance under which mankind so long bled and suffered, we have yet gained little if we countenance a political intolerance as despotic, as wicked, and capable of as bitter and bloody persecutions. During the throes and convulsions of the ancient world, during the agonizing spasms of infuriated man, seeking through blood and slaughter his long-lost liberty, it was not wonderful that the agitation of the billows should reach even this distant and peaceful shore; that this should be more felt and feared by some and less by others, and should divide opinions as to measures of safety. But every difference of opinion is not a difference of principle. We have called by different names brethren of the same principle. We are all Republicans, we are all Federalists. If there be any among us who would wish to dissolve this Union or to change its republican form, let them stand undisturbed as monuments of the safety to combat it. I know, indeed, that some honest men fear that a republican government can not be strong, that this Government is not strong enough; but would the honest patriot, in the full tide of successful experiment, abandon a government which has so far kept us free and firm on the theoretic and visionary fear that this Government, the world's best hope, may by possibility want energy to preserve itself? I trust not. I believe this, on the contrary, the strongest Government on earth. I believe it the only one where every man, at the call of the law, would fly to the standard of the law, and would meet invasions of the public order as his own personal concern. Sometimes it is said that man cannot be trusted with the government of himself. Can he, then, be trusted with the government of others? Or have we found angels in the forms of kings to govern him? Let history answer this question.

Let us, then, with courage and confidence pursue our own Federal and Republican principles, our attachment to union and representative government. Kindly separated by nature and a wide ocean from the exterminating havoc of one quarter of the globe; too high-minded to endure the degradations of the others; possessing a chosen country, with room enough for our descendants to the thousandth and thousandth generation; entertaining a due sense of our equal right to the use of our own faculties, to the acquisitions of our own industry, to honor and confidence from our fellow-citizens, resulting not from birth, but from our actions and their sense of them; enlightened by a benign religion, professed, indeed, and practiced in various forms, yet all of them inculcating honesty, truth, temperance, gratitude, and the love of men; acknowledging and adoring an overrruling Providence, which by all its dispensations proves that it delights in the happiness of man here and his greater happiness hereafter—with all these blessings, what more is necessary to make us a happy and a prosperous people? Still one thing more fellow-citizens—a wise and frugal Government, which shall restrain men from injuring one another, shall leave them otherwise free to regulate their own pursuits of industry and improvement, and shall not take from the mouth of labor the bread it has earned. This is the sum of good government, and this is necessary to close the circle of our felicities.

About to enter, fellow-citizens, on the exercises of duties which comprehend everything dear and valuable to you, it is proper you should understand what I deem the essential principles of our Government, and consequently those which ought to shape its Administration. I will compress them within the narrowest compass they will bear, stating the general principle, but not all its limitations. Equal and exact justice to all men, of whatever state or persuasion, religious or political; peace, commerce, and honest friendship with all nations, entangling alliances with none; the support of the State governments in all their rights; as the most competent administrations for our domestic concerns and the surest bulwarks against antirepublican tendencies; the preservation of the General Government in its whole constitutional vigor, as the sheet anchor of our peace at home and safety abroad; a jealous care of the right of election by the people—a mild and safe corrective of abuses which are lopped by the sword of revolution where peaceable remedies are unprovided; absolute acquiescence in the decisions of the majority, the vital principle of republics, from which is no appeal but to force, the vital principle and immediate parent of despotism; a well-disciplined militia, our best reliance in peace and for the first moments of war, till regulars may relieve them; the supremacy of the civil over the military authority; economy in the public expense, that labor may be lightly burdened; the honest payment of our debts and sacred preservation of the public faith; encouragement of agriculture, and of commerce as its handmaid; the diffusion of information and arraignment of all abuses at the bar of the public reason; freedom of religion; freedom of the press, and freedom of persons under the protection of the habeas corpus, and trial by juries impartially selected. These principles form the bright constellation which has gone before us and guided our steps through an age of revolution and reformation. The wisdom of our sages and blood of our heroes have been devoted to their attainment. They should be the creed of our political faith, the text of civic instruction, the touchstone by which to try the services of those we trust; and should we wander from them in moments of error or of alarm, let us hasten to retrace our steps and to regain the road which alone leads to peace, liberty, and safety.

I repair, then, fellow-citizens, to the post you have assigned me. With experience enough in subordinate offices to have seen the difficulties of this the greatest of all, I have learnt to expect that it will rarely fall to the lot of imperfect man to retire from this station with the reputation and the favor which bring him into it. Without pretensions to the high confidence you reposed in our first and greatest revolutionary character, whose preeminent services had entitled him to the first place in his country's love and destined for him the fairest page in the volume of faithful history, I ask so much confidence only as may give firmness and effect to the legal administration of your affairs. I shall often go wrong through defect of judgment. When right, I shall often be thought wrong by those whose positions will not command a view of the whole ground. I ask your indulgence for my own errors, which will never be intentional, and your support against the errors of others, who may condemn what they would not if seen in all its parts. The approbation implied by your suffrage is a great consolation to me for the past, and my future solicitude will be to retain the good opinion of those who have bestowed it in advance, to conciliate that of others by doing them all the good in my power, and to be instrumental to the happiness and freedom of all.

Relying, then, on the patronage of your good will, I advance with obedience to the work, ready to retire from it whenever you become sensible how much better choice it is in your power to make. And may that Infinite Power which rules the destinies of the universe lead our councils to what is best, and give them a favorable issue for your peace and prosperity.

Notes

NOTES—CHAPTER 1

[1] Jack P. Greene, ed., *The Reinterpretation of the American Revolution* (New York: Harper and Row, 1968), pp. 18-19.

[2] Clinton Rossiter, *The Political Thought of the American Revolution* (New York: Harcourt, Brace and World, 1963), p. 52.

[3] *Ibid.*

NOTES—CHAPTER 2

[1] William Bradford, *Of Plymouth Plantation*, Samuel E. Morison, ed. (New York: Modern Library, 1967), p. 25.

[2] Daniel J. Boorstin, *The Americans: The Colonial Experience* (New York: Vintage Books, 1958), p. 21.

[3] *Ibid.*, p. 24.

[4] Hugh Jones, *The Present State of Virginia* (New York: Joseph Sabin, 1856), p. 48.

[5] Quoted in Boorstin, *op. cit.*, p. 20.

[6] T. Harry Williams, *et al.*, *A History of the United States, I* (New York: Alfred A. Knopf, 1959), p. 34.

[7] Boorstin, *op. cit.*, p. 319.

[8] *Ibid.*, p. 332.

[9] Merle Curti, *The Growth of American Thought* (New York: Harper, 1951, 2nd ed.), p. 4.

[10] Robert A. Rutland, *The Birth of the Bill of Rights* (New York: Collier Books, 1962), p. 15.

[11] *Ibid.*, pp. 19-20.

NOTES—CHAPTER 3

[1] Peter N. Carroll, ed., *Religion and the Coming of the American Revolution* (Waltham, Mass.: Ginn-Blaisdell, 1970), p. xi.

[2] This is the title of a paperback version of the first part of his book, *Seedtime of the Republic*.

[3] See Perry Miller, " 'Preparation for Salvation' in Seventeenth-Century New England," *Essays in American Colonial History*, Paul Goodman, ed. (New York: Holt, Rinehart and Winston, 1967), pp. 152-183.

[4] Daniel J. Boorstin, *The Americans: The Colonial Experience* (New York: Vintage Books, 1958), p. 82.

[5] *Ibid.*, pp. 94-95.

[6] *Ibid.*, p. 43.

[7] See *ibid.*, pp. 61-62.

[8] See Alan Simpson, "How Democratic was Roger Williams?" in Goodman, *op. cit.*, pp. 188-89.

NOTES—CHAPTER 4

[1] Curtis P. Nettels, *The Roots of American Civilization* (New York: Appleton-Century-Crofts, 1963, 2nd ed.), p. 543.

[2] George B. Adams, *Constitutional History of England*, Rev. by Robert L. Schuyler (New York: Holt, Rinehart and Winston, 1962), p. 366.

[3] Nettels, *op. cit.*, p. 546.

[4] Quoted in Clinton Rossiter, *The First American Revolution* (New York: Harcourt, Brace and World, 1956), p. 103.

[5] Max Savelle, *A History of Colonial America*, Rev. by Robert Middlekauf (New York: Holt, Rinehart and Winston, 1964), p. 402.

[6] *Ibid.*

[7] Jack P. Greene, "The Role of the Lower Houses of Assembly in Eighteenth-Century Politics," *Essays in American Colonial History*, Paul Goodman, ed. (New York: Holt, Rinehart and Winston, 1967), pp. 431-32.

[8] Nettels, *op. cit.*, p. 563.

[9] Rossiter, *op. cit.*, p. 119.

NOTES—CHAPTER 5

[1] Clinton Rossiter, *The Political Thought of the American Revolution* (New York: Harcourt, Brace and World, 1963), p. 78.

[2] *The Flight from Reality* (Irvington, N. Y.: Foundation for Economic Education, 1969), p. 498.

[3] George A. Peek, Jr., ed., *The Political Writings of John Adams* (New York: Liberal Arts Press, 1954), p. 96.

[1] Lawrence H. Gipson, *The Coming of the Revolution* (New York: Harper Torchbooks, 1962), pp. 55-56.

[2] *Ibid.*, p. 58.

[3] *Ibid.*, p. 136.

[4] *Ibid.*, p. 138.

[5] See E. A. J. Johnson, *American Economic Thought in the Seventeenth Century* (New York: Russell and Russell, 1961), pp. 8-29.

[6] Curtis P. Nettels, *The Roots of American Civilization* (New York: Appleton-Century-Crofts, 1963, 2nd ed.), p. 283.

[7] *Ibid.*, p. 375.

[8] *Ibid.*, p. 434.

[9] Eugen Weber, *A Modern History of Europe* (New York: Norton, 1971), pp. 145-46.

[10] Nettels, *op. cit.*, p. 281.

[11] *Ibid.*, p. 283.

[12] *Ibid.*, p. 284.

[13] Max Savelle and Robert Middlekauff, *A History of Colonial America* (New York: Holt, Rinehart and Winston, 1964, rev. ed.), p. 261.

[14] *Ibid.*, p. 265.

[1] John Braeman, *The Road to Independence* (New York: Capricorn Books, 1963), p. 14.

[2] *Ibid.*, p. 13.

[3] Jack P. Greene, ed., *Colonies to Nation* (New York: McGraw-Hill, 1967), pp. 17-18.

[4] Merrill Jensen, *The Founding of a Nation* (New York: Oxford University Press, 1968), pp. 58-59.

[5] See Braeman, *op cit.*, pp. 17-19.

[6] John C. Miller, *Origins of the American Revolution* (Boston: Little, Brown and Co., 1943), p. 83.

[7] Jensen, *op cit.*, p. 45.

[8] Greene, *op. cit.*, p. 19.

[9] *Ibid.*, p. 24.

[10] Jensen, *op. cit.*, p. 51.

[11] Greene, *op. cit.*, p. 44.

[12] Miller, *op. cit.*, p. 101.

[13] Jensen, *op. cit.*, pp. 94-95.

[14] *Ibid.*, pp. 63-64.

[15] See Lawrence H. Gipson, *The Coming of the Revolution* (New York: Harper Torchbooks, 1962), p. 83.

[16] *Ibid.*, p. 87.

[17] Richard B. Morris, *The American Revolution* (Princeton, N. J.: D. Van Nostrand, 1955), p. 90.

[18] *Ibid.*, p. 91.

[19] Jensen, *op. cit.*, p. 113.

[20] Gipson, *op. cit.*, p. 105.

[21] Greene, *op. cit.*, p. 85.

NOTES—CHAPTER 8

[1] Merrill Jensen, *The Founding of a Nation* (New York: Oxford University Press, 1968), p. 186.

[2] *Ibid.*, pp. 207-08.

[3] Quoted in Edmund S. Morgan, "Colonial Ideas of Parliamentary Power": *The Reinterpretation of the American Revolution*, Jack P. Greene, ed. (New York: Harper and Row, 1968), p. 166.

[4] Jack P. Greene, ed., *Colonies to Nation* (New York: McGraw-Hill, 1967), pp. 88-89.

[5] This does not mean that colonists were right in everything they did in opposition to British action, nor that others at some later time would be justified in imitating their every action, even if they found themselves in analogous conditions. The rightness of a cause does not absolve people from moral and just behavior. That a cause is just is reason for working for its triumph, not for the engaging in wrongful acts.

[6] See Jensen, *op. cit.*, pp. 241-42.

[7] Forrest McDonald, intro., *Empire and Nation* (Englewood Cliffs, N. J.: Prentice-Hall, 1962), p. xiii.

[8] *Ibid.*, p. 17.

[9] *Ibid.*, pp. 43-44.

[10] See Lawrence H. Gipson, *The Coming of the American Revolution* (New York: Harper Torchbooks, 1962), pp. 185-87.

[11] Jensen, *op. cit.*, p. 253.

[12] Greene, *Colonies to Nation*, p. 143.

[13] Richard B. Morris, ed., *Encyclopedia of American History* (New York: Harper, 1953), p. 78.

[14] Jensen, *op. cit.*, p. 357.

[15] See Donald B. Cole, *Handbook of American History* (New York: Harcourt, Brace and World, 1968), p. 51.

[16] John C. Miller, *Origins of the American Revolution* (Boston: Little, Brown and Co., 1943), p. 339.

NOTES—CHAPTER 9

[1] Quoted in Merrill Jensen, *The Founding of the Nation* (New York: Oxford University Press, 1968), p. 572.

[2] Leslie F. S. Upton, ed., *Revolutionary versus Loyalist* (Waltham, Mass.: Blaisdell, 1968), p. 21.

[3] Edward Dumbauld, ed., *The Political Writings of Thomas Jefferson* (New York: Liberal Arts Press, 1955), p. 22.

[4] *Ibid.*, p. 32.

[5] *Ibid.*, pp. 19-20.

[6] Jack P. Greene, ed., *Colonies to Nation* (New York: McGraw-Hill, 1967), p. 225.

[7] See Anne H. Burleigh, *John Adams* (New Rochelle, N. Y.: Arlington House, 1969), pp. 122-29.

[8] See Jensen, *op. cit.*, p. 493.

[9] Richard B. Morris, *The American Revolution* (Princeton, N. J.: D. Van Nostrand, 1955), p. 114.

[10] John C. Miller, *Origins of the American Revolution* (Boston: Little, Brown, 1943), p. 385.

[11] See Jensen, *op. cit.*, pp. 575-78.

[12] *Ibid.*

[13] John Braeman, *The Road to Independence* (New York: Capricorn Books, 1963), p. 275.

[14] Nelson F. Adkins, ed., *Thomas Paine* (New York: Liberal Arts Press, 1953), p. 10.

[15] *Ibid.*, p. 15.

[16] *Ibid.*, p. 18.

[17] *Ibid.*, p. 34.

NOTES—CHAPTER 10

[1] Quoted in John R. Alden, *A History of the American Republic* (New York: Alfred A. Knopf, 1969), p. 243.

[2] Nelson F. Adkins, ed., *Thomas Paine* (New York: Liberal Arts Press, 1953), pp. 43-44.

[3] See Alden, *op cit.*, pp. 241-42.

NOTES—CHAPTER 11

[1] Quoted in Merrill Jensen, *The Founding of a Nation* (New York: Oxford University Press, 1968), p. 663.

[2] John R. Alden, *The American Revolution* (New York: Harper Torchbooks, 1954), p. 85.

[3] *Ibid.*, p. 86.

[4] Piers Mackesy, *The War for America* (Cambridge, Mass.: Harvard University Press, 1965), p. 36.

[5] Quoted in *ibid.*, p. 91.

[6] John R. Alden, *A History of the American Revolution* (New York: Alfred A. Knopf, 1969), pp. 203-05.

[7] Samuel E. Morison, *The Oxford History of the American People* (New York: Oxford University Press, 1965), p. 244.

[8] Douglas S. Freeman, *Washington*, abridged by Richard Harwell (New York: Scribner's, 1968), pp. 373-74.

[9] John C. Miller, *Triumph of Freedom* (Boston: Little, Brown and Co., 1948), p. 225.

[10] *Ibid.*, p. 223.

NOTES—CHAPTER 12

[1] Curtis Nettels, *The Emergence of a National Economy* (New York: Holt, Rinehart and Winston, 1962), p. 42.

[2] Quoted in Albert S. Bolles, *The Financial History of the United States*, I (New York: D. Appleton, 1896, 4th ed.), p. 208.

[3] See Nettels, *op. cit.*, p. 24.

[4] See William G. Sumner, *The Financier and the Finances of the American Revolution*, I (New York: Dodd, Mead, and Co., 1891), p. 98. Sumner indicates that one estimate runs well over $300 millions, but that it includes reissues.

[5] See John R. Alden, *A History of the American Revolution* (New York: Alfred A. Knopf, 1969), p. 255.

[6] See Bolles, *op. cit.*, pp. 150-57.

[7] Nettels, *op. cit.*, p. 24.

[8] Bolles, *op. cit.*, p. 39.

[9] *Ibid.*, p. 43.

[10] *Ibid.*, p. 39.

[11] *Ibid.*, p. 193.

[12] Nettels, *op. cit.*, p. 24.

[13] John C. Miller, *Triumph of Freedom* (Boston: Little, Brown and Co., 1948), p. 458.

[14] Sumner, *op. cit.*, p. 274.

[15] Nettels, *op. cit.*, p. 25.

[16] Samuel E. Morison, *The Oxford History of the United States* (New York: Oxford University Press, 1965), p. 230.

[17] Bolles, *op. cit.*, p. 260.

[18] *Ibid.*, pp. 121-22.

[19] Sumner, *op. cit.*, pp. 46-47.

[20] Bolles, *op. cit.*, p. 119.

[21] *Ibid.*, p. 121.

[22] Sumner, *op. cit.*, pp. 56-57.

[23] *Ibid.*, p. 61.

[24] Bolles, *op. cit.*, p. 68.

[25] *Ibid.*, p. 132.

[26] See Sumner, *op. cit.*, pp. 142-52.

[27] *Ibid.*, p. 239.

[28] Bolles, *op. cit.*, p. 139.

[29] *Ibid.*, p. 128.

[30] *Ibid.*, pp. 176-78.

[31] *Ibid.*, p. 216.

[32] *Ibid.*, p. 206.
[33] *Ibid.*
[34] Miller, *op. cit.*, p. 463.
[35] See Sumner, *op. cit.*, p. 86.
[36] *Ibid.*, pp. 94-95.
[37] *Ibid.*, pp. 152-53.
[38] *Ibid.*, p. 243.

NOTES—CHAPTER 13

[1] Jack P. Greene, ed., *Colonies to Nation* (New York: McGraw-Hill, 1967), p. 443.
[2] Howard H. Peckham, *The War for Independence* (Chicago: University of Chicago Press, 1958), pp. 109-10.
[3] Quoted in Merrill Jensen, *The New Nation* (New York: Vintage Books, 1950), pp. 26-27.
[4] John Fiske, *The Critical Period of American History* (New York: Houghton Mifflin, 1916), p. 91.
[5] Dan Lacy, *The Meaning of the American Revolution* (New York: New American Library, 1964), p. 191.
[6] Samuel F. Bemis, *The Diplomacy of the American Revolution* (Bloomington: Indiana University Press, 1957), p. 219.
[7] Greene, *op. cit.*, p. 437.
[8] Fiske, *op. cit.*, p. 34.
[9] Bemis, *op. cit.*, p. 256.
[10] Fiske, *op. cit.*, p. 111.
[11] Quoted in Douglas S. Freeman, *Washington*, abridged by Richard Harwell (New York: Scribner's, 1968), p. 506.
[12] *Ibid.*, p. 507.
[13] *Ibid.*, p. 509.
[14] Quoted in Samuel E. Morison, *The Oxford History of the American People* (New York: Oxford University Press, 1965), p. 269.

NOTES—CHAPTER 14

[1] See Merrill Jensen, *The New Nation* (New York: Vintage Books, 1950), p. 132.
[2] *Ibid.*, p. 133.
[3] John Fiske, *The Critical Period of American History* (Boston: Houghton Mifflin, 1916), p. 78.
[4] Jack P. Greene, ed., *Colonies to Nation* (New York: McGraw-Hill, 1967), pp. 399-91.
[5] Fiske, *op. cit.*, p. 71.
[6] Greene, *op. cit.*, p. 397.
[7] *Ibid.*, p. 398.

[8] See Fiske, *op. cit.*, pp. 74-75.

[9] See Robert A. Rutland, *The Birth of the Bill of Rights* (New York: Collier, 1962), p. 109.

[10] Henry S. Commager, ed., *Documents of American History*, I (New York: Appleton-Century-Crofts, 1962, 7th ed.), 107.

[11] *Ibid.*, p. 104.

[12] *Ibid.*, p. 108.

[13] Greene, *op. cit.*, pp. 472-73.

[14] Dumas Malone and Basil Rauch, *Empire for Liberty*, I (New York: Appleton-Century-Crofts, 1960), p. 196.

[15] Commager, *op. cit.*, p. 103.

[16] *Ibid.*, p. 108.

[17] See Frederick B. Tolles, "A Reevaluation of the Revolution as a Social Movement," George A. Bilias, ed., *The American Revolution* (New York: Holt, Rinehart and Winston, 1970, 2nd ed.), pp. 66-67.

[18] See Richard Hofstadter, *et. al.*, *The United States* (Englewood Cliffs, N. J.: Prentice-Hall, 1967, 2nd ed.), p. 160.

[19] Greene, *op. cit.*, p. 343.

[20] Hofstadter, *op. cit.*, pp. 159-60.

[21] Quoted in Nelson M. Blake, *A History of American Life and Thought* (New York: McGraw-Hill, 1963), p. 100.

NOTES—CHAPTER 15

[1] Samuel E. Morison and Henry S. Commager, *The Growth of the American Republic*, 1 (New York: Oxford University Press, 1942, 3d ed.), p. 265.

[2] See Andrew C. McLaughlin, *The Confederation and the Constitution* (New York: Collier Books, 1962), pp. 77-78.

[3] *Ibid.*, p. 75.

[4] Curtis P. Nettels, *The Emergence of a National Economy* (New York: Holt, Rinehart and Winston, 1962), p. 67.

[5] *Ibid.*

[6] Merrill Jensen, *The New Nation* (New York: Vintage Books, 1950), p. 303.

[7] Nettels, *op. cit.*, p. 65.

[8] *Ibid.*

[9] Jensen, *op. cit.*, pp. 247-48.

[10] *Ibid.*, p. 249.

[11] *Ibid.*, p. 250.

[12] *Ibid.*, pp. 309-10.

[13] John Fiske, *The Critical Period of American History* (Boston: Houghton Mifflin, 1916), p. 165.

[14] McLaughlin, *op. cit.*, pp. 64-65.

[15] *Ibid.*, p. 51.

[16] Fiske, *op. cit.*, p. 145.

[17] Jensen, *op. cit.*, p. 324.

[18]Forrest McDonald, *The Formation of the American Republic* (Baltimore: Penguin, 1965), p. 140.

[19]*Ibid.*, p. 147

NOTES—CHAPTER 16

[1]Quoted in Charles Warren, *The Making of the Constitution* (New York: Barnes and Noble, 1937), p. 737.

[2]*Ibid.*, pp. 55-56.

[3]*Ibid.*, pp. 99-100.

[4]*Ibid.*, p. 730.

[5]James Madison, *Notes of the Debates in the Federal Convention of 1787*, Adrienne Koch, intro. (Athens, Ohio: Ohio University Press, 1966), p. 227.

[6]*Ibid.*, pp. 653-54.

[7]Warren, *op. cit.*, p. 125.

[8]Madison, *Notes*, pp. 411-12. The present writer has taken the liberty of modernizing the spelling and using complete words rather than the abbreviations as they appear in the original.

[9]*Ibid.*, p. 447.

[10]*Ibid.*, p. 412.

[11]*Ibid.*, pp. 25-26.

[12]Jack P. Greene, ed., *Colonies to Nation* (New York: McGraw-Hill, 1967), p. 511.

[13]Quoted in Warren, *op. cit.*, p. 38.

[14]*Ibid.*, p. 44.

[15]*Ibid.*, pp. 17-18.

[16]*Ibid.*, p. 50.

[17]Madison, *Notes*, p. 159.

[18]*Ibid.*, p. 159.

[19]*Ibid.*, p. 163.

[20]*Ibid.*, p. 185.

[21]*Ibid.*, p. 455.

[22]*Ibid.*, p. 175.

[23]*Ibid.*, p. 177.

[24]*Ibid.*, p. 178.

[25]*Ibid.*, p. 233.

[26]*Ibid.*, p. 311.

[27]*Ibid.*, p. 195.

[28]*Ibid.*, pp. 193-94.

[29]*Ibid.*, p. 196.

NOTES—CHAPTER 17

[1]James Madison, Alexander Hamilton, and John Jay, *The Federalist Papers* (New Rochelle, N. Y.: Arlington House, n.d.), p. 322. Hereinafter referred to as *The Federalist*.

²*Ibid.*, p. 54.

³*Ibid.*, p. 56.

⁴James Madison, *Notes of Debates in the Federal Convention of 1787*, Adrienne Kock, intro. (Athens, Ohio: Ohio University Press, 1966), p. 653.

⁵*The Federalist*, p. 322.

⁶Richard W. Leopold, et. al., eds., *Problems in American History* (Englewood Cliffs, N. J.: Prentice-Hall, 1966), p. 134.

⁷*The Federalist*, p. 114.

⁸See Hamilton's argument in *The Federalist* No. 9, for example.

⁹Richard H. Leach, *American Federalism* (New York: Norton, 1970), p. 2.

¹⁰*The Federalist*, p. 246.

¹¹Leach, *op. cit.*, p. 1.

¹²*The Federalist*, p. 242.

¹³*Ibid.*,

¹⁴*Elliot's Debates*, Bk. 1, Vol. 1, p. 422.

¹⁵*Ibid.*, Vol. 2, p. 8.

¹⁶*Ibid.*, Vol. 3, p. 87.

¹⁷Charles Warren, *The Making of the Constitution* (New York: Barnes and Noble, 1937), p. 594.

¹⁸*Ibid.*, pp. 594-95.

¹⁹Madison, *Notes*, p. 659.

NOTES—CHAPTER 18

¹Alexander Hamilton, et. al., *The Federalist Papers* (New Rochelle, N. Y.: Arlington House, n.d.), pp. 513-14.

²Broadus and Louise Mitchell, *A Biography of the Constitution* (New York: Oxford University Press, 1964), p. 189.

³Forrest McDonald, intro., *Empire and Nation* (Englewood Cliffs, N. J.: Prentice-Hall, 1962), pp. 134-35.

⁴See Merrill Jensen, *The Making of the American Constitution* (Princeton: D. Van Nostrand, 1964), pp. 141-46.

⁵Mitchell and Mitchell, *op. cit.*, p. 196.

⁶Quoted in Robert A. Rutland, *The Birth of the Bill of Rights* (New York: Collier Books, 1962), p. 215.

NOTES—CHAPTER 19

¹Nathan Schachner, *The Founding Fathers* (New York: Capricorn Books, 1954), p. 6.

²*Ibid.*, p. 11.

³*Ibid.*, p. 12.

⁴*Ibid.*, pp. 3-4.

⁵Curtis P. Nettels, *The Emergence of a National Economy* (New York: Holt, Rinehart and Winston, 1962), p. 115.

[6]Schachner, *op. cit.*, p. 33.

[7]John C. Fitzpatrick, "George Washington," *The American Plutarch*, Edward T. James, ed. (New York: Scribners, 1964), p. 51.

[8]Allan Nevins, "Alexander Hamilton," *Ibid.*, p. 113.

[9]Morton Borden, ed., *America's Ten Greatest Presidents* (Chicago: Rand McNally, 1961), p. 4.

[10]Edward S. Corwin, "John Marshall," James, *op.cit.*, p. 164.

[11]*Ibid.*, pp. 171-72.

[12]Alfred H. Kelley and Winfred A. Harbison, *The American Constitution* (New York: Norton, 1955, rev. ed.), p. 167.

[13]Schachner, *op. cit.*, p. 46-47.

[14]John C. Miller, *The Federalist Era* (New York: Harper and Row, 1960), p. 15.

[15]Schachner, *op. cit.*, p. 63.

NOTES—CHAPTER 20

[1]Richard B. Morris, *Alexander Hamilton and the Founding of the Nation* (New York: Dial Press, 1957), pp. 290-91.

[2]Nathan Schachner, *The Founding Fathers* (New York: Capricorn Books, 1954), p. 187.

[3]John C. Miller, *The Federalist Era* (New York: Harper and Row, 1960), p. 66.

[4]*Ibid.*, pp. 68-69.

[5]Clarence B. Carson. *The American Tradition* (Irvington, N. Y.: Foundation for Economic Education, 1964), p. 212.

[6]Henry S. Commager, *Documents of American History*, I (New York: Appleton-Century- Crofts, 1962, 7th ed.), p. 172.

[7]E. James Ferguson, ed., *Selected Writings of Albert Gallatin* (Indianapolis: Bobbs-Merrill, 1967), pp. 438-39.

[8]Commager, *op. cit.*, p. 172.

[9]*Ibid.*, p. 152.

[10]*Ibid.*, pp. 172-73.

[11]Quoted in Edward S. Corwin, *The Constitution and What It Means Today* (New York: Athenaeum, 1963), p. x.

[12]Commager, *op. cit.*, pp. 193-95.

[13]*Ibid.*, p. 206.

[14]*Ibid.*, pp. 252-53.

[15]*Ibid.*, p. 253.

NOTES—CHAPTER 21

[1]Richard B. Morris, ed., *Alexander Hamilton and the Founding of the Nation* (New York: Dial, 1957), p. 610.

NOTES—APPENDIX A

[1]Jack P. Greene, ed., *Colonies to Nation* (New York: McGraw-Hill Book Company, 1967), pp. 63-65. Used by permission of the publisher.

NOTES—APPENDIX B

[1]Henry S. Commager, ed., *Documents of American History* (New York: F. S. Crofts, 1935), pp. 103-104.

NOTES—APPENDIX C

[1]Francis N. Thorpe, ed., *The Federal and State Constitutions, Vol. 7 (Washington: Government Printing Office, 1909), pp. 3873-3875).*

NOTES—APPENDIX D

[1]Frances N. Thorpe, ed., *The Federal and State Constitutions, Vol. 1 (Washington: Government Printing Office, 1909), pp. 9-17.*

NOTES—APPENDIX E

[1]James Madison, "The Federalist," from *Universal Classics Library*, Vol. 1, ed. by Oliver H. G. Leigh (Washington: M. Walter Dunne, 1901), pp. 62-70.

NOTES—APPENDIX F

[1]Frances N. Thorpe, ed., *The Federal and State Constitutions*, Vol. 1, (Washington: Government Printing Office, 1909), pp. 19-28.

NOTES—APPENDIX G

[1]Frances N. Thorpe, ed., *The Federal and State Constitutions*, Vol. 1, (Washington: Government Printing Office, 1909), pp. 29-30.

NOTES—APPENDIX H

[1]George Washington, "Washington's Farewell Address," from *Messages and*

340

Papers of the Presidents, Vol. 1, edited by James D. Richardson (New York: Bureau of National Literature, 1897), pp. 205-216.

NOTES—APPENDIX I

[1]James D. Richardson, *Messages and Papers of the Presidents*, Vol. 1, (New York: Bureau of National Literature, 1897), pp. 309-312.

Index

Boyle, Roger, 27
Brandywine, battle of, 131-132
British, 17, 27-30, 30-32, 31, 52,
66, 67, 73, 75, 79, 80, 81-82, 83,
85, 87, 89, 90, 91, 93, 94, 95,
96, 97, 101, 105, 107, 108, 109,
111, 115, 121, 124, 127, 128,
129, 130, 131-132, 135, 138,
149, 150, 151, 153, 154, 158,
160, 173, 176, 178, 179, 183,
203, 205, 211, 214, 221, 225,
226, 239, 240, 244, 247, 253,
255, 256, 260, 261
British Empire, 47, 54, 68-69, 73,
157-158
Browne, Robert, 27
Brownists, 35
Brutus, 85
Bunker Hill, battle of, 108, 129,
260
Bunyan, John, 27
Burgoyne, John, 128, 131-132, 133
Burke, Edmund, 26, 106, 108
Burr, Aaron, 261

Caesar, Julius, 85
Calvinists, 40, 43
Canada, 72, 92, 108, 129-130, 131,
150, 156, 158
Carleton, Guy, 130
Carolingian Renaissance, 58
Carroll, Charles, 123, 262
Carroll, Peter N., 16
Catholic Church, 35, 36, 37, 38,
49
Charles I, 85
Charles II, 71
Charleston, 98, 151
Christians, 20, 35-36, 38, 41, 67
Church of England, 32, 36, 37, 39,
42, 53, 79, 165, 169-170
Circular Letters, 20, 95
Clark, George Rogers, 153

Clinton, Henry, 131-132, 133, 151
Coercive Acts, 20, 98-99, 101, 102
Coke, Edward, 27
Committees of Correspondence,
86, 97, 102
Common Sense, 20, 109-111, 114,
230
Concord, 20, 107, 183
Confederation, 17, 147, 177, 178,
179, 181, 201, 226, 233, 253
Congregational Church, 35, 40-41,
165, 225
Congress of Vienna, 71
Connecticut, 86, 90, 91, 95, 107,
165, 167, 182, 187, 189, 215,
261
Conservatives, 17, 20, 25-26, 109,
262
Constitution (British), 29, 37, 46,
53, 55, 61, 64, 66, 87, 91-92, 94,
101, 105, 119
Constitution (U.S.), 16, 17, 18, 20,
33, 36, 37, 56, 117, 156, 185,
189, 190, 191, 192, 193, 198,
199-210, 211, 212-226, 217, 218,
220, 221, 222, 225, 227, 228,
229, 230-233, 237, 239, 243,
244, 246, 247-251, 257, 258,
259, 261, 263, Appendix F, 293-
305
Constitutional Convention, 16, 20,
185-198, 199, 201, 210, 215,
227, 229, 233, 244, 260, 261
Continental Army, 126, 128, 133-
134, 139, 151, 152, 158, 253,
254
Continental Association, 105
Convention of 1800, 241
Cornwallis, Lord, 128, 151, 152
Coverdale, Miles, 27
Craig, et. al v. *State of Missouri*,
250
Crisis, The, 20

Langdon, John, 197
Lansing, John, 186
Laurens, Henry, 166
Lee, Arthur, 150
Lee, Richard Henry, 107, 111, 114, 153, 192, 201, 213, 214-215, 218, 261
Letters from a Pennsylvania Farmer, 20, 94-96
Lexington, battle of, 20, 107
Liberals, 17, 109, 262
Lilburne, John, 27
Livingston, Robert, 114
Locke, John, 27, 58, 95
Long Island, battle of, 128, 130
Louis XIV, 71-72
Louisiana, 157
Loyalists, 124, 125, 132, 140, 149, 150, 158, 171, 175, 176, 177, 254
Lutheran Church, 37

McDonald, Forrest, 15
Maclay, William, 224
Madison, James, 20, 55, 154, 165, 185, 186, 187, 189, 189-190, 191, 193, 194, 195, 196, 196-197, 199, 200, 202, 204, 208-209, 210, 212, 215, 216, 217, 227, 228, 230, 232, 233, 238, 243, 244, 248, 262-263
Magna Charta, 26, 29, 211, 221
Maine, 130, 153, 225
Marbury v. Madison, 247
Marlowe, Christopher, 27
Marshall, John, 20, 215, 227, 230-231, 240, 249-251, 262
Martin, Luther, 187, 194-195
Mary, Queen, 71
Maryland, 25, 66, 94, 141, 142, 153, 154, 167, 187, 194, 196, 215
Mason, George, 165, 168, 186,

187, 191, 194, 109-110, 213, 260
Massachusetts, 24, 39, 40-41, 53, 79, 85, 95, 96, 97, 98-99, 102, 107, 129, 140, 165, 167, 168, 170, 171, 180, 183-184, 184, 187, 189, 208, 213, 215, 261
Maury, James, 81
Mayflower Compact, 61
Mennonites, 43
Mercantilism, 16, 17, 38, 65-66, 67-69, 69-70, 70-73, 73-74, 75, 169, 236
Mercer, John Francis, 196
Michigan, 157
Mifflin, Thomas, 224
Milton, John, 27
Minnesota, 157
Mississippi, 157
Molasses Act, 65, 70
Monroe Doctrine, 241
Montesquieu, 29, 59, 205
Montgomery, Richard, 129, 130
Moravians, 35, 43
More, Thomas, 27
Morgan, Daniel, 128
Morison, Samuel E., 24, 131
Morris, Gouverneur, 20, 186, 187, 188, 189, 190-191, 192, 196, 209, 262
Morris, Richard B., 15
Morris, Robert, 107, 181, 186, 262
Morton, Nathaniel, 24
Mt. Vernon, 128, 161, 224

Napoleonic Wars, 241
Natural Law, 21, 56, 58-59, 60-61, 63-64, 79, 92, 94, 105, 115, 117, 211, 255
Natural Rights, 21, 62-63, 103, 118, 167, 211-212
Navigation Acts, 69-70
Nettles, Curtis, 71, 138, 139
Neutrality Proclamation, 240

Randolph, Edmund, 186, 189, 191, 210, 234, 262
Read, George, 187, 191
Republican form of government, 21, 204, 206
Republican Party, 20, 231, 241, 243-244, 262
Revere, Paul, 19
Rhode Island, 40, 42, 90, 95, 97, 141-142, 165, 167, 183, 186, 212, 216
Rockingham, 86, 156
Rome, 19, 58, 127, 133, 195, 255
Roosevelt, Franklin D., 233
Ross, Betsy, 19
Rossiter, Clinton, 20, 21, 34, 52, 56
Rousseau, Jean Jacques, 59
Rutland, Robert A., 16

St. Leger, Baron, 132
"Salutary neglect," 48
Saratoga, battle of, 20, 132
Savelle, Max, 16
Schachner, Nathan, 16
Schuyler, Philip, 129
Scotland, 48
Second Continental Congress, 20, 107, 111, 114, 126, 137-138, 139, 140, 142, 145, 146, 151, 153, 175, 261
Senate, 30, 197, 203, 205, 206, 209, 213, 216, 217, 223, 224, 232, 233
Separation of powers, 21, 29, 63, 156, 205-206, 254, 258
Separatists, 39
Seven Year's War, 66, 73, 74, 78, 80, 108, 127
Shakespeare, William, 27
Shays, Daniel, 183
Shays' Rebellion, 20, 183-184
Shelburne, Lord, 156

Sherman, Roger, 107, 114, 187, 189, 191, 197, 260
Sidney, Algernon, 27, 58
Smith, Adam, 67
Social contract, 61
Society of the Cincinnati, 170
Socrates, 57
"Sons of Liberty," 84, 86, 89
South Carolina, 95, 140, 150, 165, 166, 187, 189, 191, 215
Spain, 72, 80, 149, 157, 158, 177-178, 214, 239, 240
Spinoza, 58
Spirit of the Laws, The, 59
Stamp Act, 20, 65, 83, 84-86, 89, 95, 103, 156, 261
Stamp Act Congress, 20, 66, 85-86
Staple Act. 69
Star Chamber, 25
Stark, John, 132
State of nature, 60
Steuben, Baron von, 20, 128, 160
Story, Justice, 231
Stuart, House of, 31, 47, 49
Suffolk Resolves, 20, 104
Sugar Act, 65, 82-83, 84, 89, 261
Sullivan, John, 183
Summary View of the Rights of British America, A, 20, 103, 114
Sumner, William G., 140
Supreme Court, 209, 231, 233, 234, 250

Talleyrand, 241
Tariff Act of 1789, 233
Tarquin, 85
Tea Act, 20, 98, 103, 261
Tennent, Gilbert, 43
Tennessee, 157
Ticonderoga, 107
Townshend Acts, 93, 94-96, 97, 103, 261
Townshend, Charles, 84, 93

Tracy, Destutt de, 135
Treaty of Paris (1763), 20, 80
Treaty of Paris (1783), 156-158, 164, 177, 239, 240
Trenchard, John, 27
Trenton, battle of, 131
Tudors, 47
Turner, Frederick Jackson, 34-35
Tyndale, John, 27

Upton, Leslie F. S., 16

Valley Forge, 19, 132, 133-134
Vane, Harry, 58
Virginia, 20, 24, 25, 42, 80-81, 85, 91, 95, 97, 103, 106, 107, 108, 140, 146, 150, 151, 153, 154, 160, 165, 166, 167, 168, 170, 172, 177, 186, 187, 189, 194, 209, 213, 214, 215, 229, 237, 262
Virginia Bill of Rights, Appendix C, 273-275
Virginia Plan, 190, 191, 193, 195
Voltaire, 59

Wales, 48
War for Independence, 15, 94, 129-134, 135, 136, 137, 149-153, 170, 229, 237
War of Jenkin's Ear, 72
War of the Austrian Succession, 73
War of the Spanish Succession, 72
Washington, George, 16, 19, 20, 107, 108, 109, 127-128, 129, 133-134, 141, 142, 143, 144, 146, 149, 151, 152-153, 158,
159-161, 180, 185, 186, 187-188, 191, 193-194, 223-224, 225, 226, 227, 228, 229, 230, 232, 233, 234, 238, 239, 240, 242-243, 245, 246, 247, 248, 254, 260-261
Washington's Farewell Address, Appendix H, 311-324
Wayne, Anthony, 128, 153
Wealth of Nations, The, 67
Wesley, John, 27
West Indies, 70, 72, 82, 83, 107, 229, 240
West Virginia, 154
Whig conception, 16
Whig Party, 77-78, 156
White, L. D., 225
Whitefield, George, 43
Williams, Roger, 42-43
William III, 47-48, 71, 72
Wilson, James, 103, 104, 107, 186, 187-188, 189, 191, 195, 196, 261
Winslow, Edward, 24
Wisconsin, 157
Wolcott, Oliver, 107
Woolens Act, 70
Writ of assistance, 78, 93
Writ of *habeas corpus*, 30-31, 168, 207, 213
Wyclif, John, 27
Wythe, George, 186, 231

XYZ Affair, 20, 241

Yates, Robert, 186-187
Yorktown, battle of, 20, 142, 151-152, 153